Creativity in Primary Education

Achieving
QTS

Creativity in Primary Education

Second edition

Edited by Anthony Wilson

LearningMatters

First published in 2007 by Learning Matters Ltd

Second edition published in 2009

British Library Cataloguing in Publication Data
A CIP record for this book is available from the British Library.

The right of Anthony Wilson, Anna Craft, Avril Loveless, Teresa Cremin, Elizabeth Wood, Tony Eaude, Liz Chamberlain, Jane Johnston, Mary Briggs, Sue Chedzoy, Paul Key, Sarah Hennessy, Hilary Claire, Richard Woolley, Dan Davies, Alan Howe, Hilary Cooper and Simon Catling to be identified as the Authors of this work have been asserted by them in accordance with the Copyright, Design and Patents Act 1988.

ISBN 978 1 84445 198 2

Cover design by Topics
Project management by Deer Park Productions, Tavistock, Devon
Typeset by PDQ Typesetting Ltd, Staffordshire
Printed and bound in Great Britain by Bell & Bain Ltd, Glasgow

Learning Matters Ltd
33 Southernhay East
Exeter EX1 1NX
Tel: 01392 215560
info@learningmatters.co.uk
www.learningmatters.co.uk

Mixed Sources
Product group from well-managed
forests and other controlled sources
www.fsc.org Cert no. TT-COC-002769
© 1996 Forest Stewardship Council
FSC

Contents

Part 3: Creativity in the foundation primary curriculum

Contributors

Anthony Wilson is Primary PGCE Programme Director at the University of Exeter. His research interests are poetry pedagogy, poetry writing by children, and creative approaches to literacy teaching. A published poet, he has worked as a primary school teacher, visiting writer in schools and writing tutor for adults. He is the co-editor of *The Poetry Book for Primary Schools* (Poetry Society, 1998).

Mary Briggs is an Associate Professor at the Institute of Education, University of Warwick where she teaches across a range of undergraduate and postgraduate programmes. Her research interests are mathematics education, early years, assessment and leadership and she has published a number of books in these areas.

Simon Catling is Professor of Primary Education, specialising in geography in primary education. From 2000-08 he was Assistant Dean of the Westminster Institute of Education, Oxford Brookes University. He taught in primary schools in London before moving into higher education. He is a Past-President of the Geographical Association. He is author of the *Mapstart* series (revised, Collins, 2009) and of *Placing Places* (Geographical Association, 2002). He has written extensively on primary geography, publishing materials for children and guidance and research for teachers and teacher educators.

Liz Chamberlain is a Senior Lecturer in English at the University of Winchester, where she coordinates English across the different courses. She is also the Strategic Consultant on the Everybody Writes project, which aims to put creativity at the heart of the writing process.

Sue Chedzoy is a Senior Lecturer in Education at the University of Exeter. Her key interests are promoting physical activity from the early years and throughout life. Her publications include: *Fitness Fun* (Southgate Publishers), *Physical Education at Key Stages 1 and 2 for Teachers and Co-ordinators* (David Fulton), *Physical Education – Access for All* (David Fulton) and *Physical Education in the School Grounds* (Southgate/Learning Through Landscapes).

Hilary Claire taught history and citizenship in ITE at London Metropolitan University. She published extensively in both primary history education and citizenship education and was the national co-ordinator of the Primary Educators Network for the Advancement of Citizenship (PENAC).

Hilary Cooper is Professor of History and Pedagogy at the University of Cumbria. Previously she taught at Goldsmiths' College, London University, and in a variety of London Primary Schools. Her doctoral research on 'Young Children's Thinking in History' was undertaken as a class teacher. She has published widely.

Anna Craft is Professor of Education at the University of Exeter and The Open University. Once a primary teacher, and with a background in national curriculum development work, Anna works with learners, teachers, researchers and policymakers to develop creativity and learning futures. She has written and edited sixteen books, co-edits the journal *Thinking*

Skills and Creativity and co-convenes the BERA Special Interest Group, *Creativity in Education*.

Teresa Cremin (formerly Grainger) is a Professor of Education at The Open University. She is currently President of UKLA, a Trustee of The Poetry Archive and of Booktrust and joint coordinator of the BERA Creativity SIG. Teresa has published widely, including *Teaching English Creatively* (2009, Routledge), *Building Communities of Readers* (PNS/UKLA, 2008), and *Creativity and Writing: Developing Voice and Verve in the Classroom* (RoutledgeFalmer, 2005).Teresa is concerned to make learning an imaginatively vital experience for all involved and seeks to foster the creative engagement of both teachers and younger learners.

Dan Davies is Professor of Science and Technology Education, Head of Applied Research and Consultancy, and leader of the Centre for Research in Early Scientific Learning at Bath Spa University.

Tony Eaude was the headteacher of a multicultural first school in Oxford. He now works as an independent research consultant and is a Research Fellow, Department of Education, University of Oxford.

Sarah Hennessy is a Lecturer in Music Education at the University of Exeter where she teaches both specialist and generalist primary music courses. She also undertakes research into music teacher education and children's musical creativity. She is author of *Music 7–11: Developing Primary Teaching Skills* (Routledge, 1995) and *Coordinating Music Across the Primary School* (RoutledgeFalmer, 1998). She is editor of *Music Education Research*, director of the International Conference for Research in Music Education (RIME) and Chair of the Orff Society.

Alan Howe is Senior Lecturer in Primary Education and Primary Science Team Leader at Bath Spa University. He is co-author with Dan Davies and others of *Primary Design and Technology for the Future – Creativity, Culture and Citizenship* (2001), *Teaching Science and Design and Technology in the Early Years* (2003), and *Science 5–11: A Teacher's Guide* (2005) all published by David Fulton.

Jane Johnston is a Reader in Education at Bishop Grosseteste University College, Lincoln where she is involved in initial teacher training and continuing professional development of practitioners. She has contributed to the development of primary science education both nationally and internationally and has a particular interest in early years education, the development of scientific attitudes and pedagogical approaches to science. Her many publications reflect her varied interests, enthusiasm for primary science and desire to develop awe and wonder in scientific learners. They include *Early Explorations in Science*, *Enriching Early Scientific Learning*, *Teaching the Primary Curriculum* and *Developing Teaching Skills in the Primary School* all published by the Open University Press and contributions to the ASE's *Primary Science Handbook*, *Laying the Foundations in the Early Years* and *The Curriculum Partnership: Early Years Handbook*. She is one of the first five science teachers to achieve the qualification Chartered Science Teacher (CSci Teach), which recognises high quality science teaching.

Paul Key is a Senior Lecturer at the Faculty of Education, University of Winchester. His interests are exploring teaching approaches which encourage imaginative and playful art and design activities for primary school children and examining the 'landscapes' of art practice and art teaching.

Elizabeth Wood is Professor of Education at the University of Exeter, specialising in early childhood. Her research interests include play in and beyond early childhood; teachers' professional knowledge and practice; curriculum, pedagogy and assessment in early childhood education, and the policy/practice interface.

Richard Woolley is a Senior Lecturer in Primary Education and Teaching Fellow at Bishop Grosseteste University College Lincoln. His interests include religious education, social justice and citizenship. He is co-author of *The Spiritual Dimension of Childhood* (Jessica Kingsley, 2008).

Acknowledgements

Teresa would like to acknowledge the work of her colleagues Jonathon Barnes and Stephen Scoffham in the Kent Creative Partnerships funded research upon which Chapter 3 draws.

Introduction
Anthony Wilson

Large numbers leave school with the bitter taste of defeat in them, not having mastered even moderately well those basic skills which society demands, much less having become people who rejoice in the exercise of creative intelligence.

Margaret Donaldson, *Children's Minds*

'Creativity' is a quality we are often made to feel we should value in our society. At the very least we feel we should be 'for' it, even if we do not know how to quantify or explain it. We may even feel slightly reluctant to define something so appealing and powerful. Like other nouns we sometimes use to signify qualities of positive value, for example, 'genius', 'poetry' or 'art', we feel we instinctively know creativity when we see it. This does not make it any easier to define.

For teachers this unease is compounded by the feeling that we should be planning for creativity and bringing to bear all of our energies on teaching towards it, including the implications this might have for planning, assessment and progression. These feelings can be complicated even further when we take into consideration the weight of curriculum orders and recommendations which teachers need to engage with, interpret and deliver.

The last word of the previous paragraph is freighted with different expectations in a context of targets and accountability. As the late Ted Wragg stated in an interview in the first edition of this book, many teachers enter into teaching not because they are passionate about 'delivery', but because they see it as a creative profession where they can develop their own creativity as well as those of their pupils. It is possible that we sign up to the idea of creativity when we begin teaching because it is emblematic of something, a quality we want to be known for, perhaps. Conversely, when we detect its absence, in curricular documentation, schemes of work, or in our own practice, we can be quick to label that as very negative. With so much support, in terms of curricular recommendations, now available to teachers, there has, perhaps, never been a better opportunity to address issues of individual and collective creativity within the profession. Anna Craft reminds us that we are most likely to feel creative about our practice when we have ownership of it. The implications of this are not easy, for it involves self-examination, honesty, risk-taking and the possibility that we may encounter failure.

How to use this book

This book is an attempt to illumine and discuss what this view of creativity means for us as primary practitioners, and how it might be put into practice across a range of curricular areas. Far from being an 'instruction manual', however, the aim of the book is to make you reconsider any preconceived notions of what creativity might be, and to ask that you reconceptualise your own responses to different subjects by trying out the suggested activities in each chapter.

You will also encounter 'Reflective Task' sections within each chapter. Please use these to reflect on the challenge to think about concepts within each subject in ways which you might not have considered before. Recording for yourself how your responses change as you read the book might be a good way of developing the four modes of creativity noted by Guy Claxton (1999) referred to in Chapter 2 by Avril Loveless: Resilience, Reflection, Resourcefulness and Relationship.

Intended audience

It is hoped that this book will be of direct interest to primary trainee teachers on all courses of initial teacher training and education in England and other parts of the UK. One of the themes running through the book is that creativity is not the preserve of the arts alone. While visual, performing and literary arts are tackled explicitly within it, the book is aimed at generalists as well as specialists on PGCE courses. The book will also be of interest to those studying creativity within educational and/or childhood and youth studies on undergraduate programmes and all primary teachers looking to reconsider the place of creativity in their practice.

Chapter details

The book is divided into three parts. Part 1 contextualises the concept of creativity and how it came to be such an important term in educational discourse. In 'Changes in the landscape for creativity in education', Anna Craft gives us an overview of how creativity came to be represented in educational thinking in the UK in three distinct 'waves'. As well as providing a historical overview, the chapter contains a summary of different models of how creativity develops, and a critique of the tensions inherent in teaching in a fast-changing world.

Avril Loveless's chapter 'Thinking about creativity' is an extremely useful summary of different models of creativity. The chapter locates its discussion of creativity much more explicitly on personal responses to questions such as: What wider role do teachers play in both being creative themselves and encouraging creativity in others? One of the central tenets of the chapter is that creative people do not work in isolation. How schools and teachers take up the challenge to draw upon local and global knowledge is exemplified by a case study showing how trainee teachers came to further their own understanding of creativity through working with children and ICT.

There follow three chapters new to this edition of the book. In 'Creative teachers and creative teaching' Teresa Cremin underlines the autonomy of each individual teacher. Truly creative teaching, she says, is one which actively models the processes of making connections and developing curiosity.

In 'Play and playfulness in the Early Years Foundation Stage' Liz Wood challenges the notion that play belongs only in the early years of education. Whilst recognising that societal and technological changes have transformed the way we think of play, the benefits of a play-based approach to creativity which takes account of pupil voice are explored for children across the whole of the primary age phase.

Tony Eaude asks us to consider how the spiritual, moral, social and cultural aspects of creativity can be developed in 'Creativity and spiritual, moral, social and cultural development'. Making links with the Every Child Matters agenda in particular, he sites the place of most influence as being individual teachers rather than government policy: 'Your most important contribution to children's personal development comes from who you are and the way of acting and interacting which you demonstrate.'

Creativity in the core primary curriculum

Parts 2 and 3 of this book tackle creativity in the core and foundation subjects respectively. In Chapter 6 Liz Chamberlain reports on schools who have taken part in the action research project 'Everybody Writes', where the key attitude of teachers was that they remained flexible in their determination to offer children real-life opportunities for writing which were practised across the whole school.

In Chapter 7 Jane Johnston asks 'What is creativity in science education?' Creative science teaching, she says, involves teachers adapting their pedagogy to suit the learning objectives, children and context they find themselves in. Promoting a view of science teaching which develops curiosity, motivation and self esteem, the chapter also reminds us that interaction with peers and supportive adults in the undertaking of exploratory and investigatory tasks are key to successful learning.

Mary Briggs's chapter 'Creative mathematics' is critical of recent curricular recommendations and challenges the reader to re-evaluate mathematics as a creative subject. The chapter argues that children need to be given open-ended and problem-solving tasks which cater for a variety of learning styles in order for their interest and development in mathematics to be sustained.

Creativity in the foundation primary curriculum

In 'Children, creativity and physical education' Sue Chedzoy gives a useful overview of how PE teaching has changed in the postwar period. She sees the key to unlocking creative potential in PE lessons as belonging to individual teachers. Being 'expert', she says, is not as important as feeling secure in setting up safe environments for children and having a basic understanding of how children learn and develop through PE.

Paul Key's chapter, 'Creative and imaginative primary art and design', asks us to consider ourselves as artist–teachers, and to base this not only on the standards set by others but on what we believe to be right. Described as a 'pathway of possibilities', this way of teaching art to children is one which demands flexibility, ambition and trust in pupils' and individuals' instincts and ideas.

Sarah Hennessy, in 'Creativity in the music curriculum', develops further the idea of the teacher as artist, a role which involves risk-taking, confidence, imagination and the mutual handing over of responsibility between teacher and pupils. Using creativity theory developed by Wallas (1926) she presents practical ideas for music teaching based on four stages of the creative process: preparation, incubation, illumination and verification.

In Chapter 12 Richard Woolley adapts the work of the late Hilary Claire to ask: 'What has creativity got to do with citizenship education?' As in previous chapters, this question requires individual teachers to place their own sense of self-esteem, confidence and identity at the core of their citizenship education. Only when we value ourselves, they argue, can we begin to value the 'worth' of others. Using the metaphor of 'journey' to describe citizenship education, teachers are encouraged to set small achievable goals on a road towards greater collaboration, responsibility and autonomy in response to global and societal issues.

In 'Creativity in primary design and technology' Dan Davies and Alan Howe challenge us not to set children artificial problems, but to support them in developing strategies that will help them to think through problems in the midst of designing and making. Synthesising the work of Csikszentmilhalyi (1997, 2002) with good classroom practice, they advocate a style of teaching design and technology which is centred on building on children's interests, identifying real opportunities and using relevant contexts for learning.

The book closes with two further new chapters: Hilary Cooper's 'Creativity in primary history' and Simon Catling's 'Creativity in primary geography'. In the latter we are challenged to 'use children's perspectives; "problematize" the topic; question the "accepted"; become aware of alternative possibilities; create personal responses and meanings; and to make judgments and decisions and justify them'. Hilary Cooper puts it slightly differently. Learning history, she says, requires us to develop and defend arguments, to listen to others and to recognise that there may be no single 'right answer' to the questions we pose in the classroom. As she says, that is part of social, emotional as well as cognitive, growth. Can the goal of education be any more important? And can the need for creative pedagogy which promotes these be any more urgent than it is now?

Anthony Wilson, 2009

PART 1
SETTING THE SCENE

1

Changes in the landscape for creativity in education
Anna Craft

Chapter objectives

By the end of this chapter you should have:

- **understood that creativity is no longer the preserve of arts education;**
- **explored how creative teaching focuses on the teacher;**
- **seen how creativity is critical for individuals to thrive in a rapidly changing world.**

This chapter addresses the following Professional Standards for the award of QTS:

Q1, Q8, Q15, Q25(a)

Introduction

In the last part of the twentieth century and the start of the twenty-first, creativity in education has increasingly become a focus in curriculum and pedagogy. It is now embedded in the Foundation Stage Curriculum and the National Curriculum for schools (England). There has been a substantial investment in staff development and the creation of teaching resources for school teachers.

This chapter explores why the landscape has altered so radically from the policy context which immediately preceded it. It also explores current concepts of creativity in use in education, and strategies used to enhance opportunity for pupils to be creative.

Finally it raises some fundamental tensions and dilemmas that face teachers fostering creativity in education.

What has changed?

The last twenty or so years have seen a global revolution so that in many places creativity has moved from the fringes of education and/or from the arts to being seen as a core aspect of educating. No longer seen as an optional extra, nor as primarily to do with self-expression through the arts, early twenty-first century creativity is seen as generative problem-identification and problem-solving, across life (Craft, 2000, 2001, 2002, 2005).

Three waves of creativity in education

We can describe the change in creativity policy as occurring in three 'waves'.

- The 'first wave' of creativity in education was perhaps in the 1960s, codified by Plowden (CACE, 1967), drawing on child-centred philosophy, policy and practice.
- The second wave began in the late 1990s, about ten years after the introduction of the National Curriculum.
- And the third is well under way in the early years of the twenty-first century.

The first wave: Plowden and beyond

The recommendations of the Central Advisory Council in Education in 1967 (which became known as the Plowden Report), formed thinking about creativity in education for the generation which followed it (CACE, 1967). Drawing on a large body of so-called liberal thinking on the education of children, it recommended that children learn by discovery, taking an active role in both the definition of their curriculum and the exploration of it. Active and individualised learning was strongly encouraged, as well as learning through first-hand experience of the natural, social and constructed world beyond the classroom. A core role was given to play.

Plowden made a significant contribution to the way in which creativity in education was understood. It influenced the early years of education but had an impact on the later primary years and secondary education, too. It provided an early foundation for the more recent move in creativity research towards emphasising social systems rather than personality, cognition or psychodynamics.

Through Plowden, creativity became associated with a range of other approaches: discovery learning, child-centred pedagogy, an integrated curriculum and self- rather than norm-referencing.

However, within the Plowden 'take' on creativity, there are several problems.

The first is the role of knowledge. For while we cannot exercise imagination or creativity in any domain without knowledge if we are to go beyond the given or assumed, Plowden nevertheless implies that a child may be let loose to discover and learn without any prior knowledge.

Secondly, there is a lack of context implied in the rationale for 'self-expression'. Plowden appears to conceive of the child's growth and expression in a moral and ethical vacuum. It has been argued more recently that encouraging children and young people to have ideas and express them should be set in a moral and ethical context within the classroom (Craft, 2000, in press; Fischmann *et al.*, 2004; Gardner, 2004).

Thirdly, Plowden suggests that play provides the foundation for a variety of other forms of knowledge and expression and in doing so appears to connect play creativity within the arts only and not with creativity across the whole curriculum.

Related to the third point is a further problem, which is that play and creativity are not the same as one another, for not all play is creative.

Such conceptual and practical problems, it has been argued (NACCCE, 1999), were in part responsible for creativity being pushed to the back of policy-makers' priorities in curriculum development. Until, that is, the late 1990s, which saw a revival of official recognition of creativity in education: the second wave (Craft, 2002, 2003a, 2004).

The second wave of creativity in education

During the late 1990s, there was a resurgence of interest in psychology and education research. This accompanied policy shifts reintroducing creativity into education.

Three major curriculum-based initiatives occurred.

The National Advisory Committee on Creative and Cultural Education Report

The report linked the fostering of pupil creativity with the development of culture, in that original ideas and action are developed in a shifting cultural context. It suggested that the fostering of pupil creativity would contribute to the cultural development of society, since creativity rarely occurs without some form of interrogation of what has gone before or is occurring synchronously. The Report proposed the idea of democratic creativity, i.e. 'all people are capable of creative achievement in some area of activity, provided the conditions are right and they have acquired the relevant knowledge and skills' (paragraph 25). This notion has some connection with Plowden, in that children's self-expression is valued and all people are seen as capable of creativity. But it *contrasts* with the Plowden approach too. First, it argues for the acquisition of knowledge and skills as the necessary foundation to creativity – reflecting the wider research context in the 'situating' of knowledge. Secondly, it has a great deal more to say on creativity than Plowden since that was its main focus. Criticisms of the NACCCE Report are very few. Since its publication, it has increasingly informed the way that creativity is being developed in the codified curriculum for Foundation Stage and beyond.

'Creative development' in Foundation Stage and Early Years Foundation Stage

The codifying of this part of the Early Years curriculum for children up to the age of five in 2000, reinforced in 2007, meshed closely with the existing norms and discourse about early education. 'Creative development' in both sets of policy guidance encompasses art, craft and design, imaginative play, music and dance, all of which have traditionally formed a core part of Early Years provision. It emphasises the role of imagination and of children developing and deepening a range of ways of responding to experiences and expressing and communicating ideas and feelings through a wide range of media and materials. In the 2007 guidance, creativity and critical thinking is seen as a core aspect of provision, allowing children to make connections, transform understanding and develop sustained, shared thinking. It involves valuing creativity and critical thinking right across the curriculum and balancing freedom with structure. In addition, creative development continues to be named as one of the six areas of learning and development and comprises being creative (responding to experiences, communicating and expressing ideas), exploring materials and media, creating music and dance, and developing imagination and imaginative play. It emphasises the need to support children in exploratory risk-taking, absorption in their activities, initiating ideas, choices and decisions, and recognising novelty in children's explorations. It includes, very significantly, offering children opportunities to 'work alongside artists and other creative adults' (DfES, 2007, card Creative Development, side 2).

Codifying creativity within the early learning curriculum has been a significant landmark; particularly in the 2007 version which acknowledges that problem-finding and problem-solving using imagination and posing 'what if?' questions occur within a whole range of domains. On the other hand there are at least two difficulties with seeing creativity in terms of 'development'.

Firstly, conceiving of creativity as something which may be 'developed' implies that there is a ceiling, or a static end-state, and that, given the appropriate immediate learning environment, children will 'develop'. Both presuppositions are problematic.

Secondly, the implication is that play and creativity are the same. As already suggested, they are not. Play may be, but is not necessarily, creative. For example, 'Snakes and Ladders', being dependent upon a mix of chance and a set structure, is not creative, but 'Hide and Seek' may well be. Similarly, imaginative play may be imitative but it may equally be highly creative.

'Creative thinking' named as a key skill in the National Curriculum

This contrasts with the Early Years formulation in seeing a *cross-curricular* role for creativity in the aims of the school curriculum, suggesting that creativity is not the preserve of the arts alone but that it arises in all domains of human endeavour.

Criticisms of the National Curriculum focused on the lack of exploration of how this skill was manifest in different curriculum areas, although at the time of writing the 2nd Edition of this text (Summer, 2008), the primary National Curriculum is under review. It seems very likely that the new formulation will reflect the 2007 formulation of the KS3 curriculum (DfES, 2007), to be implemented from September 2008. This includes six personal learning and thinking skills (PTLS), one of which is creative thinking, reflecting the NACCCE definition.

All kinds of other policy initiatives have flowed from these major developments in the second wave. These include the following:

- *Excellence in Cities*, a scheme to replace Education Action Zones and designed to raise achievement particularly in the inner city, was launched in 1999. Targeted to start with at secondary schools and then introduced to primary schools too, this programme was believed to have led to higher attainment in both GCSEs and vocational equivalents for pupils whose schools were in the scheme. Some schools and action zones focused on creativity (DfES, 2005a; OFSTED, 2004).
- For several years at the end of the 1990s and start of the 2000s, DfES Best Practice Research Scholarships and Professional Bursaries for teachers enabled teachers to research creativity in their classrooms (DfES, 2005b). From 2004 the theme was continued through the Creativity Action Research Awards offered by Creative Partnerships and DfES (Creative Partnerships, 2004).
- OFSTED took a positive and encouraging perspective on creativity through two reports published in August 03: *Improving City Schools: How the Arts Can Help* (OFSTED, 2003b) and Raising Achievement

Through the Arts (OFSTED, 2003b).
- DfES published *Excellence and Improvement* in May 2003 (DfES, 2003), exhorting primary schools to take creative and innovative approaches to the curriculum and to place creativity high on their agendas following this in 2004 with materials.
- DfES established the Innovation Unit with the brief to foster and nurture creative and innovative approaches to teaching and learning.
- DfES funded research, development and CPD initiatives including the Creative Action Research Awards (Craft *et al.*, 2007).
- The Arts Council and DCMS became integrally bound into the delivery of Creative Partnerships and associated activities (Creative Partnerships, 2005).
- A creativity strand was established within the DTI from the end of the 1990s (DTI, 2005).
- The National College for School Leadership developed the notion of Creative Leadership for fostering creativity in pupils (NCSL, 2005).
- DfES introduced 'personalised learning' (DfES, 2004a, 2004b, 2004d).
- QCA developed creativity CPD materials for Foundation Stage through to KS2 (QCA, 2005a, 2005b).

The work of the QCA in this second wave is particularly significant as a landmark. It attempted to both describe and promote creativity in schools, through its creativity curriculum development and research project launched in 2000, *Creativity: Find it! Promote it!* Drawing on the NACCCE definition of creativity, QCA added an emphasis on purposeful shaping of imagination, producing original and valuable outcomes. It aimed to exemplify creativity across the curriculum, through a framework providing early years and school settings with both a lens and strategies for finding and promoting creativity. Specifically, the QCA suggest that creativity involves pupils in thinking or behaviour involving

- questioning and challenging
- making connections, seeing relationships
- envisaging what might be
- exploring ideas, keeping options open
- reflecting critically on ideas, actions, outcomes

(QCA, 2005a, 2005b).

There are many other aspects to the framework, including suggestions for pedagogical strategies and ways in which whole schools might develop their creativity.

The model of learning which underpins the QCA framework, is found commonly in what might be called second- to third-wave work in creativity, including that which focuses on creative partnerships of a variety of kinds. For it assumes, perhaps unsurprisingly, that creativity is situated in a social and cultural context. A *situated* perspective, then, it emphasises the practical, social, intellectual and values-based practices and approaches involved in creative activities. From this perspective, 'creative learning' is seen as an apprenticeship into these, a central role being given to the expert adult, offering induction to the relative novice.

Aspects of apprenticeship include:

- **modelling expertise and approaches**
  When the adults taking a lead role in stimulating young people to work creatively are creative practitioners in their own fields, they offer novices ways into their own artistic practices. This model of

teaching and learning could be seen as quite different to that of the traditional classroom teacher in a school (Craft *et al.*, 2004).

● **authenticity of task**

The more closely the activities generated by the adult expert correspond to those that form part of their normal professional life, the greater the likelihood that pupils will be able to effectively integrate propositional and procedural knowledge, and the greater the chances of learners finding personal relevance and meaning in them too (Murphy *et al.*, 2004). This is sometimes referred to as 'cultural authenticity'.

● **locus of control**

It is very important that the locus of control rests with the young person (Jeffrey, 2001a, 2001b, 2003a, 2003b, 2004; Jeffrey and Woods, 2003; Woods 1990, 1993, 1995, 2002). Connected with this, the *quality of interactions* between adults and pupils determines, in large part, the decision-making authority.

● **genuine risk-taking**

If the locus of control resides with the pupils, this can facilitate greater and more authentic risk-taking than might otherwise have been undertaken.

When creative practitioners lead the apprenticeship, children can see work created as part of the leader's own artistic or commercial practices, and are therefore engaged in coming to understand the artist's own ways of working.

The model of creative learning as apprenticeship implies ownership by children of ideas, processes and directions, together with engagement in and motivation toward, their own creative journey. But an apprenticeship is finite. Ultimately the novice becomes a newly fledged expert, taking off without the scaffolding, travelling alone or with others, making their own map. Griffiths and Woolf (2004) document the ways in which skilful creative practitioners are sensitised to when it is appropriate to encourage young people to move to the edge of, and then beyond, the scaffolding.

There are two other issues touched on but perhaps not yet adequately explored, by the QCA framework in this particular incarnation.

● **What is the relationship between individual and collective work?**

How do the two interact? Although this question has been examined by researchers over some twenty years at least (Amabile, 1983, 1988, 1996, 1997; Craft, 1997; John-Steiner, 2000; Miell and Littleton, 2004; Sonnenburg, 2004; Wegerif, 2004), it is still not well understood.

One aspect of the individual/collective negotiation is negotiating the balance between the creative needs of the individual and the collective creative needs of a group. Nourishment and support for the individual occurs in a wider social context. Seeing how ideas are responded to is a part of this, and therefore so is evaluative two-way feedback in written, dramatic, symbol-based and other forms. The creator should be able to negotiate meaning and possible implications with evaluators.

● **Models of how creativity can be fostered**

It may not be fruitful to consider creativity as being 'triggered' in any simple or direct way. As with all social science, it is very hard to be sure of cause–effect relationships. But we do have some working hypotheses implied in some key terms: teaching for creativity, creative teaching and creative learning.

Creative teaching is focused on the teacher. Studies suggest that teachers feel creative when they control and take ownership of their practice, are innovative and ensure that learning is relevant to learners, envisaging possibilities and differences, seeing these through into action (Jeffrey and Woods, 2003; Woods and Jeffrey, 1996).

Teaching for creativity by contrast focuses on the child and is often 'learner inclusive' (Jeffrey and Craft, 2004; Jeffrey and Woods, 2003). A learner inclusive pedagogy involves giving the child many choices and a great deal of control over what is explored and how. It is, essentially, learner-centred (Jeffrey and Craft, 2004).

Research suggests that a teacher who is successful in stimulating children's creativity does some or all of the following:

- encourages development of purposeful outcomes across the curriculum;
- develops children's motivation to be creative;
- fosters the study of any discipline in depth, developing children's knowledge of it, to enable them to go beyond their own immediate experiences and observations;
- offers a clear curriculum and time structure to children but involves them in the creation of new routines when appropriate;
- provides an environment where children are rewarded for going beyond what is expected;
- uses language to both stimulate and assess imaginativeness;
- helps children to find personal relevance in learning activities;
- models the existence of alternatives while also helping children to learn about and understand existing conventions;
- encourages additional and alternative ways of being and doing, celebrating, where appropriate to do so, their courage to be different;
- gives children enough time to incubate their ideas.

(*Sources*: Balke, 1997; Beetlestone, 1998; Craft, 2000; Edwards and Springate,1995; Fryer, 1996; Halliwell, 1993; Hubbard, 1996; Jeffrey and Woods, 2003; Kessler, 2000; Shallcross, 1981; Torrance, 1984; Woods, 1990, 1993, 1995; Woods and Jeffrey, 1996.)

OFSTED (2003a, 2003b) would add to this the significance of:

- partnership;
- authentic relationships with the social, economic, cultural and physical environment.

The middle ground between creative teaching and teaching for creativity has been gradually expanded to include a relatively new term in the discourse: 'creative learning', which has been described as a 'middle ground' between teaching for creativity and creative teaching, emphasising the learner's experience (Jeffrey and Craft, 2006). So what does this term mean? European work (Jeffrey and Craft, 2006) suggests that it involves learners in using their imagination and experience to develop learning, that it involves them strategically collaborating over tasks and contributing to the classroom pedagogy and to the curriculum, and it also involves them critically evaluating their own learning practices and teachers' performance. It offers them, in many ways, a form of apprenticeship.

Nevertheless, the teaching profession and other collaborative partners still have a long way to go in characterising creative learning as distinct from other kinds of learning (Cochrane *et al.*, 2008).

During the second wave of creativity, then, there were common themes to many of the policy initiatives, for example:

- role of the arts;
- social inclusion;
- raising achievement;
- exploratiion of leadership;
- place of partnerships.

Within the research community both prior to and during the second wave, there was a matched growth. After a relatively fallow period from the 1970s until the late 1980s, the last part of the twentieth century saw greatly increased activity in creativity research as applied to education.

Research foci included the conceptualising of creativity (Craft, 1997, 2001, 2002; Fryer, 1996), exploring how creativity could be fostered and maintained (Jeffrey, 2001a, 2001b), investigation of creativity in specific domains such as information and communications technology (Leach, 2001), documenting creative teaching (Woods and Jeffrey, 1996) and exploring creative leadership (Imison, 2001; NCSL, 2005).

In common with other educational and social science research a significant direction of research into creativity, both within education and beyond it, has been to situate within it a social psychological framework which recognises the role of social structures and colla- borative practices in fostering individual creativity (Jeffrey and Craft, 2001; Miell and Littleton, 2004; Rhyammar and Brolin, 1999).

Since the 1990s, research into creativity has focused more on the creativity of ordinary people within aspects of education, what Boden calls 'p' creativity (Boden, 2001). The methodology for investigating creativity in education has also shifted, from large-scale studies aiming to measure creativity toward ethnographic, qualitative approaches to research focusing on the actual site of operations and practice, again contextualising crea- tivity in the social and cultural values and practices of both the underlying disciplines and the particular setting. There has also been a move toward philosophical discussions around the nature of creativity (Craft, 2002).

This was – and is – quite distinct from the earlier climate, in its changed emphasis on:

- characterising, rather than measuring;
- ordinary creativity rather than genius;
- complexity rather than simplicity;
- encompassing views of creativity which include products but do not see these as necessary;
- emphasis on the social system rather than the individual;
- recognitiion of creativity as situated, not 'universalised'.

The third wave: a tsunami?

The first years of the twenty-first century have, then, seen a gradual move from a second to a third wave, which goes beyond seeing creativity as universalised, to characterising it as everyday (Craft, 2001, 2002, 2005; Feldman, 1999) – seeing creativity as necessary for all at a critical period for our species and for our planet. For the children in our schools will help to shape the world in which they grow up and in which we grow old. Their ability to find solutions to the problems they inherit from us and to grow beyond the restrictions we have placed upon our own world-view will, more than in any other generation, define the future of our species and our planet.

The third wave can be viewed as a 'tsunami', or tidal wave, of change, reflecting under-pinning seismic shifts that now see creativity as fundamental to 21st century learning and living. The third wave policies all have their foundations in the second wave, and include:

- The Roberts Review (2006)
- Select Committee (2007)
- Creative Economy Strategy (2008).

The Roberts Review and the Government's response to it

The Roberts Review was perhaps the most significant of the third wave policies, in further codifying creativity in the curriculum and channelling the tsunami of change into an economic position and one which would also enhance learner engagement and inclusion. The review was established in late 2005 by the Department for Culture, Media and Sport (DCMS) and Department for Education and Skills (DfES). Led by Paul Roberts, a civil servant, it was established to consider initiatives under way to support the creative and cultural development of young people and creativity in schools since the 1999 NACCCE Report, as well as considering how creativity as a set of skills could be poised to feed the creative and cultural industries, helping to establish Britain as the world's 'Creative Hub' (Purnell, 2005).

The Roberts Review (DfES, 2006) mapped out a framework for creativity, including provision in the early years, extended schools, building schools for the future, leadership in creative teaming, initial teacher education, professional development, partnerships, frameworks of regulation and support, and introduced the idea of the individual creative portfolio, arguing creativity is a key part of the development of young citizens.

The Government's response, in late 2006, committed to the recommendations made in the Roberts Review. It emphasised the cross-curricular approach to creativity as broader than the arts, and indicated the need to retain high standards alongside creative engagement. This should include opportunities across the curriculum, some of these involving creative partnership, and creativity should be nurtured through teacher development and school leadership; support for developing these priorities was to come from both DfES and DCMS. It confirmed the QCA version of the NACCCE definition of creativity, stating:

We believe, as QCA makes clear, that:

- Creativity involves thinking or behaving – **imaginatively**;
- This imaginative activity is **purposeful**: that is, it is directed to achieving an objective;
- These processes must generate something **original**;
- The outcome must be of **value** in relation to the objective.
(DCMS/DfES, 2006, p4)

The eight areas of commitment made by Government at this point were:

- the development of a *Creative Portfolio*, in a wide range of settings and reflecting creative industries-related activities;

- a commitment to the *Early Years*, ensuring that creativity remains at the heart of the Foundation Stage, and that creative practice is encouraged and rewarded;
- development of creativity within *Extended Schools*, paying attention to supporting schools to mirror this within formal provision;
- closer attention to the development of the *Building Schools for the Future* (BSF) programme to provide inspirationally designed built environments to nurture creative engagement, involving young people in this process;
- developing further support for *Leading Creative Learning* through head teachers and other school leaders, to regard 'every subject as a creative subject', considering how both initial teacher education and continuing professional development may contribute to this;
- fostering appropriate and systemic *Practitioner Partnerships* between schools and creative industries and partnerships with particular attention to the future of the Creative Partnerships programme;
- mapping access and progression routes of *Pathways to Creative Industries*, through apprenticeship frameworks and diplomas;
- further development of *Frameworks and Regulation* such that the holistic, enquiry-based approaches of the Primary and Secondary National Strategies are supported through development of the Ofsted subject surveys and other regulatory frameworks.

A Board (The Cultural and Creative Education Board – CCEAB) was established in late 2006 to progress the recommendations of the Roberts Report and over the year of its existence, laid increasing emphasis on 'cultural learning' rather than 'creative learning'. It was perhaps unsurprising, then, that the McMaster report (2008), commissioned by the Secretary of State for Culture, Media and Sport, to explore how the public sector might encourage innovation, risk-taking and excellence, describes it as a 'cultural' rather than 'creative' learning programme, and that in February, 2008, Government launched the 'Cultural Offer', ten regional pilots for which were to sit within the Youth Culture Trust, within a slimmed-down Creative Partnerships organisation (DCMS, Feb 2008).

The Education Select Committee report (2007) and the Government's response (2008)

The House of Commons Education Select Committee (2007), was focused on creative partnership in particular. Entitled *Creative Partnerships and the Curriculum*, it argued creativity was a set of skills relevant across the curriculum, broader than the arts, and suggested there was an 'urgent' need to prioritise 'developing new methods of assessing incremental progress' stating that 'existing measures of progress which focus on the attainment of Key Stages, are unlikely to capture small but steady improvements, or progress in areas such as self-confidence, and team-working' (ibid, para 28, page 17).

The Government response to this report, recognised that 'creativity is not just about the arts … it applies across all subjects.' (House of Commons Children, Schools and Families Committee, January, 2008, Appendix, page 1), also stated that 'both Departments consider that Creative Partnerships' principal focus should remain on the arts and culture' (ibid, p3).

Creative Economy Strategy (2008)

This document, published by the Government in February 2008, shortly after the response to the Select Committee on Creative Partnerships brought together a number of aspects of creativity in relation to the economy, initiated in 2005. It focused on creativity as a set of skills to be developed in relation to careers and progression into the creative and cultural industries. As Cochrane *et al*, (2008) argue, two clear narratives were evident from it. The first focuses on 'nurturing talent' to enable young people to progress into careers and further education in the arts, cultural and creative industries. The second focuses on broader support for 'cultural learning' embedded in the Cultural Offer (Creative Partnerships, 2008).

Taken together, these three initiatives alone provide a powerful recognition of creativity and culture as embedded in education for children and young people of all ages. They emerge, too, in the context of a developing framework for ensuring that Every Child Matters, which has led to interprofessional practices to ensure that children and young people thrive. The 2007 Children's Plan identified creativity as important (albeit in terms of the economy), the (at the time of writing) current independent review of the primary curriculum is working to a remit given by the Secretary of State in January 2008, to ensure that the new curriculum both encourages creativity and inspires a lifelong commitment to learning. The DfES Manifesto to Learning Outside the Classroom (DfES, 2006) also urges the need to respond to children's curiosity and to nurture creativity.

The shift toward cultural development seems significant; at the time of writing the second edition of this book, it remains unclear whether creativity or culture, or both, will remain the main priority. Whilst the most recent shifts in England have been toward cultural development, the European Union plans to announce 2009 as the European Year of Creativity and Innovation, which shifts the emphasis back again toward creativity. What seems undisputable is that this is a period in which creativity, culture and innovation are highly valued, particularly in relation to the 'creative economy'.

Why the changing landscape?

The reasons for this resurrection of interest and the shift from a first to a second and then to a third wave of change to the landscape of creativity emerge from a mix of political, economic and social change.

The globalisation of economic activity has brought with it increased competitiveness for markets, driving the need for nation states to raise the levels of educational achievement of their potential labour forces (Jeffrey and Craft, 2001). Changes in our economy mean an increased proportion of small businesses or organisations, employing less than five people and with a turnover of less than £500,000 (Carter *et al*., 2004). Employment in no organisation is for life. We have shifted our core business from manufacturing to a situation where 'knowledge is the primary source of economic productivity' (Seltzer and Bentley, 1999, p9).

Education has, of course, a dynamic relationship with this shifting world of employment and the wider economy. In response to changes in these domains, what is considered significant in terms of educational achievement is changing.

It is no longer merely sufficient to have excellence in depth and grasp of knowledge. Critical to surviving and thriving is, instead, creativity. For it is creativity which enables a person to identify appropriate problems and to solve them. It is creativity that identifies possibilities and opportunities that may not have been noticed by others. And it is argued that creativity forms the backbone of the economy based on knowledge (Robinson, 2001).

In the wider social environment, certitudes are in many ways on the decrease. Roles and relationships in family and community structures, unchanging for centuries, are shifting fast;

a young person growing up in the twenty-first century has a much more active role than perhaps ever before in making sense of their experiences and making choices about their own life (Craft, 2001).

And alongside all this, information and communication technology plays an increasing role, both offering potential for creativity and demanding it.

All this change in the economic, political, social and technological context means that our conceptualisations of creativity, how to investigate and foster it, are changing. An aspect of the third wave in creativity is that the notion of creativity as 'universalised' is now common-place, i.e. the perspective that everybody is capable of being creative given the right environment (Jeffrey and Craft, 2001).

But the third wave also problematises creativity. It has brought with it exploration of the tensions and dilemmas encapsulated in fostering it.

Tensions and dilemmas

There are some fundamental tensions and dilemmas inherent in developing creativity. They are rather more than mere tensions between policy and practice although these too pose serious challenges in perspective, disconnected curricula and curriculum organisation to name a few.

There are at least four much more fundamental challenges, bearing in mind that in this third wave the education of children must nurture the creativity which will determine their ability to survive and flourish in a chaotic world.

Culture and creativity

There is growing evidence (for example, Ng, 2003; Nisbett, 2003) that creativity is mani-fested and defined in different cultural contexts. To what extent can and should we take account of this in a multicultural learning environment? It has been argued that it is impera-tive that we do address these possible differences in the ways that we foster creativity in the classroom (Craft, 2005). And yet, in these times when teachers and creative partners are still celebrating the relative freedoms afforded by increased policy support for creativity, and therefore not perhaps critically scrutinising their practices in ways that they might later do, there is little sign of this occurring at present.

Creativity and the environment

How does creativity impact on the wider environment? For the creativity we are experien-cing is anchored in a global marketplace that has a powerful influence on values. It is heavily marketised, so that wants are substituted for needs, convenience lifestyles and image are increasingly seen as significant and form part of a 'throw-away' culture where make-do-and-mend are oldspeak, and short shelf-life and built-in obsolescence are seen to be positive. In this marketised context, the drive to innovate ever further perhaps becomes an end in itself. And this occurs against a rising global population and an increasing imbalance between nations in the consumption of reducing world resources. How appropriate is this? What significance do we accord the evaluation of *the impact* of our ideas on others or on our wider environment? For to do so might mean seeing creativity in perhaps a more spiritual way in terms of fulfilment, individual or collective. And so it could also mean taking a different kind of existential slant on life (Craft, 2006).

Ethics

This is of course related to the environmental point. We want to encourage children's choices, but in a wider social and ethical context. What kind of world do we create where the market is seen as God? And how can we see creativity divorced from its ends? For the human imagination is capable of immense destruction as well as infinitely constructive possibilities. How do we balance these? An aspect of the teacher's role is to encourage children to examine the possible wider effects of their own ideas and those of others and to determine worth in the light of these. This, of course, means the balancing of conflicting perspectives and values – which may themselves be irreconcilable, particularly where they stem from fundamentalist beliefs (Craft, 2005).

Such fundamental challenges clearly leave us with pedagogical challenges. For example, if creativity is culturally specific how do we foster it in a multicultural classroom? And how do we rise to the direct and indirect challenges posed by creativity linked to the market? How far does creativity in the classroom reflect or challenge the status quo?

Wise creativity

Stemming from all three of the previous challenges, is the question of how creativity is fostered with wisdom in schools, since the development of policy can be seen as under-pinned by Western individualism, in relation to a globalised market economy which brings with 'blindness' to diversity in culture and values (Craft, 2008), a dissipation of trust and responsibility (Gardner, 2008) and a reluctance to consider what 'good' or 'wise' creativity might involve (Claxton, 2008). The time has perhaps come to explore how responsibility is equal to self-realisation, to recognise the intuitive and other resonances between our own actions and those of others; to recognise dispositions which may enable us to foster in the classroom creativity which dares to consider a moral role for creativity beyond current, economy-bound and habitual horizons (Craft *et al.*, 2008).

We have a challenging agenda ahead of us in education, but an exciting one.

REFLECTIVE TASK

- How familiar are the three creativity waves in your own experience of fostering creativity in education?
- How can you go about using the QCA framework to help you identify and promote creativity in learning?
- To what extent do partnership and apprenticeship form a part of your own pedagogy?
- How can you document children's perspectives about creative learning experiences?
- Which of the fundamental tensions and dilemmas could you begin to address in your own practice, and how?

A SUMMARY OF **KEY POINTS**

Changes in the landscape for creativity in education:

> No longer the preserve of the arts or arts education, creativity has moved from the fringes of educational concern to being seen as a core aspect of educating, which pertains to all aspects of human endeavour.

> Creative teaching focuses on the teacher. Studies suggest that teachers feel creative when they are in control and take ownership of their practice. *Teaching for creativity* focuses on the learner and includes giving the child many choices over what is explored and how.

> 'Creative learning' is a phrase which explores the middle ground between creative teaching and teaching for creativity. This involves learners using their imagination and experience to develop learning while strategically collaborating over tasks, critically evaluating their own teachers' practices. This mode of teaching often involves an 'apprenticeship' approach.

> In a world of rapid economic and social change it is no longer sufficient to have excellence in depth and grasp of knowledge. Wise creativity is critical for individuals to thrive and survive in the twenty-first century. This is because wise creativity enables a person to identify appropriate problems, possibilities and opportunities and to solve them in ways which others may not notice.

MOVING *ON* > > > > > > MOVING *ON* > > > > > > MOVING *ON*

In developing your own practice in fostering children's Creativity keep in mind three key questions.

What am I trying to nurture? Familiarise yourself with the NACCCE definition developed by QCA: creativity as imagination that is purposeful, leading to original and valuable outcomes. Try to be specific about how you can foster this in children you work with.

How can I do this? Consider resources, including people within and beyond school that you could work with to nurture children's creativity, enabling children in navigating choices and possibilities.

Why am I trying to develop children's creativity? How does your practice relate to the creative and cultural agenda? How far does it reflect the themes of creativity and innovation? How can you encourage children to develop 'wise' creativity in your classroom?

REFERENCES REFERENCES **REFERENCES** REFERENCES **REFERENCES** REFERENCES

Amabile, TM (1983) *The social psychology of creativity.* New York: Springer Verlag.

Amabile, TM (1988) A model of creativity and innovation in organizations, in Staw, BM and Cunnings, LL (eds) *Research in organizational behavior.* Greenwich, CT: JAI Press.

Amabile, TM (1996) *Creativity in context* (update to *The social psychology of creativity*). Boulder, CO: Westview Press.

Amabile, TM (1997) Motivating creativity in organisations: on doing what you love and loving what you do. *California Management Review,* 40:1.

Balke, E (1997) Play and the arts: the importance of the 'unimportant'. *Childhood Education,* 73:6, 353–60.

Beetlestone, F (1998) *Creative children, imaginative teaching.* Buckingham: Open University Press.

Carter, S, Mason, C and Tagg, S (2004) *Lifting the barriers to growth in UK small businesses: the FSB biennial membership survey, Report to the Federation of Small Businesses.* London: Federation of Small Businesses.

Central Advisory Council for Education in England (CACE) (1967) *Children and their primary schools, Report of the Central Advisory Council for Education in England* (The Plowden Report). London: HMSO.

Claxton, G (2008) Wisdom: Advanced Creativity?, in Craft, A, Gardner, H, Claxton, G, *et al. Creativity, wisdom and trusteeship: exploring the role of education.* Thousand Oaks, CA: Corwin Press.

Cochrane, P, Craft, A and Jeffery, G (2008) Mixed messages or permissions and opportunities? Reflections on current policy perspectives on creativity in education. Paper produced for Creative Partnerships Seminar 13 February 2008 (revised for publication April 2008).

Craft, A (1997) Identity and creativity: education for post-modernism? *Teacher Development: International Journal of Teachers' Professional Development*, 1:1, 83–96.

Craft, A (2000) *Creativity across the primary curriculum: framing and developing practice.* Abingdon: RoutledgeFalmer.

Craft, A (2001) Little c creativity, in Craft, A, Jeffrey, B and Leibling, M (eds), *Creativity in education.* London: Continuum.

Craft, A (2002) *Creativity and Early Years education.* London: Continuum.

Craft, A (2003a) Early Years education in England and little c creativity: the third wave? *Korean Journal of Thinking and Problem Solving*, 13:1, 49–57.

Craft, A (2004) Creative thinking in the Early Years of education, in Fryer, M (ed.), *Creativity and cultural diversity.* Leeds: Creativity Centre Educational Trust.

Craft, A (2005) *Creativity in schools: tensions and dilemmas.* Abingdon: RoutledgeFalmer.

Craft, A (2008) Tensions in Creativity and Education: Enter Wisdom and Trusteeship?, in Craft, A, Gardner, H and Claxton, G (2008) *Creativity, wisdom and trusteeship: exploring the role of education.* Thousand Oaks, CA: Corwin Press.

Craft, A, Chappell, K and Best, P (2007) Analysis of the Creativity Action Research Awards Two (CARA2) Programme. Final Report, October 2007. Available at http://education.exeter.ac.uk/ projects. php?id=100

Craft, A, Gardner, H and Claxton, G (2008) *Creativity, wisdom and trusteeship: exploring the role of education.* Thousand Oaks, CA: Corwin Press.

Creative Partnerships (2008) Available at: http://www.creative-partnerships.com/ (accessed January 2008).

Department for Children, Schools and Families (2007) *The children's plan.* London: The Stationery Office. Retrieved 15 April 2008 www.dcsf.gov.uk/childrensplan/downloads/The_Childrens_Plan. pdf

Department for Culture, Media and Sport and Department for Education and Skills (2006) *Nurturing creativity and young people.* London: HMSO.

Department for Culture, Media and Sport and Department for Education and Skills (2006) *Government response to nurturing creativity and young people.* London: HMSO.

Department for Culture, Media and Sport (2008) Joint DCMS/DCSF Press Release on the Cultural Offer, 13 February.

Department for Culture, Media and Sport (DCMS) Department for Business, Enterprise and Regulatory Reform (BERR) and Department for Innovation, Universities and Skills (DIUS) (2008) *Creative Britain: new talents for the creative economy.* London: DCMS.

Department for Education and Employment (DfEE) (1999a) *All our futures: creativity, culture and education.* The National Advisory Committee's Report on Creative and Cultural Education. London: HMSO.

Department for Education and Skills (DfES) (2003) *Excellence and enjoyment.* London: HMSO.

Department for Education and Skills (DfES) (2004a) *A national conversation about personalised learning.* Nottingham: DfES Publications.

Department for Education and Skills (DfES) (2004c) *High quality PE and sport for young people: a guide to recognising and achieving high quality PE and sport in schools.* London: DfES.

Department for Education and Skills (DfES) (2004d) *Personalised learning for every child, personalised contact for every teacher.* London: DfES.

Department for Education and Skills (DfES) (2005a) See website: www.standards.dfee.gov.uk/ excellence.

Department for Education and Skills (DfES) (2005b) See website: www.teachernet.gov.uk/ professionaldevelopment/resourcesandresearch/bprs/search/

Department for Education and Skills (2006) *Learning outside the classroom manifesto*. London: DfES Available at: http://publications.teachernet.gov.uk/eOrderingDownload/LOtC.pdf

Department for Education and Skills (2007) *The Early Years Foundation Stage*. London: DfES.

Edwards, CP and Springate, KW (1995) Encouraging creativity in early childhood classrooms. *ERIC Digest*. Washington, DC: ERIC Clearing House on Elementary and Early Childhood Education.

Feldman, DH (1999) The development of creativity, in Sternberg, RJ (ed.), *Handbook of creativity*. Cambridge: Cambridge University Press.

Fischmann, W, Solomon, B, Greenspan, D and Gardner, H (2004) *Making good: how young people cope with moral dilemmas at work*. Cambridge, MA: Harvard University Press.

Fryer, M (1996) *Creative teaching and learning*. London: Paul Chapman Publishing.

Gardner, H (2004) *Can there be societal trustees in America today?* Working paper, Harvard Graduate School of Education, http://pzweb.harvard.edu/eBookstore/PDFs/GoodWork43.pdf

Gardner, H (2008) Creativity, wisdom and trusteeship, in Craft, A, Gardner, H, Claxton, G, *et al.* (2008) *Creativity, wisdom and trusteeship: exploring the role of education.* Thousand Oaks, CA: Corwin Press.

Halliwell, S (1993) Teacher creativity and teacher education, in Bridges, D and Kerry, T, *Developing teachers professionally*. Abingdon: Routledge.

House of Commons Education and Skills Committee (2007) *Creative partnerships and the curriculum. Eleventh Report of Session 2006–07. Report, together with formal minutes, oral and written evidence.* London: The Stationery Office Limited.

House of Commons Children, Schools and Families Committee (2008). *Creative partnerships and the curriculum: government response to the eleventh report from the Education and Skills Committee, Session 2006–07.* London: The Stationery Office Limited.

Hubbard, RS (1996) *A workshop of the possible: nurturing children's creative development.* York, ME: Stenhouse Publishers.

Imison, T (2001) Creative leadership: innovative practices in a secondary school, in Craft, A, Jeffrey, B and Leibling, M (eds), *Creativity in education*. London: Continuum.

Jeffrey, B (2001a) Challenging prescription in ideology and practice: the case of Sunny first school, in Collins, J, Insley, K and Soler, J (eds), *Developing pedagogy: researching practice.* London: Paul Chapman Publishing.

Jeffrey, B (2001b) Primary pupils' perspectives and creative learning, *Encyclopaideia* 9, Spring (Italian journal).

Jeffrey, B (2003a) Countering student instrumentalism: a creative response. *British Educational Research Journal,* 29:4, 489–503.

Jeffrey, B (2003b) *Creative learning and student perspectives*. CLASP Report. Swindon: ESRC.

Jeffrey, B (2004a) *End of award report: creative learning and student perspectives* (CLASP) *Project,* submitted to ESRC, November 2004.

Jeffrey, B (2004b) *Meaningful creative learning: learners' perspectives*. Paper given at the ECER conference, Crete. See website: www.esrcsocietytoday.ac.uk/ESRCInfoCentre/ViewAwardPage. aspx?AwardId=2254

Jeffrey, B and Craft, A (2001) The universalization of creativity in education, in Craft, A, Jeffrey, B and Leibling, M (eds), *Creativity in education*. London: Continuum.

Jeffrey, B and Craft, A (2004) Teaching creatively and teaching for creativity: distinctions and relationships. *Educational Studies*, 30:1, 77–87.

Jeffrey, B and Woods, P (2003) *The creative school: a framework for success, quality and effectiveness*. Abingdon and New York: RoutledgeFalmer.

John-Steiner, V (2000) *Creative collaboration*. New York: Oxford University Press.

Kessler, R (2000) *The soul of education: helping students find connection, compassion and character at school*. Alexandria, VA: Association for Supervision and Curriculum Development.

Leach, J (2001) A hundred possibilities: creativity, community and ICT, in Craft, A, Jeffrey, B and Leibling, M (eds), *Creativity in education*. London: Continuum.

McMaster, Sir B (2008) *Supporting excellence in the arts: from measurement to judgement.* London: Department for Culture, Media and Sport.

Miell, D and Littleton, K (2004) *Collaborative creativity*. London: Free Association Books.

National Advisory Committee on Creative and Cultural Education (NACCCE) (1999) *All our futures: creativity, culture and education* (The Roberts Report). London: DfEE.

National College for School Leadership (NCSL) (2005) See website: http://www.ncsl.org.uk/research-index/research_activities-index/randd-activities-creativity.htm

Ng, AK (2003) A cultural model of creative and conforming behaviour. *Creativity Research Journal*, 15:2 and 3, 223–33.

Nisbett, R E (2003) *The geography of thought*. New York: Free Press.

Office for Standards in Education (OFSTED) (2004) *Excellence in cities' primary extension: real stories*, document reference HM12394. See website: www.ofsted. gov.uk

Qualifications and Curriculum Authority (QCA) (2005a) *Creativity: Find It! Promote It! – promoting pupils' creative thinking and behaviour across the curriculum at Key Stages 1, 2 and 3 – practical materials for schools*. London: Qualifications and Curriculum Authority.

Qualifications and Curriculum Authority (QCA) (2005b) See website: www.ncaction.org.uk/creativity/about.htm.

Seltzer, K and Bentley, T (1999) *The creative age: knowledge and skills for the new economy*. London: Demos.

Shallcross, DJ (1981) *Teaching creative behavior: how to teach creativity to children of all ages*. Englewood Cliffs, NJ: Prentice-Hall.

Sonnenburg, S (2004) Creativity in communication: a theoretical framework for collaborative product creation. *Creativity and Innovation Management*, 13:4, 254–62.

Torrance, EP (1984) *Mentor relationships: how they aid creative achievement, endure, change and die*. Buffalo, NY: Bearly.

Wegerif, R (2004) *Reason and creativity in classroom dialogues*. Unpublished paper based on seminar given at The Open Creativity Centre Seminar Series, Milton Keynes, UK, March 2003.

Woods, F (1990) *Teacher skills and strategies*. Abingdon: Falmer Press.

Woods, P (1993) *Critical events in teaching and learning*. Abingdon: Falmer Press.

Woods, P (1995) *Creative teachers in primary schools*. Buckingham: Open University Press.

Woods, F and Jeffrey, B (1996) *Teachable moments: the art of teaching in primary schools*. Buckingham: Open University Press.

Woods, P (2002) Teaching and learning in the new millennium, in Sugrue, C and Day, D (eds), *Developing teachers and teaching practice: international research perspectives*. Abingdon and New York: RoutledgeFalmer.

2
Thinking about creativity:
developing ideas, making things happen
Avril Loveless

Chapter objectives

This chapter will also raise some questions and discussions to help you to think about:

- **how we might recognise creativity in ourselves, in other people, in our communities and in our wider societies;**
- **how these ideas about creativity can be expressed and developed through using information and communication technologies (ICT);**
- **how we might approach our own teaching to reflect creativity for our pupils and for ourselves.**

This chapter addresses the following Professional Standards for the award of QTS:
Q1, Q6, Q7(a), Q23

Introduction

How can teachers recognise and promote creativity in their pupils, without a personal understanding of the experience of being creative themselves? This chapter will address some of the conceptual frameworks that we can use to help us recognise and think about creativity, and illustrate some of these theoretical approaches by describing creative practices in a project using ICT as a tool to develop ideas and make things happen.

What makes a person creative?

Poets, sculptors, engineers, photographers, software designers, geographers, jazz musicians, film directors, writers, theologians, political activists and teachers are not often presented together in the same list. This list represents some of the people in my immediate group of friends who I would consider to be 'creative' – but this leaves out many others who express their creativity without having a formal occupation or label. My grandmother, Alice, for example, was a 'carder'. She worked in a cotton mill and raised her children in the first half of the twentieth century, and was renowned in the family for her imaginative solutions to practical problems – such as a Heath-Robinson contraption for washing those awkward upstairs windows. Why should I be thinking about a jazz musician, a teacher and my grandmother in the first paragraph of a chapter in a book on 'Creativity'? What is it that these people have in common, yet enables them to express their individuality and difference? How do we recognise those qualities in their lives? Why do we think that we – as individuals, communities and societies – are richer for knowing such people and for being engaged by their creativity? What wider role do teachers play in both being creative themselves and encouraging creativity in others?

I believe that teaching is a creative activity that requires approaches to imagination, inspiration, preparation, engagement, improvisation and interactive relationship that the more commonly accepted 'creative' professions demand. Teachers in all stages of their professional lives, from initial teacher education to continuing professional development and postgraduate study, need to make time and space to think about creativity in their own lives, as well as in their teaching.

REFLECTIVE TASK

- Make a list – or diagram if you don't like lists – of people you know, who you would describe as 'creative', and try to identify what it is that you recognise in them.
- Make another list, or diagram, of words and phrases that help you to describe the creative 'qualities' that you see and experience in these people.

Seeing creativity as an interaction

Creativity is possible in all areas of human activity and it draws from all areas of human intelligence.

(Robinson, 2001, p138)

There are some challenging questions to consider when thinking about creativity in education:

- Where do we find creativity? Is it 'in' individual people, or groups, or societies?
- Are there conditions under which creativity can thrive more easily than others, and how does creativity express itself in, or despite, adversity?
- How might our education systems, from classrooms to national policy, provide opportunities for creative experiences which engage in the full cycle of creative interactions?

A useful way of looking at, and trying to describe and explain our understandings of, creativity is to consider it as an interaction between characteristics of people and communities, creative processes, subject domains and wider social and cultural contexts. In the 1950s to the 1970s, psychologists' interest in creativity focused on areas of personality, cognition and the stimulation of creativity in individuals, but awareness of the influence of social contexts and environments on the creativity of individuals and groups and organisations has developed in the last twenty or thirty years (Rhyammar and Brolin, 1999). *All Our Futures*, the report of the National Advisory Committee on Creative and Cultural Education, defined creativity as, 'imaginative activity fashioned so as to produce outcomes that are both original and of value' (NACCCE, 1999, p29). This definition is helpful in that it expresses five characteristics of creativity which can be considered for individual people, as well as the local and wider communities and cultures in which they act:

- *Using imagination* – the process of imaging, supposing and generating ideas which are original, providing an alternative to the expected, the conventional, or the routine;
- *A fashioning process* – the active and deliberate focus of attention and skills in order to shape, refine and manage an idea;
- *Pursuing purpose* – the application of imagination to produce tangible outcomes from purposeful goals. Motivation and sustained engagement are important to the solving of the problem. A quality of experience in the creative activities of fashioning and pursuing purpose have been described as 'flow', where the

person's capacity was being stretched despite elements of challenge, difficulty or risk (Csikszentmihalyi, 1996);

- *Being original* – the originality of an outcome which can be at different levels of achievement: individual originality in relation to a person's own previous work; relative originality in relation to a peer group; and historic originality in relation to works which are completely new and unique, such as those produced by Fermat, Hokusai and Thelonius Monk;
- *Judging value* – the evaluative mode of thought which is reciprocal to the generative mode of imaginative activity and provides critical, reflective review from individuals and peers.

Creativity and individuals

If we were asked to name our creative heroines and heroes, it is likely that we would include many exceptional, perhaps famous, individuals who have expressed creative ideas, activities and outcomes which have enabled us to experience the world differently in some way. They are recognised as contributing ideas and work that is considered to be original and of value in our society. My personal list might include such people as Norman Foster, an architect; Jane Austen, a writer; Picasso, a painter; Isambard Kingdom Brunel, an engineer; Rosalind Franklin, a scientist; Bill Evans, a jazz musician; Emeric Pressburger, a screen writer; Akira Kurosawa, a film director; Anthony Gormley, a sculptor; Anthony DeMello, a priest; and Helen Levitt, a photographer. (Such a list might say quite a lot about how I see and hear the world, and how such people have influenced me). Craft describes the creativity that we ascribe to such exceptional people as 'Big C' creativity, yet she also highlights our concern with the creative potential of all individuals: 'little c creativity' and 'possibility thinking' in a creative approach to life for everybody (Craft, 2000, p3).

There are many examples of the attempts of different writers and thinkers to recognise and describe the personal qualities of creative individuals. Shallcross (1981) described them as: openness to experience; independence; self-confidence; willingness to take risk; sense of humour or playfulness; enjoyment of experimentation; sensitivity; lack of a feeling of being threatened; personal courage; unconventionality; flexibility; preference for complexity; goal orientation; internal control; originality; self-reliance; persistence (cited in Craft, 2000, p13). Another perspective on such personal qualities is described in Sternberg and Lubart's 'confluence model', in which six resources converge: intellectual abilities; knowledge; styles of thinking; personality; motivation and environment (Sternberg and Lubart, 1999) Robinson also offers a useful approach to thinking about individuals being actively creative within a medium, in which they have control, and are able to play, take risks, and exercise critical judgement (Robinson, 2001).

Csikszentmihalyi identifies a common characteristic of creative people as *'flow'* – the automatic, effortless, yet highly focused state of consciousness when engaged in activities, often painful, risky or difficult, which stretch a person's capacity while involving an element of novelty or discovery (Csikszentmihalyi, 1996). He elaborates the description of this characteristic in identifying nine elements which such activity provides.

1. Clear goals.
2. Immediate feedback.
3. Balance between challenges and skills.
4. Merging of action and awareness.
5. Elimination of distractions.
6. Lack of fear of failure.

7. Lack of self-consciousness.
8. Distortion of sense of time.
9. Autotelic activity (enjoyment for its own sake).

Individual states of intuition, rumination, reverie, even boredom, play a role in creativity and problem-solving and some studies indicate how creativity is enhanced in a state of reverie and imagery (Claxton, 2000). Such states are not just 'letting it flow' or 'leaving it to luck', but acknowledging a way of knowing which is not necessarily conscious and draws upon resources of knowledge, skill and experience in order to make new combinations, explorations and transformations (Boden, 1992).

It is interesting that these descriptions of creative characteristics can also be recognised in discussions of what it takes to be a good learner. Alice, in her adventures in Wonderland, met the Mock Turtle and the Gryphon who told her about their lessons in Reeling, Writhing and the different branches of Arithmetic – Ambition, Distraction, Uglification and Derision. Guy Claxton speaks of a different classification of the '3Rs', indeed, he names four: Resilience, Reflection, Resourcefulness and Relationship (Claxton, 1999). Good learners, and creative people, need to be able to encounter and cope with puzzles, problems, seeming failure and disappointment, in order to learn from these experiences and demonstrate perseverance and resilience. They also develop their abilities to think about patterns and connections, and reflect upon how new situations might relate to earlier experiences or need novel solutions. They know how to draw upon a wide range of resources to help them solve problems, from materials and memories to networks of other people. They also know how to be aware of, and engage in, relationship with other people and places.

REFLECTIVE TASK

- Who would you describe as your creative 'heroines and heroes' who have enabled you to think differently about aspects of the world?
- How have they demonstrated imagination, fashioning, purpose, originality and value in their field?
- How have you been able to demonstrate various creative characteristics in your own life?
- How have you been able to demonstrate resilience, reflection, resourcefulness and relationship in your own life?

Creativity and communities

Generative ideas emerge from joint thinking, from significant conversations, and from sustained, shared struggles to achieve new insights by partners in thought.
(John-Steiner, 2000, p3)

The creativity of individuals can flourish or be stifled within the communities in which they act. These communities can be in families, peer-groups, schools, workplaces, and wider society and culture, and are also expressed in the physical as well as cultural environments in which we develop. It is, therefore, important to recognise the potential of interactions between people and their communities, and the opportunities for design of environments for nurturing creativity within those communities.

Western individualism – and romantic images of poverty-stricken artists struggling to create their work in isolated garrets – has contributed to our ideas of creativity being located within individuals. These people, however, rarely work in isolation. Their ideas and outcomes may be highly original and iconoclastic, but they are likely to have been generated through interaction with other people's ideas and reactions. It is no accident that many exceptionally creative people tell tales of their supportive families, or engaging network of friends, or group of like-minded people in studios or laboratories. Vera John-Steiner's work with creative people explores the essential nature of their collaborations with others, in which they can challenge, discuss and try out their ideas (John-Steiner, 2000). She discusses the influences upon creative work of the intimate relationship between partners such as Simone de Beauvoir and Jean-Paul Sartre, or Pierre and Marie Curie; and highlights the patterns of collaboration between artists such as Picasso and Braque who encouraged and challenged each other, learned from each other and were transformed by working together. As well as these 'Big C' creative collaborations, she notes a large number of groups who work together and acknowledge the shared nature of their thinking and knowing – from writing plays to scientific discoveries.

An interesting focus of her work is on the importance of mentorship and inter-generational creative collaborations, in which senior participants provide continuity, guidance and a 'new embodiment' of complex knowledge by working with younger people with energy and fresh approaches to questions in the field. Our traditions of 'apprenticeship' are rooted in this type of collaboration in which experts think and work with novices to mutual benefit, and provide interesting models for the relationships between teachers and pupils as 'expert' and 'novice' learners.

Of all the communities and places in our society, one would expect that schools would be creative and enriching learning communities. We are, however, sadly familiar with experiences of schools in which approaches to active learning and the development of creativity have been lacking in the general ethos, the physical environment, the organisation of the curriculum and the appropriation of the pressures for improvement measured by attainment in a narrow range.

One example of a school which addresses these issues and expresses its identity as a creative community is Coombes County Infant and Nursery School. Jeffrey and Woods (2003) offer an inspiring account of the Coombes' ethos, described through the themes of dynamism, appreciation, captivation and care which permeates the learning and teaching activities. The everyday knowledge of the wider community is drawn upon and celebrated in the activities of the school that are grounded in the cycles of the natural world, and local and global communities. The learning environment encompasses all the space, both inside and outside the school. It draws upon the imaginative development of the school grounds as extensions to the physical space of the classrooms, corridors, resource areas and meeting halls, attaching the curriculum to the cycles and connections of natural life on the doorstep and in the wider world. The spaces in the school are 'Aladdin's caves', representing the range of activity and experience through resources and displays which provoke responses, questions, enquiry, development of ideas and celebration of the pupils' achievements.

> *What matters is not just the substantive knowledge, but the maze-like structure of the knowledge and the interdependence of its many different parts and forms.*
> (Jeffrey and Woods, 2003, p94)

PRACTICAL TASK PRACTICAL TASK **PRACTICAL TASK** PRACTICAL TASK **PRACTICAL TASK**

- Think about the different communities in which you have lived, worked and engaged with other people. What were the characteristics of those you felt encouraged your creativity, and what were the characteristics of those you felt inhibited your creativity?
- How would you envisage developing the physical spaces in your own classroom and school to promote a creative learning environment?

Creative processes

Anthony De Mello described an image of God's relationship with creation developed in Hindu India as God 'dancing' creation.

> *He is the dancer, creation is his dance. The dance is different from the dancer; yet it has no existence apart from him. You cannot take it home in a box if it pleases you. The moment the dancer stops, the dance ceases to be.*
>
> (De Mello, 1984, p14)

Creativity can be thought of as the 'dance', which does not exist separately from the people who are performing the dance. Creative processes are an expression of the individuals and groups engaging in them, not activities that are independent of them. They can be modelled, encouraged, and nurtured, rather than transmitted. Being able to take risks is the next level in which the person engages in the 'creativity cycle' of preparation, letting go, germination, assimilation, completion and preparation. Robinson emphasises the need to recognise that creativity involves *'doing something'* – in different subject areas, with different media and materials: 'Whatever the task, creativity is not just an internal mental process: it involves action. In a sense, it is applied imagination.' (Robinson, 2001, p115). These processes express, shape and encourage creativity as an approach to life.

Trying to identify creative processes helps us to think about how we recognise when creativity 'is going on'. We can't lift off the tops of people's heads to see if they are thinking more creative thoughts at one time rather than another; but we can see and discuss how they express creativity through their behaviours, activities, experiences and outcomes. The NACCCE definition of creativity encompasses processes of imagining, fashioning, pursuit of purpose, and evaluation of originality and value. We can also overlay these processes with behaviours of questioning and challenging, making connections and seeing relationships, envisaging what might be, playing with ideas, representing ideas and evaluating the effects of ideas (QCA, 2004).

Thus people and communities engage in these processes using a wide variety of tools and media to express and fashion their imaginative ideas. A musician, a mathematician, or a marine biologist would each approach their endeavours by asking 'what's going on here and what would happen if . . .'; playing with ideas and materials; paying close attention to cause and effect; practising and refining techniques and skills; standing back and evaluating the outcomes; and learning from experiences in order to engage in the processes in new situations. Sculptors might work with stone; engineers with steel; photographers with film; multimedia designers with pixels – each is working and fashioning with chosen media to represent and express their imaginings. Digital technologies can be used as tools in creative activity in physical and virtual learning environments, and for developing ideas; making connections; creating and making; collaboration and communication and evaluation (Loveless, 2007a).

PRACTICAL TASK PRACTICAL TASK **PRACTICAL TASK** PRACTICAL TASK **PRACTICAL TASK**

- Think of a variety of creative outcomes or artefacts – from a dance to a design for a new toothbrush – and imagine how the 'creators' engaged in a range of creative processes in order to realise their ideas.
- List the different media and tools that were used to create these outcomes.
- When do you have the opportunities to pose a problem and apply your imagination?

Creativity in subject domains

Where is the life we have lost in living?
Where is the wisdom we have lost in knowledge?
Where is the knowledge we have lost in information?

T.S. Eliot 'The Rock', 1934)

Creativity is, of course, not confined to particular subject domains, such as art, drama, music and design and technology, but can be expressed in all areas of our knowledge and 'ways of knowing'. Our understandings of 'learning domains' as 'subjects' are related to our under-standings about the nature of knowledge. It is possible to distinguish four perspectives on the nature of knowledge within the UK education system and traditions. A 'rationalist' view, described by writers such as Hirst and Peters, identifies subject areas as distinguishable by different ways of thinking and the kinds of methods and evidence used in enquiry within the subjects. In the National Curriculum the clear identification of subject boundaries is related to this view (DfEE, 1999B). An 'empiricist' perspective draws attention to the structuring of knowledge through active engagement in the environment, that is the application of the intellect to experience. Such an approach is grounded in a constructivist, Piagetian view of learning. An 'interactionist' approach to the nature of knowledge focuses on a social-constructivist perspective expressed by theorists such as Vygotsky and Bruner, in which knowledge is constructed through social interaction and agency. An 'elitist' view, described by writers such as Bernstein, would highlight the role of powerful social groups defining the status and appropriateness of certain types of knowledge. Discussions of learning domains will therefore reflect a variety of approaches to knowledge, concepts, skills, philosophies, communities, ways of working, cognitive demands and ways of knowing (see Pollard, 2002).

The structure of the National Curriculum and the training of teachers to offer a 'subject specialism' in their teaching, indicates how school curriculum and assessment systems are rooted in a view of 'subject knowledge'. Pupils also learn from people with recognised subject expertise beyond school settings and many schools offer opportunities to engage with 'experts' or 'practitioners'. These 'experts', such as artists, musicians, scientists, engi-neers, writers, historians, sportsmen and -women, can model their own high levels of practice which draw upon their deep conceptual understanding, knowledge and skills within authentic contexts in the subject area. This approach to learning from the expertise of others is reflected in theories of learning in 'communities of practice' and by apprentice-ship in 'legitimate peripheral participation' (Lave and Wenger, 1991).

It is argued that creative individuals within subject domains demonstrate knowledge and understanding of the concepts and traditions within the domain while knowing how to 'break the rules' in order to present original combinations of ideas. This can be illustrated in the ways a jazz musician, for example, can improvise to high levels when grounded in the history, philosophy, technique and practice of jazz (Humphreys and Hyland, 2002; Loveless, 2007b; Nachmanovitch, 1990). The conceptual understanding of subject 'experts' enables them to make decisions about the appropriate use of tools and technologies to support and explore creative processes of imagination, fashioning, pursuing purpose, being original and judging value within the field. Looking closely at how 'experts' are creative in their different areas offers vivid illustrations of the relationship between subject knowledge and creative processes. In my own work in teacher education I have had the opportunity and privilege to work with scientists, artists, photographers, sculptors, film-makers and writers who work alongside pupils and teachers in schools. We have often witnessed how these practitioners – who are immersed in, and passionate about, their practice – can represent and draw out a deeper conceptual understanding from the pupils in their creative work (Hawkey, 2001; Loveless, 1999a, 1999b; Loveless and Taylor, 2000).

REFLECTIVE TASK

- Who are the creative heroes and heroines in your own favourite subject areas?
- What have they contributed to our knowledge and practice in these domains?

Creativity in social and cultural contexts

Heavier-than-air flying machines are impossible.
Lord Kelvin (1824–1907), ca. 1895, British mathematician and physicist

The wider contexts in which we promote and reward, or stifle and disregard creative people and practices, act as 'gateways' to recognition or marginalisation of creative activities in our societies. Teachers who are interested in developing creativity need to be able to 'read the world' in order to recognise not only the subject and local contexts in which creativity can be expressed and acknowledged, but also the wider cultural, political and economic spheres in which creativity is encouraged.

Recent research in communities of practice also presents a view of learning as social, situated and characterised by interaction and communication between individuals (Wenger, 1998). Leach (2001) cites examples of creative individuals, such as Nobel Prize winners who benefit from association with other creative people within their communities which supported and celebrated the creative process. Feldman, Csikszentmihalyi and Gardner (1994) propose that creativity arises from the interaction between the 'intelligence' of *individuals*, the *domain* or areas of human endeavour, disciplines, crafts or pursuits, and the *field*, such as people, institutions, award mechanisms and 'knowledgeable others' through which judgements of individual performances in society are made.

Csikszentmihalyi develops his discussion of the *field* as a component of creativity wherein other individuals act as 'gatekeepers' to a domain by recognising, preserving and remembering creative outcomes (Csikszentmihalyi, 1996). He presents a systems model in which creativity is in the interaction between a person's thoughts and actions, their knowledge and skills within a domain and a sociocultural context which can encourage, evaluate and reward. In such a systems model, the recognition and value of creativity is related as much to the wider context of *domains* and *fields* as to *individuals*. This has important implications for thinking about creativity and learning, where the context could be a school classroom, education system or a large corporation that can either nurture or dismiss the development of creative individuals, groups and communities. There can be a tension, however, between the current policy of promoting creativity in education that can be linked to political and economic imperatives, and the place of creative people and communities who can be challenging and disruptive to the status quo.

Creativity is currently a term used often in policy and practice of education in the UK. After many years of concern about lack of creativity in the curriculum (Kimbell, 2000; NACCCE, 1999; Robinson, 2001), government agencies engaged in consultation and policy development to include national initiatives to develop materials to promote pupils' creativity (QCA, 2004), and a national Primary Strategy, named 'Excellence and Enjoyment', for teaching to improve standards in pupil attainment, measured in national testing arrangements (DfES, 2003). Creativity is therefore now discussed as 'a good thing', promoting both personal expression and enhancing opportunities to engage in the complexities of problem-solving in the economic and cultural landscape of the twenty-first century.

There are, however, concerns that both the definition of creativity and the practical experience of creative processes become simplistic, unproblematic and unable to reflect the complexities and challenges of developing creativity in the wider spheres of curriculum and pedagogy for the twenty-first century. There are dangers of creativity being used as a complex and slippery concept leading to confusions and contradictions which do not help educators to focus on the purpose and possibilities of creative processes in the curriculum (Prentice, 2000). Hartley draws attention to the ways in which government and business are attending to creativity and emotional literacy in education, attaching them to 'practice which remains decidedly performance-driven, standardised and monitored' (p16), and harnessing them for instrumental purposes in the knowledge and service-based economy (Hartley, 2003; Troman, Jeffrey, and Raggl, 2007). Craft also acknowledges the tensions and dilemmas which creative processes can raise within teachers' professional practice and development, such as the culturally specific nature of creativity; the desirability of perpetual innovation in a consumerist economy; the potential challenges to the status quo; the organisation of the curriculum; the role of the teacher and 'professional artistry' in a centralised pedagogy; and the tensions between teaching for creativity, creative teaching and creative learning (Craft, 2003, 2005).

Being creative is not easy or straightforward, indeed, not always desirable in every situation. In our work with creative practitioners, teachers, children and policy makers engaged in a variety of 'creative experiences' in projects, workshops and consultations in recent years, we have been aware of the dangers of creativity being perceived as just the elements of 'having good ideas' or 'making pretty things', rather than the challenging, and often painful or frustrating, experience that characterises the practices of creative people – the 'hard fun' and the 'flow' (Csikszentmihalyi, 1996; Papert, 1993). Teachers who wish to promote creativity in the lives of their pupils need to be able to model and share the range of creative experiences from their own lives – as individuals working in communities which are shaped by engagement in, and resistance to, the wider social, economic, cultural and political arenas in which education takes place.

Craft, Claxton and Gardner have drawn our attention to the desirability of creativity being characterised and enriched by wisdom and trust within our wider community and society, providing a foundation for Good Work which is excellent, creative and ethical in our lives with others (Craft, Claxton, and Gardner, 2008).

- How does a view of creativity as an interaction between people and communities, creative processes, subject domains and wider social and cultural contexts help you to understand your own creative experiences and possibilities?
- How would you like to describe yourself as a creative teacher?

Creativity in context: Student teachers working with children

I feel that I have been able to engage with creative processes in ways that I haven't had the opportunity to do before. I feel that being able to work in small groups during session one and then in pairs during session two, allowed me to be creative with my peers. I have been able to use my imagination to develop my ideas and to be creative with other people's ideas. I feel that I have also seen that creativity is a process rather than simply one activity. I have seen that there is a process from developing an idea to working with that idea and then developing it further with the technology.

(Jan, student teacher, 2004)

If it is useful to think about creativity as an interaction between people and communities, processes, subjects and the wider social and cultural contexts, what might that look like in a real case study for teacher education? The following example focuses, not on the technologies used, but on the underlying creative processes that bring the activities to life. The Creativity and Professional Development Project at the University of Brighton focused on student teachers, and one of the aims of the project was to develop a conceptual framework for looking at creativity in the context of the use of ICT in Primary classrooms. The students were given opportunities to experience working to a creative brief at their own level, as well as working with young children in school (Loveless, Burton, and Turvey, 2006).

The framework for creativity and ICT attempted to describe the interaction between three elements of creative practices with ICT:

- creative processes – for example, using imagination, fashioning, pursuing purpose and evaluating originality and value;
- the features of ICT – for example, provisionality, interactivity, capacity, range, speed, automatic functions, multimodality (see Sharp, Potter, Allen, and Loveless, 2002);
- and ICT capability as an expression of elements of higher order thinking – for example, finding things out, developing ideas and making things happen, exchanging and sharing information, and reviewing, modifying and evaluating work as it progresses, through a breadth of study (see Department for Education and Employment, 1999a).

The study focused on the experiences of a group of 16 student teachers, all ICT specialists in primary education, working collaboratively in using digital technologies to support creative digital video activities in primary schools. They worked with ten 'digital media labs' of portable ICT resources which included a laptop, digital video camera, digital camera, music keyboards and software for image and sound editing and manipulation. The student teachers were given two days to familiarise themselves with the resources by investigating what the hardware and software could do, working in groups of four. Firstly, they were shown the key features of the DV cameras and editing software, and then given two hours to make a mini-movie to a brief of getting someone through a door in only 10 shots. The following week they were asked to work with digital still cameras and music composition software to create a slideshow that evoked memories of childhood toys.

After another two half-days of visiting schools and planning, the groups spent two days working in small groups in two Primary schools – one class of 5-year-old children and one class of 10-year-old children. Each group of children worked on making a digital movie from starting points emerging from the children's ideas – from stories shared in class to music videos and original dramas. Half a day was spent in viewing and evaluating the outcomes from all the groups, and a final half-day was used as an exhibition of the groups' work and critical reflections. Group feedback from this exhibition informed the students' individual presentation of their module assignment.

By engaging with the project and analysing their experiences, the student teachers reflected upon their personal understandings of creativity, the contribution of ICT as a tool, and their own professional development. Their own definitions of creativity were wide-ranging, from creative qualities in all individuals, to a focus on having ideas, or the making of tangible products. Many discussed the experience of being engaged in activities that they thought were creative, and emphasised not only the ideas and outcomes, but also on the feelings in that engagement. They described enjoyment, enquiry, excitement which led to their greater involvement, and desire to follow things through. Many focused on the opportunities, and frustrations, of working in groups to develop creative ideas. They commented on the experience of offering their ideas to the group and learning how to adjust them, rethink and develop new ideas through discussion. One group highlighted the word 'compromise' in describing this experience, and acknowledged the difficulty of having to put aside, or compromise their personal ideas within the group activity. After the presentation of all the work, the students remarked upon their feelings of pride and achievement in what they had done. They later observed that their own experiences of generating ideas in groups, excitement and frustration in shooting and editing images, and enjoyment and pride in exhibiting the final movies were echoed in the children's experiences. They also recognised that their earlier experiences with playing and exploring with the equipment had enabled them to support the children's ideas in a more flexible manner. All recognised how they personally had engaged with a cycle of creativity activities and processes, from developing initial ideas, through fashioning and reworking, to presentation and evaluation.

In considering how they thought the technologies have helped or hindered them in being creative in these activities, they highlighted the affordances of ICT to try out lots of ideas, revise and make choices. They described how they felt that they had used their imagination and collaborated to produce a mini video story. In order to do this they had to master the use of the technology, collaborate, pool ideas, discard ideas that did not work, edit their work and show it to their colleagues. The provisionality of the technology enabled them to try things, then discard or edit them easily. The immediacy of seeing their work in progress, without the constraints of limited film footage, allowed them to move on quickly to produce an acceptable product. There were, of course, feelings of frustration and impatience in learning to use new techniques with unfamiliar technology, but the groups developed strategies to share their knowledge with each other.

The focus on creativity and ICT afforded the opportunity to practise and advance their ICT capability in a context that was more challenging than many of their previous school placements. As well as learning to work with colleagues, they acknowledged the need for teaching strategies to support creative and collaborative group work for the children. Despite being experienced and successful student teachers nearing the end of their training, they recognised that they had learned much by working with small groups of children.

An important aspect of the project was the challenge it raised for the students working within the wider context of systems of primary schools and teacher education. They recognised the usual constraints of timetable, curriculum and assessment targets – for the children and for themselves. Designing opportunities for student teachers to experience, model and evaluate creativity in their practice is a challenge in the context of a schooling and teacher training system characterised by centralised pedagogy, monitoring and inspection, and aspirations focused on standards of achievement in a limited range of 'measures'. A conceptual framework for creativity and ICT must describe not only the interaction in the activities themselves, but also the interactions between the activities and the wider contexts of policy and practice as they affect people, and communities. By engaging in creative practices within the C&PD project, the student teachers experienced tensions and resolutions that helped them to 'read the world' in which they were acting in a more informed and interrogative manner.

REFLECTIVE TASK

- Look back at your own experiences of being creative in your life. What have you learned from those experiences? How will you take this into your own teaching?

- How would you like to express and develop your own creativity and creative habits of mind? What practical steps can you take to make that happen? How can you build a network of like-minded people to support and encourage each other?

A SUMMARY OF KEY POINTS

> A useful way of looking at creativity is to consider it as an interaction between characteristics of people and communities, creative processes, subject domains and wider social and cultural contexts.

> Creativity can be described as combining the following five characteristics: using the imagination; a fashioning process; pursuing purposes; seeking originality; and judging values.

> Good learners, and creative people, need to be able to encounter and cope with puzzles, problems, seeming failure and disappointment, in order to learn from these experiences and demonstrate perseverance and resilience. They also develop their abilities to think about patterns and connections, and reflect upon how new situations might relate to earlier experiences or need novel solutions.

> Creative people rarely work in isolation. Their ideas and outcomes are likely to have been generated through interaction with other people's ideas and reactions.

> A challenge for schools to think creatively in this regard is to draw upon the everyday knowledge of local and global communities; and to promote imaginative use of school environments as extensions to the physical space of classrooms.

> Being creative is not easy or straightforward, indeed, not always desirable in every situation. Tensions can arise when pursuing creativity: for example, between individual teachers, who challenge the status quo of pedagogical and curricular recommendations, and their schools.

> Teachers who wish to promote creativity in the lives of their pupils need to be able to model and share the range of creative experiences from their own lives.

MOVING *ON* > > > > > > MOVING *ON* > > > > > > MOVING *ON*

In order to develop your understanding and expression of teaching as a creative act, and yourself and your pupils as creative people, you should think about how you might:

- realise creativity in your own life experiences;
- recognise and engage with other people in your community and networks who can inspire, support and sustain creativity;
- identify creative 'niches' and environments in which pupils' creativity can be fostered;
- draw upon creative connections within and between subjects;
- understand the wider social and cultural contexts for creativity beyond the boundaries of classroom and school.

REFERENCES REFERENCES **REFERENCES** REFERENCES **REFERENCES** REFERENCES

Boden, M (1992) *The creative mind*. London: Abacus.

Claxton, G (1999) *Wise up*. London: Bloomsbury.

Claxton, G (2000) The anatomy of intuition, in Attention, T and Claxton, G (eds) *The intuitive practitioner*. Buckingham, Philadelphia, PA: Open University Press.

Craft, A (2000) *Creativity across the primary curriculum: framing and developing practice*. Abingdon: Routledge.

Craft, A (2003) The limits to creativity in education: dilemmas for the educator. *British Journal of Educational Studies*, 51:2, 113–27.

Craft, A (2005) *Creativity in schools: tensions and dilemmas*. Abingdon: Routledge.

Craft, A, Claxton, G and Gardner, H (eds) (2008) *Creativity, wisdom, and trusteeship*. Thousand Oaks, CA: Corwin Press.

Csikszentmihalyi, M (1996) *Creativity: flow and the psychology of discovery and invention*. New York: HarperCollins.

De Mello, A (1984) *The song of the bird*. New York: Doubleday.

Department for Education and Employment (1999a) *The National Curriculum for England: information and communication technology.* London: DfEE.

Department for Education and Employment (1999b) *The National Curriculum. Handbook for primary teachers in England. Key Stages 1 and 2.* London: DfEE.

Department for Education and Skills (2003) *Excellence and enjoyment*. Retrieved 3 May 2004, from http://www.dfes.gov.uk/primarydocument

Feldman, DH, Csikszentmihalyi, M and Gardner, H (1994) *Changing the world: a framework for the study of creativity.* Westport, CT and London: Praeger.

Hartley, D (2003) The instrumentalisation of the expressive in education. *British Journal of Educational Studies*, 51:1, 6–19.

Hawkey, R (2001) Science beyond school: representation or re-presentation? in Loveless, A and Ellis, V (eds) *ICT, pedagogy and the curriculum: subject to change*. Abingdon: Routledge.

Humphreys, M and Hyland, T (2002) Theory, practice and performance in teaching: professionalism, intuition and jazz. *Educational Studies*, 28:1, 5–15.

Jeffrey, B and Woods, P (2003) *The creative school: a framework for success, quality and effectiveness*. Abingdon and New York: RoutledgeFalmer.

John-Steiner, V (2000) *Creative collaboration*. New York: Oxford University Press.

Kimbell, R (2000) Creativity in crisis. *The Journal of Design and Technology Education*, 5:3, 206–11.

Lave, J and Wenger, E (1991) *Situated learning. Legitimate peripheral participation*. Cambridge: Cambridge University Press.

Leach, J (2001) A hundred possibilities: creativity, community and ICT, in Jeffrey, CAB and Leibling, M (eds) *Creativity in education*. London: Continuum.

Loveless, A (1999a) *Art on the net evaluation – report to South East Arts, Lighthouse and DCMS*. Brighton: University of Brighton.

Loveless, A (1999b) A digital big breakfast: the Glebe School Project, in Sefton-Green, J (ed.) *Young people, creativity and new technology: the challenge of digital arts*. Abingdon: Routledge.

Loveless, A (2007a) *Creativity, technology and learning: a review of recent literature* (update). Bristol: Futurelab.

Loveless, A (2007b) Preparing to teach with ICT: subject knowledge, Didaktik and improvisation. *The Curriculum Journal*, 18:4.

Loveless, A, Burton, J and Turvey, K (2006) Developing conceptual frameworks for creativity, ICT and teacher education. *Thinking Skills and Creativity*, 1:1, 3–13.

Loveless, A and Taylor, T (2000) Creativity, visual literacy and ICT, in Leask, M and Meadows, J (eds) *Teaching and learning with ICT in the primary school* (pp65–80). Abingdon: Routledge.

NACCCE (1999) *All our futures: creativity, culture and education*. Sudbury: National Advisory Committee on Creative and Cultural Education: DfEE and DCMS.

Nachmanovitch, S (1990) *Free play: improvisation in life and art*. New York: Jeremy P Tarcher/ Putnam a member of Penguin/Putnam Inc.

Papert, S (1993) *The children's machine: rethinking school in the age of the computer*. New York, London, Toronto, Sydney, Tokyo and Singapore: Harvester Wheatsheaf.

Pollard, A (2002) *Reflective teaching*. London: Continuum.

Prentice, R (2000) Creativity: a reaffirmation of its place in early childhood education. *The Curriculum Journal*, 11:2, 145–56.

QCA (2004) *Creativity: Find it! Promote it! Retrieved 22 January 2005 from http://www.ncaction.org.uk/creativity*.

Rhyammar, L and Brolin, C (1999) Creativity research: historical considerations and main lines of development. *Scandinavian Journal of Educational Research*, 43:3, 259–73.

Robinson, K (2001) *Out of our minds: learning to be creative*. Chichester: Capstone Publishing Ltd.

Sharp, J, Potter, J, Allen, J and Loveless, A (2002) *Primary ICT: knowledge, understanding and practice* (2nd edition). Exeter: Learning Matters.

Sternberg, RJ and Lubart, TI (1999) The concept of creativity: prospects and paradigms, in RJ Sternberg (ed.) *Handbook of creativity*. Cambridge: Cambridge University Press.

Troman, G, Jeffrey, B and Raggl, A (2007) Creativity and perfomativity policies in primary school cultures. *Journal of Education Policy*, 22:5, 549–72.

Wenger, E (1998) *Communities of practice: learning, meaning and identity*. Cambridge: Cambridge University Press.

3
Creative teachers and creative teaching
Teresa Cremin

Chapter objectives

By the end of this chapter you should have:

- **widened your knowledge of theory and practice about creative teachers and creative teaching;**
- **considered your own personal qualities and emerging pedagogic practice in relation to creativity;**
- **reflected upon specific features of creative pedagogic practice and identified ways forward.**

This chapter addresses the following Professional Standards for the award of QTS:
Q1, Q2, Q4, and Q27.

Introduction

What are the key features of creative teachers' pedagogical practice and just how do teachers teach creatively and teach for creativity, thus fostering children's creative learning? This chapter seeks to respond to these questions putting forward a three-dimensional model in which creative practice is seen as a product of the dynamic interplay between the teacher's personal qualities, the pedagogy they adopt and the ethos developed in the class and school. A number of key features of creative practice are highlighted including: curiosity, making connections, autonomy and ownership as well as originality. These are explored and the difference between good teaching and creative teaching is examined.

Exploring creative teaching

Although in the late 90s the literacy and numeracy strategies in England (DfEE, 1998; DfEE, 1999) heralded a move towards increasingly centralised conceptions of classroom pedagogy over the last decade many teachers have exercised their professional artistry and sought to teach more creatively and nurture children's creativity (Jeffrey and Woods, 2003; Grainger, Goouch and Lambirth, 2005; Craft, Cremin and Burnard, 2007). They have been encouraged in their endeavours by numerous government reports and recommendations (DfES, 2003; OFSTED, 2003) as well as support materials (QCA, 2005a, 2005b) which have tried to encourage teachers to adopt more creative approaches to the curriculum and to teach for creativity as well as teach creatively.

Distinctions between creative teaching and teaching for creativity tend to highlight the teacher orientation of the former and the learner orientation of the latter. Creative teaching is seen to involve teachers in making learning more interesting and effective and using imaginative approaches in the classroom. Teaching for creativity by contrast is seen to involve teachers in identifying children's creative strengths and fostering their creativity.

The National Advisory Committee on Creative and Cultural Education suggests that the first task in teaching for creativity is 'to encourage young people to believe in their creative potential, to engage their sense of possibility and to give them the confidence to try' (NACCCE, 1999, p90). The same challenge might well be set your education department lecturers who need to help new entrants to the profession like you to recognise and believe in your own creative potential and enable you to take risks as you learn to teach creatively and teach for creativity. In the process they will be developing your professional awareness, understanding and capacity for making connections between your own creativity and that of the children you teach.

There has been considerable research into creative teaching, some of which focuses on people's perceptions of creative educators, and tends to result in long lists of particular character traits and propensities which such teachers possess (e.g. Fryer, 1996; Beetlestone, 1998). Other research makes use of close observation and analysis of creative teachers, resulting in case study accounts of individuals' classroom practice (e.g. Jeffrey and Woods, 2003; Grainger, Barnes and Scoffham, 2004, 2006; Cremin, Burnard, and Craft, 2006). The research work of Woods and Jeffrey has been particularly influential in this area in documenting the creative response of primary professionals to the changing face of education (Woods, 1995; Woods and Jeffrey, 1996; Jeffrey and Woods, 2003; Jeffrey, 2006) and in identifying features of creative teaching, namely relevance, ownership, control and innovation.

In seeking to become a creative teacher you will want to widen your understanding of your own creativity, and the imaginative approaches and repertoire of engaging activities that you can employ in order to develop the children's capacity for original ideas and action. You will also want to exert your professional autonomy, learning to be flexible and responsive to different learners and diverse learning contexts. For as Joubert (2001, p21) observes:

> Creative teaching is an art. One cannot teach teachers didactically how to be creative; there is no fail-safe recipe or routine. Some strategies may help to promote creative thinking, but teachers need to develop a full repertoire of skills which they can adapt to different situations.

In a study of creative teachers, funded by Creative Partnerships Kent, the university-based team sought to investigate the presence of commonalities between teachers who were identified as highly creative professionals in both primary and secondary schools (Grainger, Barnes and Scoffham, 2006). This case study research, acknowledging the close relationship between teacher and learner creativity, focused on the nature of creative practice. It proposed an emergent creative teaching framework, highlighting three interrelated dimensions of creative practice: namely teachers' personal characteristics, their pedagogy and the class/school ethos (see Figure 3.1). Research in the field of creative teaching has highlighted different aspects of these dimensions and this is now explored, before a closer examination is made of the core features of creative teachers' practice.

REFLECTIVE TASK

Consider the many teachers whose practice you have observed in your training so far. Which do you consider to be the most creative teacher and why? Discuss your reasons with a colleague. What does your discussion tell you about how you currently perceive creative teachers? Is there a tendency for us to assume creative teachers are extroverts, flamboyant professionals? There is no evidence to suggest this is the case.

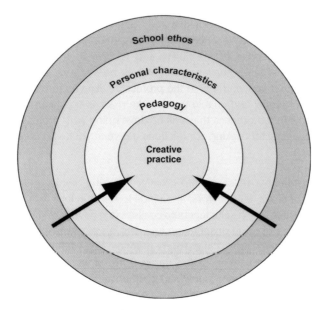

Figure 3.1 Diagram to represent a framework for creative teaching

Personal qualities

It is extremely difficult to identify the personality characteristics of creative individuals, although some researchers have sought to list features, including for example: curiosity, independence in judgement and thinking, intuition, idealism, risk taking and a capacity to become preoccupied with tasks (Torrance, 1965). In drawing together the findings from a number of studies, Stein (1974) again notes curiosity, independence, the capacity to become preoccupied, persistence and assertiveness, as well as domain expertise and unconventional tendencies.

Research in educational contexts reveals that confidence, enthusiasm and commitment are common qualities in creative teachers (Beetlestone 1998; Jones and Wyse, 2004; Grainger *et al.*, 2004) and that a sense of the self as a creative being is an important aspect of this (Sternberg, 1997). There is also some agreement that a key source of teacher self-confidence is secure subject knowledge (Gardner, 1999; QCA, 2003).

Creative teachers are noted by many writers to be comfortable with risk-taking in both their private and professional lives (Boden, 2001; Craft, 2001; Ofsted, 2003). Arguably they are at ease with demonstrating their own creative engagement and exposing the ambiguity and uncertainty inherent in creative endeavour (Halpin, 2003), and are likely to perceive failure as a learning opportunity. Several writers also emphasise the combination of childlike play and exploration with adult-like self awareness, and stress that such teachers are individuals who are curious (QCA, 2005a; Richart, 2002). In addition, Woods and Jeffrey (1996) highlight the humanist approach of creative teachers, their openness to emotions and feelings, and their strong moral and political investment in their work.

In noting personal creative characteristics from the research literature, however, we must remember that creativity can also be collaborative since ideas emerge from joint thinking and interaction (John-Steiner, 2000).

In order to foster creativity in the children you will want to model and share a range of creative experiences from your life, during which you engaged in using your imagination and developed ideas with others. Consider what insights you have learnt from problem-solving contexts for example, when you had to find and shape unexpected solutions. How might you share these? Bear in mind children need to know that creativity can involve challenge and even discomfort as well as pleasure and play, and that perseverance plays a part.

Pedagogic practice

Creative teachers' pedagogic practice is seen to be most effective when they help children find relevance in their work either through practical application or by making emotional and personal connections (Abbs, 2002; Woods and Jeffrey, 1996). Although it might be argued emotional engagement is a requirement of all good teaching, creative teaching depends upon it more because creativity is, as Csikszentmihalyi (2002) observes, a 'central source of meaning in our lives'. Identifying the purpose and relevance of work may help prompt 'flow', which Csikszentmihalyi notes is a common characteristic of creative people.

Practice which fosters children's self direction and agency as learners is also recognised as central (Grainger *et al.*, 2006; Jeffrey and Woods, 2003), this arguably arises most effectively from a pedagogy which seeks to involve them as a co-participants, offering work that is of personal significance and ensuring there is time and space to experiment. Such an inclusive approach (Jeffrey and Craft, 2004) expects and fosters independence from the very earliest years of schooling (Cremin *et al.*, 2006).

Flexibility of style and pace is another recorded characteristic of a creative pedagogy (Grainger *et al.*, 2004; Halpin, 2003; Nickerson, 1999). Government documents agree that varying the tempo, allowing time for students to have their say, a willingness to be spontaneous and the desire to give each child an opportunity to excel, mark out those who are called creative (DfES, 2003; QCA, 2005a). Research into possibility thinking as the engine of creativity suggests that teachers pausing to stand back and observe learner engagement is another potent pedagogical tool (Cremin *et al.*, 2006).

Another strategy seen as common is the frequent use of open-ended questions, the promotion of speculation and the generation of possibilities (Craft, 2001; Robertson, 2002). It is suggested that teachers who reflect back questions asked of them will be developing a more generative and open stance in children (Cremin *et al.*, 2006). Fostering persistence and resourcefulness is also seen as important (Claxton, 1997; QCA, 2005a), as is providing time for reflection and refinement, and helping children make connections. There are many ways in which creative teachers use metaphor, anecdote and analogy to promote connection making (Jensen, 1996).

The English Qualifications and Curriculum Authority (QCA) creativity policy framework, identifies certain pedagogical approaches which it suggests enable creativity. While not reflecting all the available evidence noted above, they suggest:

- *establishing criteria for success;*
- *capitalising on the unexpected without losing sight of the original objective;*

- *asking open questions;*
- *encouraging openness to ideas and critical reflection;*
- *reviewing work in progress.*

(QCA, 2005a, 2005b)

REFLECTIVE TASK

REFLECTIVE TASK

Can you identify a recent curriculum activity which you believe led to learner creativity, prompting the children to offer more unusual or innovative ideas and connections or ask questions and generate possibilities to pursue? How relevant was the task to them personally and/or emotionally? What degree of control did the children have over the activity? Was time and space offered for open exploration? What was it about the pedagogy that supported their creativity?

Ethos

While ethos is central to a consideration of what makes a creative teacher, the dividing line between creative pedagogy and ethos is inevitably blurred, because of the links between creative teaching and learning and emotional security (Halpin, 2003; Jeffrey and Woods, 2003). Positive, trusting relationships and a high degree of emotional safety are seen as necessary to ensure a creative ethos (Shayer and Adey, 2002). Such relationships are likely also to be mirrored among staff (Barnes, 2003) since the institutional ethos will affect the ethos created by each teacher (Amabile, 1988). In terms of the physical and social environment, creative professionals appear to provide children with a range of resources, and the space and time to experiment with these purposefully (Cremin *et al.*, 2006).

The core features of creative teachers' practice

Research into the three major dimensions of creative practice suggests a diverse range of personal qualities and pedagogical strategies as well as different kinds of ethos are present in the classrooms of creative teachers. But attempting to encompass all of these is unrealistic, so what are the core features of such practice which as a trainee teacher you will want to adopt and develop more explicitly?

In examining the personal qualities, pedagogy and ethos of the classrooms of creative teachers, recent research with teachers of 4–16 year olds, revealed that five core characteristics were in evidence in each of these three dimensions of creative practice (Grainger *et al.*, 2006). These included: curiosity and a questioning stance, connection making, originality, autonomy and ownership, and a developing sense of themselves as creative people and creative educators, educators who consciously use their own creative capacity in the classroom context. It is clear that creative teachers in both their planning and teaching are alert to the potential mental connections between imagination and personal/professional experience and attribute high value to curiosity and risk taking, to ownership and autonomy and to the development of imaginative and unusual ideas in both themselves and in their children.

So to become a creative teacher, pedagogically conscious of trying to teach for creativity, you will want to work to attend to these core features (detailed further below) and become more creatively involved yourself. For as Sternberg (1997) points out, those who work most creatively, identify and reward creativity in others and in addition, young people's creative abilities are 'most likely to be developed in an atmosphere in which the teacher's creative abilities are properly engaged' (NACCCE, 1999, p90). You will find considerable pleasure and satisfaction in being creatively engaged as a role model in the classroom as you seek to promote creativity in the children. Developing your awareness of yourself as a creative being is therefore an important first step, for with a flexible and creative mindset you will be able to teach creatively and foster creativity in the young.

PRACTICAL TASK PRACTICAL TASK **PRACTICAL TASK** PRACTICAL TASK **PRACTICAL TASK**

Seize the opportunity to become better acquainted with your own creativity in various ways. Perhaps you already engage at your own level as a creative artist (a writer, web-designer, musician, dancer, etc.) and could connect this to your work in school (Cremin, 2006), or you could seek to work in institutions with a creative frameset or instigate partnerships with the cultural/creative sector or research your own creative practice as you train. Plan a way forward to harness and enrich your creativity.

Curiosity and a questioning stance

Personal qualities: Creative teachers demonstrate curiosity and genuine desire to learn. Such individuals are likely to have a wide range of personal interests and passions and knowledge of the wider world and are likely to share their enquiring stance with the learners, pondering aloud and reflecting on issues in classroom conversations in a genuinely open and interested manner. They are also interested in and curious about the children as people and as learners.

Pedagogically: Creative teachers make extensive use of large framing questions and employ a speculative stance in the classroom regardless of the subject domain or the age of the learners (Chappell *et al.*, 2008).Their questioning perspective demonstrates that the formulation of a problem is as important as the resolution of one, and they make use of generative questions, creating further interest, enquiry and thinking. Such teachers explicitly encourage children to identify and share their own questions, through brainstorms, partner work on puzzlements and recording questions on Post-it notes for example, as well as by providing opportunities for the learners to take responsibility for undertaking research based on their own enquiries in small groups. When invited to respond to children's problems, such teachers frequently employ reverse questioning passing back the responsibility for resolving difficulties to the learners, enquiring for example 'What can you do about this problem?'

Ethos: Being able and willing to express partial knowledge and show a genuine interest in issues through asking questions and generating possibilities involves taking risks, and is only possible in safe and affirmative environments, in which individuals feel supported and do not expect to be judged. It is evident that the ethos created by creative teachers tends to be positive, secure and inclusive, encouraging the articulation of tentative and reflective questions in whole-class and small-group conversational contexts. Furthermore, creative teachers appear to profile and give status to children's speculations, affirming these and expressing genuine interest in them.

For example, in a project on ancient Egyptians, a class of 8–9-year-olds grouped into research teams, each generated and selected a theme (food, daily life, clothes) to investigate, later presenting their findings to the class. Teams began by sharing their provisional knowledge and brainstorming questions and issues to research. Over time they used a range of resources (books, artefacts, internet sites and photographs) to respond to their enquiries. The focus on 'identifying open, interesting and unusual questions' and the challenge to, '...dazzle us with your new knowledge' resulted in a buzz of research activity, which was sustained and developed through feedback and their teacher's genuine interest in their insights. As new enquiries and possibilities emerged, their most intriguing questions were highlighted and celebrated. At one point the teacher observed '...you've become research-ers just like me – I wonder if you too will find questions you just can't really answer – we'll have to wait and see...'.

Making connections

Personal qualities: Creative teachers perceive making connections as central both to the craft of teaching and to themselves as individuals. They are often committed to personalising teaching and model the process of sense-making through making multiple imaginative connections in whole-class and small-group contexts. For example, in a poetry session, one teacher read aloud from a personal AA Milne collection and showed the children an old holiday photograph of herself in East Sussex at 'Pooh Sticks' bridge. They later brought in favourite first books and recalled when and where they had read them, or who had read them. Creative teachers know a great deal about their children's interests and passions and see this as essential knowledge in order to make connections.

Pedagogically: Creative teachers seek to avoid the limiting nature of subject boundaries, and make frequent references to other subjects and to the world beyond the school gate. They provide time to revisit prior knowledge, make links and offer multiple opportunities for children to work collaboratively in order to widen their perspectives. Such teachers encou-rage children to link their learning between subjects and within subjects and often prompt connections with the children's lives outside school. This appears to increase the relevance of the curriculum to the learners. As one teacher observed 'If they can't connect to what we're learning – can't make it personal – or relate it to what they know already, then they'll never retain it'.

Ethos: Creative teachers although aware of the requirements of the curriculum, often appear to give precedence to children's social and personal learning intentions over subject outcomes, and strongly defend their right to shape the curriculum in response to the lear-ners. As a consequence the classroom ethos reflects considerable respect for the children whose emotional comfort and engagement is planned for, thus enabling them perhaps to perceive themselves as individuals first and pupils second, making connections to their lives as well as their learning.

Autonomy and ownership

Personal qualities: Creative teachers show a considerable degree of ownership with regard to planning, teaching and assessment. They exert a strong sense of professional autonomy in the classroom and demonstrate both flexibility and confidence, asserting their desire to create a co-constructed curriculum which builds on the learners' interests and their social/cultural capital, as well as curriculum requirements.

Pedagogically: Creative professionals focus explicitly on the development of children's autonomy. They seek to share ownership of the educational agenda and expect the young-sters to identify areas for enquiry and possibilities to investigate and review. They demonstrate considerable trust, interest and respect for children's ideas and set group tasks which the children have to organise for themselves, engendering both self-direction and offering scope for collaborative creativity. Creative teachers thus provide freedom and frame challenges so that, as one teacher noted, 'they make their own decisions, get organised and take ownership of their learning'.

Ethos: The classroom ethos of creative professionals also reflects this sense of autonomy as children are expected to take shared responsibility for shaping their own learning. They are trusted and viewed as co-participants who have to make decisions for themselves, use of available resources and complete their work in the time available. In viewing classrooms as the children's spaces, creative teachers share responsibility for the environment, and encourage voting on the role-play area or the organisation of the reading corner for example.

Fostering originality

Personal qualities: We are all creative in different ways in our personal lives, although you may not be used to thinking of yourself as creative. Creative teachers are prepared to take risks, and remain open to new ideas, sharing any particularly inventive practices they trial or develop. Through involvement in the creative process of generating and evaluating ideas, creative teachers seek to develop their creative dispositions and enhance their ability to be inventive educators.

Pedagogically: Creative teachers model creativity and take part as learners in the classrooms; they experiment with resources, engage in problem-solving, take up different roles, and generate and critique their ideas. Such teachers demonstrate considerable flexibility and model creativity by being innovative, acting spontaneously, and shifting the focus of sessions in response to children's interests and questions, thus tempering the planned with the lived. In perceiving children as creative thinkers, they leave space for uncertainty and the unknown and show considerable creative assurance in building on unexpected contributions or enquiries, fostering the autonomy of the learners in the process.

Ethos: Creative teachers pay attention to unusual ideas or novel elements evident in children's work and celebrate and affirm these in order to help them appreciate the development of their creative thinking. Such teachers also seek to profile and make public the children's original and alternative work in displays, presentations and assemblies.

Creative teachers

Professionally independent and curious, creative teachers are aware of themselves as creative beings, although for some this may be a relatively new insight. They model, demonstrate and foster a questioning stance and the making of connections, and a marked degree of autonomy and ownership; in the process they value and nurture originality and the generation/evaluation of ideas. Through such practice they seek to develop the creative dispositions of their students.

Recognising and exercising personal creativity appears to be an important part of creative teachers' professional and personal meaning-making. So perhaps the difference between being a good teacher and being a creative one is one of emphasis and intention. Although good teachers recognise the importance of inventiveness, creative teachers see the development of creativity and originality as the distinguishing mark of their teaching. They recognise their own creativity and seek to develop such a creative mindset in the children.

The creative teacher, it is suggested, is one who is aware of, and values, the human attribute of creativity in themselves and seeks to promote it in others. The creative teacher has a creative state of mind which is actively exercised and developed in practice through the four core features of creative practice (see Figure 3.2). These features are closely interrelated and are fostered in schools which profile creativity, expect the unexpected and encourage the professional autonomy of the teaching staff, enabling them to take supported risks as they collaborate with one another and the children on their learning journeys.

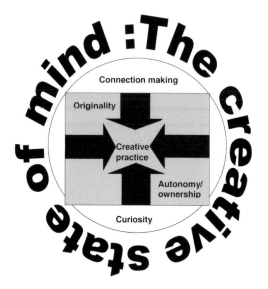

Figure 3.2 A model of creative practice and a creative state of mind

PRACTICAL TASK PRACTICAL TASK PRACTICAL TASK PRACTICAL TASK PRACTICAL TASK

To widen your confidence and efficacy as a creative professional, consider the core features of creative pedagogical practice and identify one which you wish to develop further. Plan how you might nurture this capacity in yourself as well as in your teaching and learning; how might you make it more explicit in your pedagogy and classroom ethos? Discuss your plan with other trainees, and decide whether you will be able to profile this element of creative teaching in a forthcoming serial practice.

A SUMMARY OF **KEY POINTS**

> **Creative teachers are aware of and value the human attribute of creativity in themselves and seek to foster such a mindset in the young.**

> **Creative practice is multilayered; it encompasses the three dimensions, namely personal qualities, pedagogy and ethos, each of which has a distinctly creative orientation.**

> **Creative teachers personally, pedagogically and in their classroom ethos, both demonstrate and develop children's curiosity, their connection making, autonomy, ownership and originality.**

> **Creative teachers are autonomous professionals, who actively model their own creative engagement in the classroom and seek to nurture this in children.**

> While all good teachers reward originality, creative ones depend on it to enhance their well-being and that of their pupils; they see the development of creativity and originality as the distinguishing mark of their teaching.

MOVING *ON* > > > > > > MOVING *ON* > > > > > > MOVING *ON*

In order to develop and sustain your own creative state of mind, your flexibility, collaborative capacity, optimistic and creative disposition as an individual and as creative practitioner you should seek to:

- prize a questioning stance and foster children's curiosity through offering them the chance to undertake their own enquiries;
- make personal and professional connections;
- exert your professional autonomy and co-construct the curriculum with the children, thus increasing their ownership and autonomy;
- encourage, profile and celebrate originality in both yourself and the children;
- continue to read and reflect upon your growth as a creative professional and research your own and the children's creative learning within and beyond the classroom.

REFERENCES REFERENCES **REFERENCES** REFERENCES **REFERENCES** REFERENCES

Abbs, P (2002) *Against the flow*. Abingdon: Routledge.

Amabile, TM (1988) A model of creativity and innovation in organizations, in Staw, BM and Cunnings, LL (eds) *Research in organizational behaviour.* Greenwich, CT: JAI.

Barnes, J (2003) Teachers' emotions, teachers' creativity. *Improving Schools*, 6:1, 39–43.

Beetlestone, F (1998) *Creative children, imaginative teaching*. Buckingham: Open University Press.

Boden, M (2001) Creativity and knowledge, in Craft, A, Jeffrey, B and Liebling, M (eds) *Creativity in education*. London: Continuum.

Chappell, K, Craft, A, Burnard, P and Cremin, T (2008) Question posing and question responding: the heart of possibility thinking in the early years. *Early Years: An International Journal of Research and Development*, 28:3, 267–86.

Claxton, G (1997) *Hare brain, tortoise mind: why intelligence increases when you think less*. London: Fourth Estate.

Craft, A (2001) Little c Creativity, in Craft, A, Jeffrey, B, and Leibling, M (eds) *Creativity in education*. London: Continuum, pp45–61.

Craft, A, Cremin, T, Chappell, K and Burnard, P (2007) Possibility thinking and creative learning in Craft, A, Cremin, T and Burnard, P (eds) *Creative learning 3–11*. Stoke-on-Trent: Trentham.

Craft, A, Cremin, T and Burnard, P (2007) (eds) *Creative learning 3–11*. Stoke-on-Trent: Trentham.

Cremin, T, Burnard, P and Craft, A (2006) Pedagogies of possibility thinking. *International Journal of Thinking Skills and Creativity*, 1:2, 108–19.

Cremin, T (2006) Creativity, uncertainty and discomfort: teachers as writers. *Cambridge Journal of Education*, 36:3, 415–33.

Cziksentmihalyi, M (2002) *Flow: the classic work on how to achieve happiness*. London: Rider.

Department for Education and Employment (1998) *The National Literacy Strategy framework for teaching*. London: DfEE.

Department for Education and Employment (1999) *The National Curriculum: handbook for primary teachers in England*. London: HMSO.

Department for Education and Skills (2003) *Excellence and enjoyment: a strategy for primary schools*. Nottingham: DfES Publications.

Fryer, M (1996) *Creative teaching and learning*. London: Paul Chapman Publishing.

Gardner, H (1999) *The disciplined mind: beyond facts and standardized tests, the K-12 education that every child deserves*. New York: Simon & Schuster; New York: Penguin Putnam.

Grainger, T, Barnes, J and Scoffman, S (2004) A creative cocktail: creative teaching in initial teacher education. *Journal of Education and Teaching*, 38:3, 243–53.

Grainger, T, Barnes, J and Scoffham, S (2006) *Creative teaching for tomorrow.* Research report for creative partnerships.

Grainger, T, Goouch, K and Lambirth, A (2005) *Creativity and writing: developing voice and verve in the classroom.* Abingdon: Routledge.

Halpin, D (2003) *Hope and education.* Abingdon: Routledge.

Jeffrey, B and Woods, P (2003) *The creative school: a framework for success, quality and effectiveness.* Abingdon: RoutledgeFalmer.

Jeffrey, B (ed.) (2006) *Creative learning practices: European experiences.* London: Tufnell Press.

Jeffrey, B and Craft, A (2004) Teaching creatively and teaching for creativity: distinctions and relationships. *Educational Studies,* 30:1, March.

Jensen, E (1996) *Brain-based learning.* Del Mar: Turning Point.

John-Steiner, V (2000) *Creative collaboration.* New York: Oxford University Press.

Jones, R and Wyse, D (eds) (2004) *Creativity in the primary curriculum.* London: David Fulton.

Joubert, MM (2001) The art of creative teaching: NACCCE and beyond, in Craft, A, Jeffrey, B and Liebling, M (eds) *Creativity in education,* London: Continuum.

NACCCE (1999) *All our futures: creativity, culture and education.* Report of the National Advisory Committee on Creative and Cultural Education. Sudbury: DfEE.

Nickerson, RS (1999) Enhancing creativity, in Sternberg, R (ed.) *Handbook of creativity.* Cambridge: Sternberg.

Office for Standards in Education (OfSTED) (2003) *Expecting the unexpected: developing creativity in primary and secondary schools,* HMI 1612. E-publication, available at www.ofsted.gov.uk

Qualifications and Curriculum Authority (2003) *New directions in spoken English: discussion papers.* London: Qualifications and Curriculum Authority.

Qualifications and Curriculum Authority (QCA) (2005a) *Creativity: Find it! Promote It! – promoting pupils' creative thinking and behaviour across the curriculum at Key Stages 1, 2 and 3 – practical materials for schools.* London: Qualifications and Curriculum Authority.

Qualifications and Curriculum Authority (QCA) (2005b) website: http://www.ncaction.org.uk/creativity/about.htm

Richhart, R (2002) *Intellectual character: what it is and how to get it.* NY: Basic Books.

Robertson, I (2002) *The mind's eye.* London: Bantam.

Shayer, M and Adey, P (2002) *Learning intelligence: cognitive acceleration across the curriculum from 5–15.* Buckingham: Open University Press.

Stein, M (1974) *Stimulating creativity,* vol. 1. New York: Academic.

Sternberg, RJ (1997) *Successful intelligence.* New York: Plume.

Torrance, EP (1965) *Rewarding creative behaviour.* Englewood Cliffs: NJ Hall.

Woods, P (1995) *Creative teachers in primary schools.* Buckingham: Open University Press.

Woods, P and Jeffrey, B (1996) *Teachable moments: the art of creative teaching in primary schools.* Buckingham: Open University Press.

4

Play and playfulness in the Early Years Foundation Stage

Elizabeth Wood

Chapter objectives

By the end of this chapter you should have:

- **understood how children's lives are constrained;**
- **explored the benefits of play in childhood;**
- **recognised the need for teachers to maintain a sense of playfulness.**

This chapter addresses the following Professional Standards for the award of QTS:
Q1, Q10, Q15, Q18

Introduction

The aim of this chapter is to consider how teachers can develop playful attitudes towards teaching and learning, and how play activities can contribute to children's creativity, learning, development and to all aspects of their well-being (emotional, social, physical, cultural and intellectual). Play is considered to be a natural disposition and orientation to activity in human beings – we are, after all, the most complex primates on the planet, and our ability to play is part of this complexity. Play is amongst the many ways in which human beings learn new skills and knowledge, adapt to their cultures and environments, create and solve problems, and build their sense of identity as individuals and members of different communities. Play involves lateral thinking, symbolic activity, creativity and transformational capabilities. So while play and creativity are not synonymous, there are some shared characteristics. Becoming a master player is a lifelong journey, and educational communities have an important role in developing children's ludic intelligence and capabilities.

The value of play is recognised in social policies, including the Children Plan (DCSF, 2007), Every Child Matters (DfES, 2004) and the four UK Play Councils (Play England, Play Scotland, Play Wales and PlayBoard Northern Ireland). Improving the quality and quantity of play provision is linked to the Extended Schools initiative, as well as to community play developments, with a focus on improving well-being, physical fitness, mental health, and social cohesion. Play is also central to the Early Years Foundation Stage (DfES, 2007) and is seen as a key way in which children learn and develop. However, this outcomes-focused agenda is controversial since it seeks to manage and control play, and to impose adults' views of what play should be, and what play should do for young people. Therefore it is essential that teachers should sustain the magical, mythical and metaphorical qualities of play that draw on children's creativity, inventiveness and imagination. Teachers need to take a knowledgeable and critical approach to their provision, and to liaise with colleagues across the key stages to ensure continuity and progression in play provision (NUT, 2007).

In this chapter, I will outline some of the main definitions and characteristics of play, and summarise recent research that links play with learning. I will then examine the current policy context, and the issues that this presents to teachers, in theory and in practice. In the final section, I will outline some practical ways in which teachers can develop play and playfulness, drawing on case studies of children at play in education settings.

Defining play

It is perhaps not surprising that there is no agreed definition of play (Wood and Attfield, 2005), given the wide variety of activities that are typically labelled as play, for example, free-flow play; organized games with rules; theatrical performances such as plays, films, panto-mime and comedy acts; leisure activities ranging from informal street football and cricket to extreme sports and Olympic contests. Play is often ephemeral, transitory, and may not result in immediate, tangible or measurable outcomes (which is why play poses such challenges within education settings). Play, imagination and pretence are often seen as less credible and less valuable than work (which is the serious business of life). However, the distinctions between play and work, or play and not play, are not clearly delineated, because many aspects of our lives can be infused with the spirit of playfulness. There is some agreement (Wood and Attfield, 2005) about the *characteristics* of play, which make connections between *what play is*, and *what play does* for the playing child.

- Play is chosen by children, based on their ongoing ideas, interests, hobbies, and personal dispositions.
- Play is personally motivated by the satisfaction that is gained from playing.
- Play is invented by children and enables them to explore ideas, materials, roles and events that are new or unfamiliar to them. They transform reality according to their own wishes and intentions. Play is free from outside rules, but children may create and modify their own internal rules.
- Play enables children to develop and express an inner sense of self, which has moral, spiritual and ethical dimensions.
- Play is pretend (non-literal), but is done 'as if' the activity were real: children weave between real and pretend actions, making cognitive and symbolic transformations (making one thing stand for another). Children attach their own meanings in play (a piece of material can be a blanket, a magic cape, a surfboard). Imagination is more complex than pretence (which is often dismissed as merely making things up), for it involves image-making – calling images into mind, and transforming them into meaning and activity.
- Play is fun and enjoyable: it is done for its own sake, and for the satisfaction of the players. The process is more important than outcomes, although children may produce an outcome if they so wish, such as performing a play or dance; making artefacts to use in their play.
- Play requires active involvement, engagement and participation of the players, including minds, bodies and spirits.

These characteristics relate predominantly to free, imaginative play. However, children may also choose structured play activities such as games with rules (snakes and ladders, ludo, chess, football) or create their own games with rules (skipping and clapping games).

REFLECTIVE TASK
REFLECTIVE TASK

What forms of play did you engage in as a child? Who did you play with? How much freedom did you have from adult control? What do you think are some of the main differences between your own play lives, and those of young people today?

Because play activities are difficult to accommodate within a school environment it is helpful to distinguish between truly free play and educational play. Those who take a purist view that only *free play* is *real play* contest the concept of educational play because it changes and distorts the essential nature of play. I take the pragmatic view that play in educational settings will always be structured by rules, routines, structures and cultures of learning. What typically distinguishes play is children's freedom to choose and control their activities without undue interference from adults (Broadhead, 2004). The need for some degree of freedom is understandable, given the extent to which children's lives are controlled and regulated in and out of school. However, such freedom poses challenges to teachers, because 'truly free play' can be messy, chaotic, exuberant, mischievous, wild, noisy, subversive, and even anarchic. Allowing children to make their own choices and rules often invites challenges to established rules, and may result in choices that are not approved, such as war games, superhero and rough and tumble play (Holland, 2003; Tovey, 2005). However, teachers need to take a pragmatic view of what is possible in their settings, because they have to justify play in the context of national policy frameworks (though this is the only justification for high quality play provision). A pragmatic approach to play is preferable to little or no play at all: preschools and schools can provide diverse and imaginative spaces for play activities which may otherwise not be available to children. Similarly, all adults can imbue their practice with a sense of playfulness, humour and fun in order to maintain the essence or spirit of play.

Justifying play

Inevitably, teachers may be asked to justify their approaches to play to parents, colleagues, inspectors, and students. Although play is often justified according to the developmental needs of young children (Chazan, 2002) there is no definitive research that demonstrates the efficacy of play as *the* medium for learning (Smith 2005). Play is one of *many* ways in which children learn and develop, and can offer qualitatively different ways of thinking, learning and being in the world. Some of the evidence regarding the value play is summarized below, drawing on contrasting disciplinary perspectives.

In the psychoanalytical and therapeutic traditions, play is important for healthy social and emotional development (Chazan, 2002). Children's patterns of play activity can reveal how they experience themselves as individuals, how they build and manage their identities, how they experience others in relation to themselves, and how they adapt and manage their internal and external realities. Play enables children to develop strategies for coping with and adapting to life, especially as they can play with powerful emotions such as anger, anxiety, jealousy, fear, shame, indifference, dread, aggression, protest, humiliation, loss and abandonment. It is normal (and desirable) for children to feel positive as well as negative emotions: imaginative play helps children to understand that such feelings can be experienced, managed and accepted. Play can have therapeutic self-healing and self-actualising potential, by enabling children to rationalise difficult experiences and feelings, and release tension and anxiety (Wood, 2008a). Resilience and coping abilities stem from the capacity to develop a coherent narrative of the experience, to create meaning, and to make sense of traumatic events, transitions and dislocations. Children also learn to express sympathy and empathy in imaginative contexts, and to transfer those insights into other social contexts and relationships, thereby contributing to social affiliation. These perspectives are relevant to the well-being agenda in Every Child Matters (DfES, 2004): positive play experiences can contribute to children's social, cultural and emotional well-being.

In terms of cognitive development, play incorporates creativity, adaptability, problem-creating and problem-solving, and flexibility, all of which are essential to learning. Through imagination and fantasy, play activities enable children to reach beyond everyday realities, and to create potential spaces, potential selves and infinite possibilities. Thus play has a transcendental quality because children are able to play in and with their real/not real boundaries. Within the flow of play, children transform themselves and their co-players, along with materials and resources, to their immediate needs, wants and desires. Cognitive flexibility can be seen in these transformational processes, especially their use of everyday resources and tools, and the symbolic meanings they convey: a cardboard tube becomes the microphone for the *X Factor* contestants; a length of fabric becomes a Roman toga; a box of counters becomes the pirates' golden treasure.

Research evidence shows that play integrates children's discipline-based knowledge (Wood and Attfield, 2005). Worthington and Carruthers (2003) present detailed case studies of children's mark-making and meaning-making in mathematics. They found evidence of mathematical knowledge, language and activity in children's self-initiated play, especially where they had the opportunity to solve real, everyday problems. Anning and Ring (2004) focus on the processes and content of children's drawings, emphasising the importance of 'multi-modal communication'. Children communicate their ideas and knowledge in many different ways, such as through doodling, drawing, painting; modelling with dough and clay; making collages, plans and layouts, as well as through dance, drama, physical activity and gestures. Multi-modality is important for all children, and particularly for boys, who often have difficulty with formal ways of recording. They also argue that drawing should not be seen as a 'pre-writing' skill, but should be valued as a means of creative expression in its own right.

Twenty-first century children are developing remarkable technological skills. Marsh (2005) presents a range of perspectives on children's literacy practices in the new media age, many of which are inherently playful, as they engage with popular culture, computer games, social networking sites, text-messaging via computers and mobile phones, as well as making their own movies, using interactive television and engaging in virtual worlds. The worlds that children inhabit are becoming increasingly complex, increasingly virtual, and almost without borders in terms of their flexibility and potential (Yelland, 2007). Technological play spaces have infinite transformational possibilities, whether players represent their everyday worlds, or fantasy worlds. The challenge to teachers is to integrate new media technologies into their practice in ways that are consistent with children's rapidly developing capabilities, and to see these as valuable tools for play and playful activity.

REFLECTIVE TASK

Carry out some observations of children at play in different contexts (constructive play, water play, role play, outdoor play). Observe a child or group of children for 10 minutes each day for a week, noting down their actions and interactions. Try to include their spoken language, gestures, facial expressions (use a video or digital camera as an aide mémoire). With your teaching team, review and discuss these episodes in terms of what they tell you about the children as players and learners. Ask some critical questions:

- Who leads or dominates the play?
- Who play together?

- What are the patterns and themes of the play?
- Who is included or excluded?
- Consider play in relation to diversity and dimensions of difference (ethnicity, gender, ability/disability, religious affiliation, social class, special or additional educational needs, sexual orientations). Are there any issues regarding equity and inclusion?
- How can you use this knowledge to inform your practice?

Play and policy frameworks

While many research studies provide good justifications for play in relation to children's learning, there remain a number of unresolved dilemmas that teachers need to consider when developing their own beliefs, values and practices. The curriculum frameworks for early childhood in England reflect a pragmatic approach to play, and have been influenced substantially by the subject orientation of the National Curriculum. The Early Years Foundation Stage (EYFS) (DfES, 2007) is designed for children age birth–5 in all types of preschool provision. The EYFS is organised around six areas of learning: personal and social education; communication, language and literacy; mathematical development; creative development, knowledge and understanding of the world, and physical development. The key principles that underpin a play-based pedagogy include well-planned play; continuity between adult-directed and child-initiated activities; responding to children's spontaneous play in ways that extend specific areas of learning; extending children's language and communication in their play; and assessing children's learning through play.

Many of these recommendations are informed by the findings of a government-funded study on Effective Provision for Preschool Education (EPPE), which endorse play as an integral characteristic of effective pedagogy and high quality provision (Siraj-Blatchford and Sylva, 2004). The findings state that effective pedagogy includes both 'teaching' and the provision of instructive learning and play environments and routines. The most effective settings provide both teacher-initiated group work and freely chosen yet potentially instructive play activities. Those settings that were judged to be excellent achieved a balance between adult-led and child-initiated interactions, play and activities. These findings do not propose that play-based learning activities are more appropriate than those which involve teacher direction and direct instruction. Rather it is the mix of activities that contributes to pedagogical effectiveness and child outcomes.

On the basis of these recommendations, teachers may use play predominantly as a means of covering curriculum content and achieving defined earning outcomes. But play is not necessarily the best means of achieving these purposes because of its unpredictable and free-flow nature. Moreover, in terms of diversity and difference, play may not be the leading or dominant activity in children's homes. Children's orientations to play will be influenced by their home cultures and child-rearing practices, and they will be at different points when they enter a children's centre or school (Brooker, 2008). Therefore, teachers need to maintain a reflective and critical stance on policy-driven research, and continuously question their play provision in relation to dimensions of difference.

REFLECTIVE TASK

REFLECTIVE TASK

On the basis of your observations and experiences in Early Years Foundation Stage settings, consider some of these questions. Discuss your beliefs, values and ideals with members of the team.

- Who takes responsibility for planning play provision within the overall curriculum?
- How much responsibility do children have?
- To what extent are adults responsive to children's ideas, interests and themes?
- Is there a balance between child-initiated and adult-directed learning?
- Whose purposes are being served (the child, the adult, the curriculum)?
- What forms of knowledge are being privileged (curriculum-based knowledge, or children's wider home-based knowledge)?
- Are adults tuned into multi-modal communication when they observe children at play?
- What choices are children making, and what implications do these have for others?
- In what ways are children planning and participating in play, and how does this vary according to dimensions of difference?

Developing an integrated pedagogical approach

One of the main areas of contention around play is the role of adults. Much research (including the EPPE findings) advocates a proactive approach to creating play/learning environments, alongside responsiveness to children's agendas and interests. The key to being a sensitive co-player is the ability to realise the magical and transformative power of play, and to avoid inappropriate interventions, which may destroy the flow. When adults do become involved in play, it should always be on the basis of discrete observation, leading to informed and intuitive actions, usually with the permission or invitation of the players. Wood (2008b) argues that early childhood teachers need to develop an integrated pedagogical model, which combines activities in the following areas.

1. **Child-initiated/child-directed activities** incorporates freely chosen play and other activities, which reveal individual and collaborative engagement, interests and motivations. These activities are flexible, open-ended, and develop mainly under the control and direction of the children. Play activities may be spontaneous, or may be planned by the children to build on previous themes and activities. They make the rules, choose the players and resources, and, if possible, where play will take place (indoors or outdoors). There may be no tangible products from these activities, but children can make their own decisions about products and outcomes (building a spaceship to play in, creating a drama to present to the class).
2. **Child-initiated/adult-responsive activities** are initiated by children, and may provoke 'potentially instructive' responses from teachers and adults in the setting. Adults observe closely as children's interests, agendas and themes develop over time, and respond to their prompts or requests for involvement (making resources and costumes to enhance play, using video and still images to record a drama).
3. **Adult-initiated/child-responsive** activities involve intentional teaching, structure or direction, and are linked to learning outcomes. Such activities incorporate playful orientations, with flexibility for unplanned developments based on children's

responses, for example the teacher chooses a story (fact or fiction) to create a structured role play or drama. Children respond with their own ideas and there is some flexibility to take the activity in unplanned directions.

4. **Teacher-initiated and -directed activities** are defined as non-play or work because they involve little choice or flexibility, and are linked to specific learning outcomes. There may be elements of imagination and fun in how the activity is presented in order to engage and interest the children. The adult maintains control and direction of the activity.

Exploring play and playfulness – some case studies

Throughout childhood, play activities typically become increasingly complex, more organised and industrious, more rule-bound, and more focused on ends as well as means. As children become skilled players, their play also becomes more sustained, with increased attention to structures, problem-solving, intentional activities and outcomes (Broadhead, 2004). They display many positive dispositions that are considered essential to lifelong learning, such as planning and organisation, taking risks, creating challenges, problem-creating and problem-solving, concentration, persistence on task, engagement, involvement, participation, and metacognitive capabilities. Therefore it can be argued that the integrated pedagogical model outlined above is equally relevant to children across the Early Years Foundation Stage, Key Stages 1 and 2 (and beyond).

In the following section, I present narrative descriptions of children's play to support the case for continuity and progression in schools. The narratives reveal different ideas about the nature of play across childhood, and challenge how we think about play, including our own beliefs, values and practices. They also exemplify the importance of close observation of children at play in order to understand their meanings and intentions.

CASE STUDY
Garden play

Joshua (age 23 months) is in the garden with his grandfather, Tony. Following heavy rain, the wheelbarrow is half full with water. Tony gets out Joshua's small wheelbarrow and tools, and Joshua begins to use the watering can to empty water from the big barrow. At first he concentrates intently on this sensory and exploratory activity: watering the grass and flowerbeds, feeling the water as it flows from the spout, and sloshing about in the water in the barrow. He is just beginning to use short sentences to comment on his own and other people's actions, such as 'water cold; Josh wet; fill it up; all gone'. He is fully engaged, concentrates deeply, and pays attention to his self-chosen tasks. As Joshua sprays water from his watering can, he wets Tony's shoes. 'Oh no, Joshua, don't wet my shoes.' Joshua immediately changes his body language. He laughs (making a 'play face' to signal 'this is play'), and starts to chase Tony, with the watering can. Tony runs backwards but allows Joshua to catch him with the water. They are both laughing as they get wet. Joshua spends the next hour going between his focused, solitary activity and his social play activity. Tony responds to Joshua's cues, repeating 'Oh no, Joshua, don't wet my shoes' when Joshua starts the chasing/wetting game.

This episode shows how playfulness emerges in a young child, with Joshua playing with rules, materials and ideas. We learn how to play by being with playful people, who are able to initiate and respond to play signals. Play can be socially constructed between an adult and a child, with the defining quality being intersubjective attunement – that is, the players tune in to the cues and signals that 'this is play'. Joshua has some agency and creativity in this episode – he is able to direct both his own exploratory activity, and the more playful chasing game. His grandfather makes sure that the game is successful by running away, but allowing himself to be caught.

CASE STUDY

School play (Reception)

Abigail is a creative and playful teacher, who believes in the importance of stimulating children's imagination, and allowing them to take her planned activities in their own directions. In her PGCE year she is prepared to take some risks with her teaching, and to explore her own ideas about the kind of teacher she wants to become. She uses stories in a playful way, encouraging children to go beyond the original and create their own characters, plotlines, and endings. In the traditional story of 'The Three Little Pigs', the children are visited by the local community police officer, who asks for a report of the wolf's bad behaviour, a description of him, and some ideas about where he might be hiding. The children collaborate in designing 'Wanted' posters, with some inventive ideas about the wolf's habits and characteristics. A teaching assistant takes a different tack and presents the children with a report from the planning committee which identifies all the problems with illegal house construction, and sets out what they have to do to get planning permission for well-built houses. These stimuli result in many different ideas and activities, which the children are able to develop in groups. Abigail uses the integrated pedagogical model to balance teacher-led and child-initiated activities, ensuring that she builds in time to respond to their ideas, provides appropriate resources, and allows free play for the children to develop roles and themes in their own ways.

Developing play in Key Stage 2

Early years teachers may have the opportunity to take on the role of the school's play co-ordinator, which is likely to become an increasingly important role in light of the policy emphasis on play in extended provision. Therefore I have included two narratives of play in Key Stage 2 to exemplify progression and continuity.

In response to developing the new Foundation Phase in Wales, the management team of a large primary school decided to implement an action research project to develop a whole-school approach to play and playfulness. The school community was very diverse, with 87% of the children from a wide range of ethnic backgrounds, and with around 27 community languages (typically 6–7 different languages in a class). I worked with the staff over one school year, visiting the school each term to discuss progress, and supporting their ideas. The following case studies report the action research projects for Year 4 and Year 6, and provide evidence that drama, structured play, and free play are integral to effective practice, and can provide continuity with the more flexible pedagogies in the early years.

CASE STUDY
Developing drama and writing in Year 4

Miriam teaches a Year 4 class, is concerned about the motivation and performance of some of the boys in her class, and considers that they are underachieving and underperforming. She decides to explore role play and drama in the context of their History/English project on the Romans to see if she can stimulate their interest and engagement, and improve their literacy skills. The project develops over half a term and includes a wide range of activities.

The children research the Romans on the internet and in text books, with a focus on everyday life (for a slave girl, a gladiator, a centurion and a rich family). They begin to create stories about their chosen characters, taking care to use correct historical facts, thinking about what they would say and do. Their scripts reveal empathy with the characters (putting themselves in someone else's life, thoughts and feelings) and include dramatic events such as being captured, flogged and starved as a slave, learning how to fight as a gladiator, being brave in adversity.

Miriam gives the children video blue cameras to record their developing dramas. They use them responsibly and with great enthusiasm. Some of the children choose to rehearse during playtimes, recording on video, then writing and editing their scripts. They use lengths of fabric as costumes to help them get into their roles. When they are satisfied with their script, they rehearse formally, and then present their dramas during a whole-school assembly. At the end of the project, Miriam highlighted the improvement in their interest and motivation, particularly among the low-performing boys, which became evident in the quality and creativity of their writing, and in their literacy levels.

CASE STUDY
Year 6 as action researchers – improving playtime

Following an in-service session on action research methods, the Year 6 team decided to cascade these ideas to the children, and give them the choice of the research topic. A specific area of concern was the use of the playground (typically by boys) for football, which limited other activities. The children became the action researchers and were involved in each stage of the study, exploring a range of strategies and activities that would improve collaboration and interaction between children during playtimes. Their research included interviews with children in Key Stages 1 and 2, identifying 'problem' areas, and generating solutions; researching games and playgrounds on the internet; designing their own PowerPoint presentations to feedback their research findings; making games; considering appropriate play spaces/activities for children with special educational needs. A half-day workshop was provided by the team to teach the children how to use/play the games they had either found on the internet, or made themselves. Children brought in ideas for play activities from their families and home cultures, which led to culturally diverse games.

The project was particularly beneficial for Sama, who had little vision, and felt excluded from play; she was afraid of being knocked over by the footballers, and there was nothing for her to do. Sama co-operated with her peers to make a sensory play box containing a range of games and activities that she could use on her own or with friends. When she transferred to secondary school, Sama insisted on leaving the box for other children to use. The teaching team found that active playtimes provided continuity of learning through purposeful activity, which led to exploration, experimentation, developing independence and collaboration, self-esteem, creativity, imagination, social relationships, language, cognitive and physical skills, and improved behaviour.

A SUMMARY OF **KEY POINTS**

> Children's play lives are being constrained by a wide range of social trends, such as increased sedentary activity, lack of play spaces, and the reluctance of parents to allow children to play freely outdoors. At the same time, technological play spaces are creating new possibilities.

> Such changes continue to demand playful engagement with and in the world, and for the world to be a playful place in which humans can learn and develop.

> Constraining play within and beyond early childhood may deny its many benefits, including opportunities for children to become master players, to develop well-being and emotional resilience, and to develop the flexibility and creativity needed now and in the future.

> A shared responsibility is to maintain a sense of what it means to be a playful teacher in the twenty-first century.

MOVING *ON* > > > > > > MOVING *ON* > > > > > > MOVING *ON*

- What are your own beliefs and values regarding children's play? Discuss with colleagues your attitudes towards risky play (such as rough-and-tumble, war games).
- In what ways do you create playful approaches to teaching and learning in your setting? Discuss your definitions of playfulness with colleagues and members of the teaching team.
- What are the key messages about the value of play that you would give to colleagues and parents?

REFERENCES REFERENCES **REFERENCES** REFERENCES **REFERENCES** REFERENCES

Anning, A and Ring, K (2004) *Making sense of children's drawings.* Maidenhead: Open University Press/McGraw-Hill.

Broadhead, P (2004) *Early years play and learning: developing social skills and co-operation.* Abingdon: RoutledgeFalmer.

Brooker, L (2008) *Supporting transitions in the early years.* Maidenhead: Open University Press/McGraw-Hill.

Chazan, S (2002) *Profiles of play.* London: Jessica Kingsley.

Department for Children, Schools and Families (2007) *The Children Plan.* London: HMSO.

Department for Education and Skills (2004) *Every Child Matters.* London: HMSO.

Department for Education and Skills (2007) *The Early Years Foundation Stage.* Nottingham: DfES Publications http://www.standards.dfes.gov.uk/primary/foundation_stage/eyfs/

Effective Provision for Preschool Education (EPPE) http://www.ioe.ac.uk/projects/eppe

Holland, P (2003) *We don't play with guns here: war, weapon and superhero play in the early years.* Maidenhead: Open University Press.

National Union of Teachers (2007) *Time to play.* London: National Union of Teachers.

Marsh, J (2005) (ed) *Popular culture, new media and digital literacy in early childhood.* Abingdon: Routledge.

Siraj-Blatchford, I and Sylva, K (2004) Researching pedagogy in English pre-schools. *British Educational Research Journal*, 30:5, 713–30.

Smith, PK (2005) Play: types and functions in human development, in Ellis, B and Bjorklund, D (eds) *Origins of the social mind: evolutionary psychology and child development*. New York: Guilford Press.

Wood, E (2008a) Everyday play activities as therapeutic and pedagogical encounters. *European Journal of Psychotherapy and Counselling,* 10:2.

Wood, E (2008b) Conceptualising a pedagogy of play: international perspectives from theory, policy and practice, in Kuschner, D (ed.) *From children to red hatters: play and culture studies*, vol. 8, (in press). Westport, CT: Ablex.

Wood, E and Attfield, J (2005). *Play, learning and the early childhood curriculum* (2nd edition). London: Paul Chapman Publishing.

Worthington, M and Carruthers, E (2003) *Children's mathematics, making marks, making meaning.* London: Paul Chapman Publishing.

Yelland, N (2007) *Shift to the future: rethinking learning with new technologies in education.* Abingdon: Routledge.

5
Creativity and spiritual, moral, social and cultural development
Tony Eaude

Chapter objectives

By the end of this chapter you should:

- **understand more about spiritual, moral, social and cultural development and how these are linked to creativity;**
- **recognise the importance of the learning environment in enhancing both SMSC and creativity;**
- **have reflected on the importance of process rather than content in encouraging children's creativity across all subject areas.**

This chapter addresses the following Professional Standards for the award of QTS:
Q1, Q4, Q8, Q10, Q30

CASE STUDY

Leigh was a rather troubled and disorganised six-year-old, often late for school and with little self-belief. In a project on electricity, we made working models. He designed and built a lighthouse. The children checked at least once a day that the models still worked. And every day they were reminded to break the circuit. For some weeks afterwards, first thing, Leigh would dash into the classroom. Before anything else he would reconnect the wires to see that his lighthouse still worked. It was not just the light that shone. The beam on his face was even brighter.

Introducing creativity

This chapter considers the relationship between creativity and spiritual, moral, social and cultural development (SMSC). The word 'creativity' is used with different meanings, as is SMSC, often without being associated closely with creativity. So I start with a definition of creativity and then explore, in turn, spiritual, moral, social and cultural development and how these relate to creativity. Finally, I consider the features of a learning environment to encourage these and the implications for teachers.

All Our Futures, often called the Robinson Report, defines creativity as 'imaginative activity fashioned so as to produce outcomes that are both original and of value.' (NACCCE, 1999, p29). Think about Leigh and his lighthouse. His work involved:

- imagination (planning the wiring);
- activity (making the model);

- an outcome (something tangible);
- originality (something different); and
- value (at least we thought so).

If you are wondering whether young children can be original, consider the NACCCE's (p30) distinction between **historic, relative and individual** originality. The first is confined to a few geniuses. Relative originality occurs when a child takes an approach or arrives at an outcome which is original compared to other children's. Individual originality relates to the child's previous work, so that a child trying out unfamiliar ways of applying paint or discovering a mathematical pattern new to him- or herself can be seen as original. Relative and individual originality roughly correspond with what Craft (Craft *et al.*, (2001), pp45-62) call 'little c creativity', with 'Big C creativity' reserved for historic originality. So young children can be creative in making a discovery that is original – to themselves – but this requires a divergent approach, not just following someone else's ideas. To achieve a successful outcome requires knowledge and skills, but imagination and divergent thinking come first.

This definition, in my view, misses out one important aspect of most creative activity – that the exact outcome changes between the planning and the performance stages. A choreographer does not know quite how the dance will be. A website designer will experiment with the structure and the look of the site. Writers, starting out, are unsure what the final text will look like. Creativity involves imagining the outcome, without this being too definite at the outset.

REFLECTIVE TASK

What qualities do you, or a child, need to be creative? Add your own to my list:

flexibility				curiosity
		openness	imagination	

Approaching spiritual, moral, social and cultural development

SMSC occupies an important place in legislation, from the 1944 to the 1988 and 1992 Education Acts and the Children Act (2004), based on the Green Paper 'Every Child Matters'. This is reflected in the Ofsted Framework for Inspection, although in practice inspectors tend to focus heavily on measurable outcomes.

It may help to think of spiritual, moral, social and cultural as four facets of personal development. Who we are has many facets, such as emotional, intellectual, physical, mental and social. The emphasis on these four does not mean that others are not important – after all, each of us is one person, with different facets. An educated person, in my view, is one who integrates these.

The current emphasis of education is strongly on cognitive and intellectual ability, where attainment can be measured, so that personal development is seen as something separate – even having its own subject heading: personal, social, health and citizenship education (PSHCE). However, Pollard, in a conference talk, described attainment and personal development as being like two strands of a rope intertwined and dependent on each other. Too much focus on 'personal development' may lead to a lack of mental and intellectual challenge, while too little may result in children not learning life-skills and how to relate to other people. We all need both.

My guess is that you feel fairly comfortable with what social, and probably moral, development are all about, a bit less sure about cultural and fairly puzzled about, or perhaps hostile towards, spiritual development. I discuss each of them in more detail in Eaude (2007), but the next four sections explore what is distinctive about each and how they link to creativity. It will help to think of them as overlapping but with:

Spiritual		*Meaning*
Moral	*mainly related to*	*Action*
Social		*Interaction*
Cultural		*Belonging*

My perspective is similar to Pollard's (1985, px) when he writes that

> *[I]ndividuals are thought to develop a concept of 'self' as they interpret the responses of other people to their own actions. Although the sense of self is first developed in childhood, ... it is continually refined in later life and ... provides the basis for thought and behaviour. Children's spiritual, moral, social and cultural development involves children creating their own selves: being, in Goodman's phrase, world-makers, with 'worldmaking always start(ing) from worlds already on hand: the making is a remaking.*

Spiritual development and creativity

Spiritual development is a very elusive idea, and hard to define. Your immediate response probably relates it to religion. Historically, this link has been very close, and many people still argue that spiritual development depends on involvement in a religious tradition. However, the view that 'spiritual' is wider than 'religious' is more common. Hyde (2008), for instance, identifies four aspects: the felt sense, integrating awareness, weaving the threads of meaning and spiritual questing; while Hay and Nye (1996) write of awareness sensing, mystery sensing, and value sensing.

REFLECTIVE TASK

Think (ideally with someone else) about other connotations. Add your own to these that teachers often mention:

	awe and wonder	relationships to each other and/or to God		beyond the ordinary
reflection/prayer	evocative/favourite places/experiences			mystery

My research (Eaude, 2007) sees it as primarily about questions related to meaning, such as:

- Who am I?
- Where do I fit in?
- Why am I here?

These are the sorts of question that religion tries to answer, but they are universal. They are asked repeatedly at any age, not necessarily frequently and never answered easily, quickly or finally. They require space and time and regular re-visiting. They involve making sense of puzzling and difficult experiences, as well as joyous ones; and realising that much of what gives meaning to our lives is intangible, rather than material possessions.

You may think that young children do not ask such questions. Of course, they may use different language, and are (often) more centred on themselves than adults are. However they often wonder:

- who they are (think of their fascination with mirrors and puppets);
- whether they belong (think of the importance of their family and groups they are part of); and
- why things are as they are (think of how children ask questions about what they do not understand).

REFLECTIVE TASK
REFLECTIVE TASK

One remarkable thing about spiritual development, taught in many religious traditions, is that children have qualities that are lost, or at least inhibited, in adults: for example, openness, capacity for joy and an ability to live in the here and now. Can you think of others? Put the book down and spend a few minutes thinking about what children can teach us.

So, how is spiritual development linked to creativity? Music, poetry, drama, worship, the direct experience of nature may come to mind as routes into spiritual development; but it can occur in any subject area. Remember for now the importance of children making sense of the world and creating personal meaning, a process involving questions and space and time to explore these.

Moral development and creativity

Moral development is often seen as children learning the difference between right and wrong and behaving well. This seems to me too simple. The problem is not one of knowing but of acting appropriately and living what Oakeshott calls the good life; and internalising this, so that actions are based on positive dispositions and motives, rather than fear or reward. Moral development is something wider, and more profound, than behaviour management. To use a rather old-fashioned term, it is about building character – the sort of person one is or becomes.

Character consists of a range of qualities and dispositions, some intrapersonal, some interpersonal, which help in living the good life. Often, these are called values, though I prefer 'virtues', because 'values' is used about cultures and societies as well. Which virtues help us to lead the good life are not just a matter of individual choice, but reflect the different traditions and cultures we come from: the home and school, wider society and faith communities.

REFLECTIVE TASK

REFLECTIVE TASK

Think what virtues you value in a child – again I have started you off.

			Courage	
Tolerance				
	Honesty			Thoughtfulness

You may see these as universal, but I suggest that, while there is a lot of overlap, they vary between cultures. For example, compassion and respect appear to be fairly universal, but modesty, or humility, or patriotism more contested. For each, one needs a balance – neither too much, nor too little – of each, and this requires individual judgement.

Consider how children learn these rather abstract qualities. The most important way is through example, and habituation; that is, by role modelling and by practice, with positive re-inforcement. Talking about what they involve is valuable, but internalising requires a subtle mixture of example, habituation and conscious deliberation. Remember the importance of stories, an insight which religious traditions recognise in emphasising the stories of faith: because stories engage children of all ages and their open-endedness encourages them to think about characters' actions and motives. Such a process helps develop a sense of self – and what is sometimes called a coherent personal narrative (see Bruner, 1996).

You may worry that if children are not given clear rules they will not know how to act. But too didactic an approach or too limiting a structure discourages children's intrinsic motivation – doing something because it is right, rather than because of reward or punishment. Children need both guidance and the chance to internalise these virtues, to understand what they mean and to live them, to determine for themselves how to act and to be able to navigate a way through confusion and fragmentation that often results from mixed messages. So, adults who provide a good example and the opportunity for children to reflect on how they have acted, and how they should, help children create their own character.

Social development and creativity

Social and emotional development are closely linked. Indeed, as Gerhardt (2004) indicates, babies learn to regulate their emotional impulses and responses through interaction and feedback. From the start, identity and sense of self are created.

Anxiety leads to aggression or to withdrawal. Put simply, it is very hard to be creative if you are feeling unsafe. However, creativity also requires challenge and an element of risk-taking. So, the culture and the mood of the classroom has to offer the right balance of safety and challenge; for all children, but especially so those who find learning difficult because:

- the expectations at home clash with those at school; or
- previous experience, such as rejection, or their current situation, such as poverty or domestic responsibilities, make them too anxious.

Emotional intelligence involves learning to respond to, and regulate, the whole range of emotions – anger, grief and envy as well as joy – and occurs not just in particular lessons. Remember that, just as personal development and attainment are interdependent, emotional development is interwoven with the whole range of learning.

Part of the challenge of learning is to build on what is familiar and to learn about similarity and difference. So, children benefit from a range of experiences which take them beyond their current state of knowledge, moving them away from being centred on themselves, by recognising the feelings and needs of others.

Good learners can act both independently and interdependently. Learning is both an individual and a collective activity. Of course, many learning activities require individuals to work on their own. But think, for example, of how in activities like singing as a group or playing team sport, discussing a scientific experiment or being quiet together a group experience creates more than the sum of its parts. By co-operating with others, children both learn the skills of interaction and extend the range of their learning. Social development involves more than children knowing how to get on with each other. It entails learning how to co-operate and negotiate, working with others, as well as on one's own. Our sense of self, or identity, is social as well as individual, because we become ourselves only as part of something bigger than ourselves.

Cultural development and creativity

In Eagleton's (2000, p131) words, 'culture is not only what we live by. It is, also, in great measure, what we live for. Affection, relationship, memory, kinship, place, community, emotional fulfilment, intellectual enjoyment, a sense of ultimate meaning': areas where the four facets of SMSC overlap.

However, 'culture' is one of the most complicated words in English, with several different meanings. The section in *All Our Futures* (NACCCE, pp40–53) is excellent on this. Two relevant meanings relate to:

● cultural background, identity and belonging; and
● 'high' and 'low' culture.

Children come to school with what is often called 'cultural capital': expectations and beliefs influenced by their background and previous experience. These result from many factors, including family, social class, and ethnicity. Where these expectations and beliefs clash with the school's, children may be confused or anxious, for instance about how to respond to other children or adults, or about dress or diet. Remember the importance of feeling safe. So, taking account of children's cultural capital helps them to belong, for example by valuing the knowledge brought from home and being sensitive to what they are encouraged (or forbidden) to do there. Where children feel that they do not belong, or feel excluded, their learning suffers.

Identity depends on belonging, being part of a whole range of different groups, each with its own culture: family, nursery, class, voluntary or sporting groups, and, for some, faith community; and in other ways such as supporting a football club or wearing a particular brand of clothes. These cultures may protect or challenge, guide or inhibit, at different stages of our lives, but all contribute to the 'narrative' that each of us tells of ourselves, which is always a mixture of different, often conflicting, stories about who we are.

The second meaning of culture relates to the arts, what is often called 'high' culture, and is often linked to creativity. Particular sorts of experience help us to understand ourselves better – and to improve ourselves (though this is a hotly debated area). The arts – music, drama, visual art, poetry – are wonderful ways of learning about different people and about ourselves. Visits to a concert, a museum or a farm, hearing a poet or working with an artist can help expand children's cultural horizons both in experiencing other people's creativity and developing their own.

Like Leigh, creative activity can help to create or reinforce our identity. However, like SMSC, this depends on *how* children approach tasks and experiences, rather than *what* these are, as such. So, it is more like a way of learning than located within any particular experience or subject. And this is where you as a teacher can open up possibilities by the culture, the environment and the expectations that you create.

Creating environments to encourage creativity

Think back to the story of Leigh. Making the lighthouse was a creative activity, where his imagination and activity helped him complete the task. However, it appeared to be more than that. The lighthouse was *his,* almost a part of him. In re-creating it each day, he was, in a sense, re-creating himself and re-affirming the possibility of his own creativity.

Although the four facets of SMSC have been treated separately, they overlap and depend on an environment very similar to that which encourages children's creativity. In this section, I consider features of such an environment.

For children to be creative requires both **safety** and **challenge**. How much of each will differ according to background, experience, confidence, and task. It may change from day to day, or between subject areas. Think of your own strengths and weaknesses and how these depend on where you are and how you feel. Meeting new people, or performing in public, may energise or panic you. What you can do easily on your own may become next to impossible in a group – or vice versa. However, we all thrive on challenge as long as we remain in control. Too often, adults assume that children are not capable, rather than creative learners and lateral thinkers; and in assuming this, we may help to make them so. Being in control helps to build children's growing sense of agency, in both their academic and personal development.

Creativity and SMSC both entail a mixture of **structure** and **freedom**. Children require both guidance to be creative (at least in a focused way) and the chance to:

- generate their own ideas;
- ask questions and pose and solve their own problems;
- try out new experiences and ways of working, including taking risks and making mistakes;
- engage in open-ended activities, adopting different approaches and making unusual connections.

A third feature is the chance **to play** and **to be playful**. Look at a young child playing (seriously) and consider Winnicott's words (1980, p63): 'It is in playing and only in playing that the individual child or adult is able to be creative and to use the whole personality. It is only in being creative that the individual discovers the self.' Similar opportunities may occur most obviously in drama or dance, but also through literature, planning a presentation or solving a problem. These provide opportunities for children to explore their own, and other people's, feelings and beliefs, involving qualities such as empathy, imagination and lateral thinking.

A fourth feature is **space**. At times, expecting children to work quickly is appropriate; but an environment to encourage creativity and SMSC requires space for thinking, imagining, planning, exploring and reflecting. This space may be physical and emotional, or both, sometimes individual, sometimes in a group. Remember how busy and cluttered many children's lives are and the pressure they are under. Space enables children (and adults) to reflect, slow down and allow the unconscious to work, as Claxton (1997) discusses, and so gives children the chance to make sense of, and to answer for themselves, life's more profound and difficult questions. What is often called experiences of 'awe and wonder' may help children gain a sense of something beyond themselves, and of perspective. This can involve language but symbols, times of quiet and stillness and direct experience of nature offer alternative, often more accessible, opportunities for this.

PRACTICAL TASK PRACTICAL TASK **PRACTICAL TASK** PRACTICAL TASK **PRACTICAL TASK**

What other features of an environment to encourage creativity would you highlight? Think back to those areas where you are creative and what helps (or inhibits) your own creativity.

Teaching for creativity

Many of the implications for teachers follow directly from the sort of environment described. This section considers some less obvious implications.

All Our Futures (NACCCE, 1999, p89) distinguishes between teaching creatively and teaching for creativity. Nurturing and demonstrating your own creativity will enhance your children's creativity, as well as ensuring that you look after yourself. However, it is possible to teach creatively without encouraging creativity. What appears to be creative teaching may leave some children without enough structure. Teaching for creativity implies empowering, encouraging and enabling children to be in control of activities. Children's learning benefits from more opportunities to exercise creativity than they often receive, but no-one can foster creativity all the time. Dictating exactly what sort of picture, model or piece of writing is required, while not encouraging creativity, may at times be appropriate.

Other chapters in this book explore creativity within specific subject areas. Although 'the arts' may present more obvious opportunities than maths or geography, possibilities exist in every subject area. While circle time or PSHCE may help you focus on social and emotional development, this can happen in any situation.

You may be thinking that teaching for creativity presents a big challenge. It does, especially given the strong emphasis on content coverage, tightly defined learning objectives and measurable outcomes. But:

- think more about *how* children learn (by imagining, questioning and creating) than *what* they learn;
- plan carefully, but give some space for flexibility and exploration; and
- recognise that many important questions cannot be answered definitively, though adults who provide answers which are too definite inhibit children's ability to live with uncertainty and mystery, ambiguity and paradox.

The culture of your school influences how you teach, just as the classroom culture you create affects how children learn. Many primary schools, especially in the early years, are very good at encouraging and enabling teaching for creativity. For example, the Early Years Foundation Stage Curriculum encourages creative development as one of six areas of learning, although this is represented as occurring only in some subject areas; but such a curriculum based on areas of learning rather than definite boundaries between subjects makes it easier to adopt an approach conducive to children's SMSC.

The stronger emphasis on curriculum content and what can be measured often evident in Key Stage 2 makes it harder, but hopeful signs include:

- the growing recognition, since Excellence and Enjoyment (DfES, 2003), that creativity and enjoyment are ways of helping children learn better, two sides of one coin, or two strands of the same rope;
- the Every Child Matters agenda, which encourages schools to consider a broader range of outcomes, such as health (both physical and mental); and
- the growing interest in formative assessment, asking open questions and encouraging and expecting children to be reflective, which are widely recognised as good teaching and which encourage children's creativity.

However, children's creativity and SMSC is enhanced more by what you do and who you are than by any government policy. You can make a huge difference by encouraging, rather than inhibiting, creativity and divergence and by having expectations which are high but realistic. Remember that children do not have one fixed, inherent level of ability but:

- bring tremendous experience of active, creative learning; and
- have a range of what Gardner (1993) calls multiple intelligences and (often untapped) gifts and talents.

Your most important contribution to children's personal development comes from who you are and the way of acting and interacting which you demonstrate. By displaying qualities such as openness, courage and flexibility, you will encourage children to adopt these. The relationships you make can ensure the right balance of re-assurance and of challenge. Your identity, as a learner and as a person, will help shape your children's. And your ability to be reflective, to be curious and to address difficult questions thoughtfully will be an example for children who, very often, lack such a model.

Ofsted (2004, p4) were right to say that 'most teachers would see (pupils' SMSC development) as the heart of what education is all about – helping pupils grow and develop as people'. In exercising their creativity, children, like Leigh, are not just making things, but are helping to shape themselves and their future; and teachers who enable this are engaged in one of the most exciting creative processes of all.

A SUMMARY OF **KEY POINTS**

> Spiritual, moral, social and cultural development are four important, but elusive, facets of personal development;

> Personal development and attainment are closely interlinked;

> An environment which enables SMSC is similar to one that encourages creativity;

> Teaching for creativity depends more on process than content and can happen in all subject areas.

MOVING *ON* > > > > > > MOVING *ON* > > > > > > MOVING *ON*

Points to consider for practice
Think about how:

- the classroom environment where you teach can encourage children to be creative and questioning.
- you can plan and assess, allowing for some flexibility and taking account of children's responses.
- the relationships you form can provide both security and challenge.
- your own (often natural) actions and responses set an example for children.

REFERENCES REFERENCES **REFERENCES** REFERENCES **REFERENCES** REFERENCES

Bruner, J (1996) *The culture of education.* Cambridge, MA.: Harvard University Press.

Claxton, G (1997) *Hare brain, tortoise mind: why intelligence increases when you think less.* London: Fourth Estate.

Craft, A, Jeffrey, B and Leibling M (eds) (2001) *Creativity in Education.* London: Continuum.

Department for Education and Skills (2003) *Excellence and Enjoyment.* Nottingham: DfES.

Eaude, T (2007) *Children's spiritual, moral, social and cultural development: primary and early years.* Exeter: Learning Matters.

Eagleton, T (2000) *The idea of culture.* Oxford: Blackwell.

Gardner, H (1993) *Frames of mind: the theory of multiple intelligences.* London: Fontana.

Gerhardt, S (2004) *Why love matters.* Abingdon: Routledge.

Hay, D with Nye, R (1998) *The spirit of the child.* London: Fount.

Hyde, B (2008) *Children and Spirituality.* London: Jessica Kingsley.

National Advisory Committee on Creative and Cultural Education (1999) *All our futures: creativity, culture and education.* London: DfEE.

Ofsted (2004) *Promoting and evaluating pupils' spiritual, moral, social and cultural development.* www.ofsted.gov.uk/publications

Pollard, A (1985) *The social world of the primary school.* London: Cassell.

Winnicott, D (1980) *Playing and reality.* London: Penguin.

PART 2
CREATIVITY IN THE
CORE PRIMARY CURRICULUM

6
Creativity and literacy
Liz Chamberlain

Chapter objectives

By the end of this chapter you should:

- **have an understanding of the links between speaking and listening, reading and writing;**
- **have considered the literacy environment in your own classroom;**
- **have gained an awareness of the importance of a creative approach to writing;**
- **have reflected on your role in motivating children to write;**
- **have planned a writing session with a real purpose and audience.**

This chapter addresses the following Professional Standards for the award of QTS:

Q7, Q8, Q14, Q15, Q30

Introduction

This chapter outlines how schools are adopting more creative approaches to literacy and how, by using exciting stimuli, the whole school is talking about writing.

Getting the whole school writing

Imagine a child going home and telling a parent that today, school had been a bit different, and that when they had arrived at school they were a little surprised to discover that an alien spaceship had crashed-landed in the school playground. What, I wonder, would the reaction be? But this is precisely the approach that many schools are taking to engage the whole school in writing. What they have realised is that children need something to write about – something they are interested in, something they have experienced and, more importantly, something that has a real audience and in essence gives children a sense of ownership over the writing (Graves, 1983). In the case of this school, children from Reception to Year 6 were all involved in creating the world's biggest newspaper, which was then displayed in the school hall for parents and children to enjoy. To add to the authenticity of the experience, the English Subject Leader invited a journalist from the local newspaper to talk to the children about how to 'write' their articles.

With the recent implementation of the *Primary Framework for Mathematics and Literacy* (DCSF, 2006) schools, more than ever, are taking advantage of this tide of change in the teaching of English. Teachers are being encouraged to learn the lessons from the *National Literacy Strategy* (1998) and rather than view the planning of English activities in discrete units, to consider speaking and listening, reading and reading as inter-related and that when planning for one, to consider how to plan for all (Cremin, Goouch, Blakemore, Goff and Macdonald, 2006). This is especially true of writing, which over the last 10 years many believe has been reduced to a series of word, sentence and text level objectives rather than as an essential means of communication that children need to engage with and to see as relevant to their lives (Cremin, *et al.*, 2006). What this chapter aims to do is to outline some of the innovative approaches schools are adopting when considering English activities in their school and how, as a writing teacher (Bearne, 2002), rather than a teacher of writing, your role is vital.

REFLECTIVE TASK

Think of the best writing lesson you have seen. What was it that made it such a good lesson? List the key factors that made this lesson so effective.

Consider:

- the role of the teacher;
- what the children were being asked to do;
- the aim of the writing;
- the audience for the writing.

Who is writing for?

As previously suggested, in recent years some teachers may have suggested that the aim of writing was to introduce children to a range of different genres, both fiction and non-fiction, with a sprinkling of poetry (Cremin *et al.*, 2006). As a Year 6 pupil, this would have been reduced to being able to identify key features of different genres and to be able to use them, confidently, within their own writing. What effective teachers of literacy have always done is to be able to place the audience and purpose at the heart of any writing activity (Medwell, 2002; Hall and Harding, 2003). The children in the alien spaceship scenario were motivated not only by the experience but also by the idea that they needed, somehow, to capture this moment and to share it with as many people as possible. This is the aim of writing – it is the way that we share our innermost thoughts with others and it is this very fact that makes writing so difficult not only technically but socially. For some children the idea that their writing, which somehow represents them as a person, and is laid bare for others to see, to comment on and possibly judge, is a very vulnerable position to be in. You might identify with this as you hand in an assignment and it is important to keep this in mind when you set children writing tasks. As Margaret Meek reminds us, 'To read is to think about meaning; to write is to make thinking visible as language. To do both is to become both the teller and the told in the dialogue of the imagination.' (1991, p48)

As a Year 5 pupil who has good initial ideas but has poor handwriting, I may find it hard to write things down. Conversely the Year 3 pupil who writes reams and reams about best friends and favourite pets and always brings a narrative element to any genre of writing also needs support in their writing. As a teacher, it is important to know whether it is the content or the physical aspects of writing that need developing.

Stainthorp (2002) suggests that 'writing is hard' and, as you sit to write another assignment, you may well agree. She draws on a 'simple view of writing' suggested by Berninger *et al.*, (2002) which, in its most basic form, involves a child being able to draw on their long- and short-term memory, to employ skills of encoding, an understanding of sentence structure, an ability to present their work legibly and neatly which Smith (1994) would describe as the 'secretarial skills' of writing. As practitioners, these are the areas of writing that we are more confident about teaching; we can comment on the handwriting, correct the spelling and make mention of the effort involved (Black and Wiliam, 2003). However, the missing part of the writing equation is the development of authorship skills, the aspects of the writing that contain the thoughts and ideas – the bit you want to tell people about (Smith, 1994; Latham, 2002). This is harder to teach, as it is not as easy to give children an imagination or to provide them the words for them. However, it **is** your job to give children experiences that they want to write about. In essence, if a child does not have anything to write about, then writing is going to remain hard. However, if you offer children exciting experiences both within and beyond the classroom, they will be more motivated to write. Stainthorp (2002) proposes that if the transcription elements, the spelling and the handwriting, are secure then there is more capacity for children to translate their ideas onto the page. Conversely it could be argued, that if children have the ideas, then the heavy demands placed on the working memory will be significantly freed up, and if they are not working so hard to think of something to write, then it will be easier to draw on the transcriptional skills and quality writing has a chance.

Having generated a reason or purpose for writing, writing also needs an audience. Children need to know not only what the writing is about but who the writing is for (Graves, 1983). This goes beyond knowing what genre to write in and the appropriate language and layout features but knowing who the audience will be, i.e. who is going to read the writing. In the case of the alien spaceship, all the children knew they were creating an article for a news-paper that would be read not only by other children but by parents and the wider community. This influenced the style of their writing in terms of using the conventions of a newspaper report, but it was the purpose and audience that drove the activity, not the genre.

However, setting children real reasons for writing should be approached with caution as teachers sometimes get it wrong. Year 5 pupils are often asked to compose a piece of persua-sive text, convincing the Headteacher that school uniform should be banned or to stop the school hall being knocked down to make way for a housing development. These might be real situations but if the task simply pretends to be for a real audience then there is no emotional investment for children. Instead, ask the children to write about something that is important to them, something that they feel strongly about and compare the quality of the writing.

REFLECTIVE TASK

Think of a child who is a good writer. What are you basing this judgement on? How would you describe them as a writer? Consider what secretarial and authorship skills they bring to the process and how you would support them in the next stage of their writing journey.

Creating a landscape of language

The average 5-year-old, in the UK, spends five hours a day in the classroom; over the course of a year that is a total of 950 hours (Smith and Call, 2003). Your classroom therefore needs to be a place that is interesting and inspiring to be in, not just for the children, but also for you. When you walk into your own classroom for the first time, take stock of how it feels. Is this a place where reading and writing are valued?

If we want children to enjoy learning, then reading and writing need to be everywhere. It needs to be obvious to them what topic they are learning about through wall and practical displays. You can also scaffold children's learning by ensuring you have word walls that children can refer to when writing, by displaying 'tricky' words as a reminder when spelling, or choose a poem, write it out, put it up and let children respond (Rosen, 2007). Let children explore your classroom and see it as a place where there is always something new to discover. Have a book of the week, nominate a child to bring in their favourite book from home, display it in a prominent place. Let children explain why the book is important to them and allow other children to respond. If, as James Britton stresses, 'reading and writing float on a sea of talk' (1970), then time must be made for it.

Ensure your book corner is well-stocked. All children, whether Reception or Year 6 need to have access to a range of reading material: quality literature, poetry, non-fiction, magazines, annuals or comics. Ask the children to help plan the book corner; let them decide on the theme and what to include; they might choose cushions, chairs, a listening station, boxes of books or a special entrance. Not only will this encourage children to read for pleasure, it will also help them as writers, as Vygotsky reminds us 'reading and writing are two halves of the same process' (as cited in Barrs, 2004: 267; Flynn and Stainthorp, 2006).

Find a table, have a range of stationery and writing implements available and call it a writing area. This is a common feature of Key Stage 1 classrooms but increasingly Key Stage 2 teachers are realising the benefits of children being able to write with sparkly pens on different kinds of paper. Let children re-discover the pleasure of physically writing. Themed role-play areas create exciting opportunities for all kinds of English activities; in speaking and listening children play in role, use puppets and props and are engaged in a range of problem-solving activities. As highlighted in the Rose Review young children need a broad and language-rich curriculum where the explicit nature of learning to read sits along-side stories, songs and drama (2006, p29).

Create a literate role-play area so that children can engage in appropriate writing activities (Bayley and Palmer, 2004). For example:

A garden centre   Writing labels for plants, instructions for growing vegetables, listing opening times, designing seed packets.

A café   Compiling menus, taking orders, creating recipes, replying to letters of complaint, writing a restaurant review.

Even Key Stage 2 can enjoy role play and by using Helen Bromley's idea of *Storyboxes* they can enter an imagined world of Ancient Egypt, a pirate ship or even learn more about the experience of an evacuee from World War II. By using artefacts included in the box, children can engage in high-level discussion and collaborative talk where they are genuinely respond-ing to a shared experience (Mercer, 2000). Imagine the writing that would follow from exploring the following:

Evacuee's Storybox	A ration book, a letter from a grieving mother, a watch, a train ticket, a medal, a torn family photograph.
Alex Rider's Storybox	A stopwatch, torch, a fading photograph of his parents, carabiner and rope, invisible ink, mobile phone, envelope with coded letter.

Rather than the teacher determining the genre, allow children the opportunity to choose how they would like to respond, through poetry, a diary entry, a historically accurate report, or through an exciting narrative. Cremin *et al.* (2006) would argue that teachers should refrain from determining the genre and allow children to 'seize the moment' to write and their research suggests that when children take ownership of the writing, the quality improves.

REFLECTIVE TASK

Consider what essential elements you are going to include in your classroom so that visitors will know that yours is a classroom rich in language, where books are celebrated and children's writing is valued. How will children know that you are a writing teacher?

Planning for writing

As previously highlighted, children who have a sense of ownership in their writing, who are writing about topics that they have chosen, are more motivated writers (Graves, 1983). For some teachers there is an apparent conflict between the demands of the curriculum and the opportunity to be imaginative but effective teachers of literacy know that by adopting a creative approach to writing, children engage and therefore succeed in writing (Hall and Harding, 2003). Indeed the revised Framework (DfES, 2006) allows teachers the opportunity to be more flexible with their planning and it is up to you to look for ways that will motivate children to write.

PRACTICAL TASK PRACTICAL TASK PRACTICAL TASK PRACTICAL TASK PRACTICAL TASK

The following units of work are from the Primary Framework for Literacy.

(For clarity, some outcomes have been combined.)

As you read the learning outcomes, consider what you know about children's learning and the need for a real audience for writing. What kind of creative approaches could you take to the following units of work?

Year group, unit of work, genre	Learning outcomes
Year 1 Unit 1 – Traditional tales and fairy stories Narrative	• Children can identify and re-tell the main events in traditional tales, sequencing them in chronological order, using story language. • Children can discuss the appearance, behaviour, characteristics and goals of characters to create a character profile. • Children can discuss how narratives on audio-tape or video are presented and express an opinion about the different versions. • Children can read a simple play-script aloud using appropriate expression and identify how it differs to the story version. • Children can write their own version of a traditional story, using a series of complete sentences organised into chronological order.

Suggestions:
Create a role-play area of favourite fairy tales with a range of props, puppets and storybooks, and make a story throne with a crown for the storyteller. As a teacher tell stories and encourage children to learn them by heart, send stories home to practice. Use video cameras to capture stories, create freeze-frames, use role on the wall to find out more about the characters. Be creative with the character profile – who is it for? Is it a 'Wanted' poster for the Big Bad Wolf, a letter of complaint about Goldilocks, a census for Old King Cole of all the characters in the land? Host a ball, teach children to dance, send invitations, interview the guests whilst they entertain the Prince.

Year 3 Unit 2 – Instructions Non-fiction	• Children can recognise the structure and language features of an instructional text. • Children can express a view clearly as part of a class or group discussion. • Children can orally produce instructions, evaluate their effectiveness and develop them into a chronological sequence. • Children can write an instructional text using selective adverbial language, sequenced imperative statements and presentational features such as bullet points or numbering.

Suggestions:
Create a kitchen role-play area, watch TV clips of cookery programmes, write instructions for making fruit salad for Sports Day and hand out pre-prepared instructions for parents to make it at home. Upload onto the school web-site and encourage parents to leave comments about the success of the instructions. Create a podcast to capture the experience of all those attending Sports Day. (With thanks to DT.)

www.standards.dfes.gov.uk/primaryframework/literacy/planning/

Ideas for meaningful writing activities

You are entering teaching at a time of change, and with documents such as *Excellence and Enjoyment* (DfES, 2003), *All Our Futures: Creativity, Culture and Education* NACCCE (1999), teachers, more than ever, are being encouraged to ensure that creativity is at the heart of English activities. Having read this chapter you should have a better understanding of the many demands placed on children when engaging with writing (Stainthorp, 2002). You realise the importance of children needing to be inspired and have experiences to write about but you are also aware of the tensions that can arise with the demands of the National Curriculum (2000) and the Primary Framework (2006). So, how do schools manage to offer a creative approach while balancing the demands of the curriculum?

Two schools involved in *Everybody Writes*, a web-based project aimed at celebrating innovative approaches to writing, decided to take a fresh look at the writing opportunities within their own school and how they could bring a creative element to their planning.

CASE STUDY 1
Letter writing for the whole school
Forest School were introducing the Primary Framework for Literacy and wanted to review their letter-writing unit of work for Year 5. The school decided to get the whole school writing with Year 2 sending love letters to parents on Valentine's Day, Nursery children writing letters of apology from Goldilocks while Year 4 children designed stamps for letters they really posted and sent messages in balloons.

However, Year 5 took things a little further:

'Wanted. Young, skinny, wiry fellows. Not over 18. Must be expert riders.
Willing to risk death daily. Orphans preferred.'

Intrigued by the above advert, children were inspired by the exciting but short-lived Pony Express and enjoyed the thrill of finding out about the lone horse riders that raced across the United States in the time of the Wild West. This is in itself inspired discussion but the school went a step further and made contact with the Pony Express Museum in Missouri who put the school in touch with a local school. This then led to email contact and the children in Forest School being able to learn more about a far-off country and make a host of new friends. So from a very modest approach to writing within school, the international link added a new and exciting element.

CASE STUDY 2
Townhill Primary School

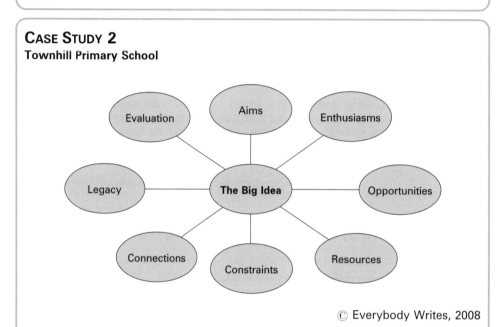

© Everybody Writes, 2008

Townhill Primary School were keen to raise the profile of writing within their school and the **aim** was to encourage pupils to see writing as something fun that they *chose* to engage with. The school ran a very successful gardening club and therefore identified nature and gardening as **enthusiasms** that could be drawn on. The school held an annual Arts Week in June and saw this as an **opportunity** to undertake a cross-curricular project involving writing. Their **big idea** then was to hold an Everybody Writes Day during Arts Week, collapsing the curriculum for the day and involving all pupils in transforming the outdoor space into a poetry playground.

Pupils were involved in generating poems that hung from the trees in the playground, lined the borders of the gardens, stretched across footpaths, with favourite words carved onto stepping-stones. In transforming an under-used corner of the playground into a new outdoor theatre space, children now had a place where poetry could be performed, plays acted, and speeches delivered. The playground was saturated with language and poetry with pupils keen to use the outdoor space during playtimes. The biggest **resource** they had was staff giving up their time and finding ways to involve the whole school community, the Headteacher, teaching assistants, site manager and parents. As with any project there were funding **constraints** and, as this was a whole-school project, this was solved by the Headteacher. However, this was an ambitious project and the ideas are easy to adapt. In using established **connections** the school involved a local artist and poet to bring an additional creative element to the project. The school now has a lasting **legacy** in the shape of a poetry playground with children who enjoy playing with language and see writing as relevant to them.

More inspirational ideas for using the school grounds:

- create a writing space;
- explore secret spaces;
- read stories under a story tree;
- find a space for a stage;
- plant a word garden;
- inspire with pebble poetry;
- go on a poetry journey.

A SUMMARY OF **KEY POINTS**

> Ensure your classroom is a language-rich classroom, with role-play areas, a writing space (indoors or outdoors), a well-stocked book corner, a classroom rich with words to support writing and poetry to enjoy.

> When planning, consider how to combine speaking and listening, reading and writing activities.

> Be aware that writing is hard and makes many demands on children and ensure you are flexible with time but be realistic about learning.

> Writing involves secretarial and authorship elements.

> Look for creative opportunities when planning writing for a real audience.

MOVING *ON* > > > > > > MOVING *ON* > > > > > > MOVING *ON*

As teachers reflect on what they know about effective literacy teaching, a more flexible approach is being adopted but with an emphasis on high expectations about what children can achieve. By slowing down the writing process, time can be planned in for pre-writing activities where ideas can be generated through talk, drama and discussion and will result in an experience that needs to be captured (Bearne, 2002). Pie Corbett talks about teachers inspiring children in such a way that they are on the edge of their seats 'wondering what writing task will come their way' (2005, p6). Just as Bruner suggested that 'knowing is a process not a product' (1966, p72), creativity should also be viewed as a process, not a one-off event (Grainger, Goouch and Lambirth (2005, p16). This should be at the heart of your thinking when you start to plan for English activities within your own class. What will your legacy be?

REFERENCES REFERENCES **REFERENCES** REFERENCES **REFERENCES** REFERENCES

Barrs, M (2004) The reader in the writer, in *The RoutledgeFalmer reader in language and literacy*. Abingdon: RoutledgeFalmer, pp267–76.

Bayley, R and Palmer, S (2004) *Foundations of literacy*. Stafford: Network Educational Press.

Bearne, E (2002) *Making progress in writing*. Abingdon: RoutledgeFalmer.

Berninger, V, Vaughan, K, Abbott, R, Begay, K, Coleman, K, Curtain, G, Hawkins, J and Graham, S (2002) Teaching spelling and composition alone and together: implications for the simple view of writing. *Journal of Educational Psychology*, 94:2, 291–304.

Black and Wiliam (2003) *Assessment for learning: putting it into practice*. Buckingham: Open University Press.

Britton, J (1970) *Language and learning*. Oxford: Heinemann.

Bromley, H (2007) *50 exciting ideas for storyboxes*. Lawrence Educational Publishers. www.foundationstageresources.com

Bromley, H (1998) in Bearne, E (1998) *Use of language across the primary curriculum*. Abingdon: RoutledgeFalmer.

Corbett, P (2005) *How to teach fiction writing at Key Stage 2*. London: David Fulton.

Cremin, T, Goouch, K, Blakemore, L, Goff, E and Macdonald, R (2006) Connecting drama and writing: seizing the moment to write. *Research in Drama Education*, 11:3, 273–91.

Department for Children, Schools and Families (2006) *Primary framework for mathematics and literacy*. London: HMSO.

Department for Education and Employment (1998) *The National Literacy Strategy: framework for teaching*. London: DfEE.

Department for Education and Skills (DfES) (2000) *The National Curriculum for England and Wales*. London: HMSO.

Department for Education and Skills (DfES) (2003) *Excellence and enjoyment*. London: HMSO.

Flynn, N and Stainthorp, R (2006) *The learning and teaching of reading and writing*. Chichester: John Wiley & Sons Ltd.

Grainger, T, Goouch, K, Lambirth, A (2005) *Developing voice and verve in the classroom*. Abingdon: Routledge.

Graves, DH (1983) *Writing: teachers and children at work*. London: Heinemann Educational Books.

Hall, K and Harding, A (2003) A systematic review of effective literacy teaching in the 4 to 14 age range in mainstream schooling. *Research evidence in education library*. London: EPPI Centre, Social Science Research Unit, Institute of Education.

Latham, D (2002) *How children learn to write: supporting and developing children's writing in school*. London: Paul Chapman Publishing.

Medwell, J, Wray, D, Poulson, L and Fox, R (2002) *Teaching literacy effectively in the primary school*. Abingdon: Routledge.

Meek, M (1991) *On being literate*. London: The Bodley Head.

Mercer, N (2000) *Words and minds: how we use language to think together*. Abingdon: Routledge.

National Advisory Committee on Creative and Cultural Education (NACCCE) (1999) *All our futures: creativity, culture and education* (The Robinson Report). London: DfEE.

Rose, J (2006) *Independent review of the teaching of early reading*. Nottingham: DfES.

Smith, A and Call, N (2003) *The ALPS approach.* Stafford: Network Educational Press.

Smith, F (1994) *Writing and the writer*. NJ: Lawrence Erlbaum Associates.

Stainthorp, R (2002) Writing is hard. *Psychology of Education Review*, 26, 3–11.

Useful websites

www.everybodywrites.org.uk – with more details about the alien space ship crash-landing, letter writing to the Pony Express, Poetry Garden.

www.michaelrosen.co.uk/poetryfriendly.html – Michael Rosen's poetry-friendly classroom.

7
What is creativity in science education?
Jane Johnston

Chapter objectives

The purpose of this chapter is to help you:

- **to understand the nature of creativity in science education;**
- **to understand the importance of creativity in science teaching on learning and learners;**
- **to understand and overcome the difficulties of being creative in teaching and learning.**

This chapter addresses the following Professional Standards for the award of QTS:
Q10, Q14, Q22, Q25(a), Q25(b), Q25(c), Q25(d)

Introduction

Science is not often thought of as creative, but rather as a body of certain and unchanging knowledge. This narrow view does not acknowledge the tentative nature of scientific theories and the creativity of scientific discoveries, which broaden our understanding of the universe, changing the way we think and the way we view the world. Children's pictures (see Figure 7.1), show scientists as white, male and white-coated, although the addition of 'thought bubbles', exclamation marks and the use of words such as 'Eureka!', indicate an element of invention, discovery and innovation if not creativity. The reason for this seeming anomaly is that creativity is not only difficult to define and is used synonymously (Childs, 1986) with words such as originality, but also has different meanings in science and technology than when used in the context of the arts.

Figure 7.1 A stereotypical picture of a scientist
(Johnston, 1996, p33)

REFLECTIVE TASK

REFLECTIVE TASK

What picture comes into your mind when you think of science?

How would you draw a picture of a scientist?

Do you think the stereotypical image of science and scientists is outdated?

It is necessary to extend our understanding of creativity in order to see how science can be creative and we should include creativity of thinking and problem-solving (de Bono, 1992), as well as discovery and innovation. Creativity is not exclusively an artistic attribute (Prentice, 2000) and is described in dictionaries (Macdonald, 1972) as concerned with bringing into being or making something new, a definition that can be applied to science with ease. Beetlestone's (1998) six-part definition of creativity,

1. learning;
2. representation;
3. productivity;
4. originality;
5. thinking creatively/problem-solving;
6. universe/creation-nature;

can be applied to science and acknowledges the multifaceted and all-encompassing nature of creativity in science. However, there is not a clear definition of creativity or agreement of what creativity is (Gibson 2005; Prentice 2000).

Historically, science has been innovative, involving discovery and creative thinking and with creative scientists as risk takers. Leonardo da Vinci is considered to one of the greatest artists and scientists, producing significant works of art and scientific ideas, which have been used to support understanding (human anatomy) and technological advances (aircraft design). Newton, Archimedes and Curie demonstrated creativity of thought which led to improved understanding of our world (Newton extended understanding of gravitational force and light) and technological advances (Archimedes's ideas led to the use of levers to help lift heavy objects and Curie's discoveries led to radiotherapy). Other scientists, such as Darwin and Galileo, took great risks in communicating their ideas to a world that was unwilling and unready to accept them, and faced public humiliation and incarceration.

Our science education has an important influence on our perception and understanding of science. Differences in understanding appear to result from societal emphasis (Ofsted, 2003; Osborne and Dillon, 2008), views of the world (Kahn, 1999) and science education (Johnston *et al.*, 1998), although a contrasting view is offered in a review of curricula as part of the Primary Review (Hall and Øzerk, 2008). It may be that whereas different countries may have similar curricula, the emphases may be different. For example, sometimes primary science education has a biological and geographical emphasis (Finland, Bosnia), with chemistry, physics and mathematics being taught as secondary sciences, is mainly knowledge-based and curriculum-focused (England post National Curriculum, Macedonia and Japan), or skills-based and child-centred (England pre-National Curriculum).

PRACTICAL TASK PRACTICAL TASK PRACTICAL TASK PRACTICAL TASK PRACTICAL TASK

Learning about scientists and their discoveries can help develop a better understanding about the nature of science and scientific discoveries.

- Try learning about Leonardo da Vinci through reading extracts from his notebooks and explore gravitational force by making paper helicopters. Explore what happens when you use different types of paper/card or different sizes or add extra paperclips or fold the wings the opposite way.
- Read the story of Darwin's voyage on the Beagle and sort pictures of animals or collections of plants according to observable features. Look at teeth, skull shapes, leaf shape or seeds and think what this tells us about the animal/plant.
- Retell the story of Archimedes and then explore how different objects affect the water level of a tank of water (Johnston and Gray, 1999). Does the weight or size make a difference?

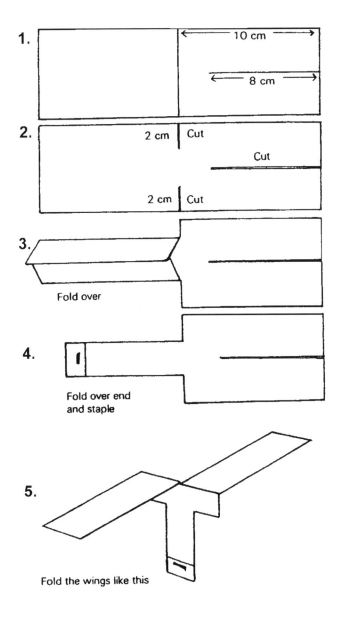

Figure 7.2 Making a paper helicopter

What is creativity in science education?

Creative science education is a complex inter-relationship between science and education; made difficult because of the different natures of science and education. Science is commonly viewed as a body of empirical, non-political knowledge. Education is felt to reflect changes in society and views, is inherently political and values all knowledge and under-standing and is therefore less static in its development than science. Science education sits somewhat uncomfortably between science and education and is viewed differently depend-ing on whether viewed, initially, from a science or education strength. Where science is the stronger partner, then progress in science education can be slowed by the empirical view of the nature of science. Science education in our present national curriculum (DfEE, 1999) has focused on factual learning of the views of science, although creativity is increasingly more valued by society (Osborne and Dillon, 2008) and emphasised in recent government drives (DfES, 2003; QCA, 2003) and journals (see for example, *Teaching, Thinking and Creativity*, an on-line journal of articles on creative teaching).

Making connections is considered (Duffy, 1998) to be an important aspect of creativity and creativity in science education involves making connections between aspects of learning across the curriculum (DfES, 2003). In this way science education will not focus solely on the acquisition of limited scientific knowledge, but involve the development of scientific under-standing, skills and attitudes, integrating other subjects through real-life contexts so that knowledge and skills can be applied in real situations; that is, the development of scientific literacy.

Creative science education involves practitioners with subject and pedagogical knowledge who adapt their teaching to suit the learning objectives, children and context. Creative science education does not follow rigidly imposed methodologies such as implied by the introduction of some primary strategies (DfEE, 1998 and 1999). Such changes in education are thought to have affected pedagogical practice (Cullingford, 1996; Johnston, 2002) and reduced the practical component of much science teaching (ASE, 1999) so that many science lessons are not structured sufficiently to effectively develop scientific learning objec-tives (Osborne and Dillon, 2008). Creative science education is active and child-centred, involving individual problem-solving and exploration and not those passive learning approaches which published schemes, CD-ROMs and schemes of work (e.g. QCA, 2000) appear to advocate. Creative science practitioners make their own decisions about teaching styles and learning experiences, producing novel ideas for achieving objectives to the bene-fit of the children's learning (DfES, 2003; QCA, 2003). They are enthusiastic about science education and balance the needs of the whole curriculum with those of children's creative development (Boden, 2001). Excellent science practitioners have been identified (Fraser and Tobin, 1993) as those who manage their classrooms effectively, use teaching strategies which focus on the children's understanding, provide learning environments which suit the children's learning preferences, have a strong content knowledge and encourage chil-dren's involvement in classroom discussions and activities. More recently, excellent science teachers have been recognised by Chartered Science Teacher Status (see Association for Science Education and Science Council websites) as those whose teaching is informed by the personal scholarship and research identified by the Children's Plan (DCSF, 2007).

REFLECTIVE TASK

Look at Figure 7.3 and decide what you think is good teaching and learning in science.

Pedagogical approaches in science can fall along two continua, constructivist/positivist and traditional-ist/post-modernist (Longbottom, 1999) as seen in Figure 7.3.

Highly structured teacher-led approaches are ones in which the teacher imparts scientific knowledge, demonstrates concepts and instructs pupils in the use of equipment. These approaches fall within the traditionalist/positivist sector and are the least creative type of approaches. More creative are teacher-led explorations, where the teacher sets up and structures explorations and investigations to enable pupils to construct their own scientific conceptions and develop skills. These fall into the traditionalist/constructivist sector. Even more creative science education involves exploration and discovery where teachers guide pupils and support the construction of understandings through scientific challenge and discourse. These type of approaches fall into the constructivist/post-modernist sector. Other creative approaches engage pupils in the discussion and argumentation of scientific understanding and abstract ideas and these fall into the positivist/post-modernist sector.

TRADITIONALIST
Emphasis on authority, dissemination, imparting knowledge and training skills

Highly structured teacher-led instruction/ demonstration	Teacher-led exploration
Structured teacher-led instruction/ demonstration	Structured teacher-led exploration

POSITIVIST   **CONSTRUCTIVIST**
       Constructing understanding from experience

Pursuit of knowledge as a truth

          Exploration

Debate/discussion/argumentation   Discovery

POST-MODERNIST
Emphasis on engaging with issues/ideas and challenging interpretations

Figure 7.3 How pedagogical approaches fit into the constructivist/positivist and traditionalist/ post-modernist continua (Longbottom, 1999)

Student and teacher views of creativity in science education

In one piece of research (Johnston and Ahtee, 2006), I compared 98 student teachers' attitudes towards teaching physics activities with their attitudes towards teaching their mother tongue (English), mathematics and science using a previously validated semantic differential questionnaire with 20 bipolar adjective pairs (Ahtee and Rikkinen, 1995; Ahtee and Tella, 1995). The semantic differential (SD) is a method of observing and measuring the connotative meaning of concepts (Osgood *et al.*, 1967). The scoring adopted was +2, +1, 0, −1, −2 with high positive scores signifying a positive attitude. The bipolar adjectives were grouped in four broad categories with five pairs in each.

- *Level of Difficulty* (easy/difficult, self-evident/abstract, commonplace/mystical, simple/complicated, productive/trivial);
- *Level of Interest and Involvement* (interesting/boring, gripping/undesirable, active/passive, social/individual, practical/theoretical);
- *Perceived Nature* (free/compulsory, open/closed, creative/non-creative, cheerful/sad, broadening/ constricting);
- *Perceived Value* (valuable/worthless, profound/superficial, wise/foolish, selfish/unselfish, sublime/ ridiculous).

PRACTICAL TASK PRACTICAL TASK **PRACTICAL TASK** PRACTICAL TASK **PRACTICAL TASK**

Decide for yourself which of the bipolar adjectives (as above) you feel describes science.
Compare your results with the students in Figure 7.4.

The results as seen in Figure 7.4, show that science education is viewed as less creative than English teaching, but physics education is not viewed as creative and mathematics (sometimes referred to as the purest of sciences) is considered to be the least creative educational subject.

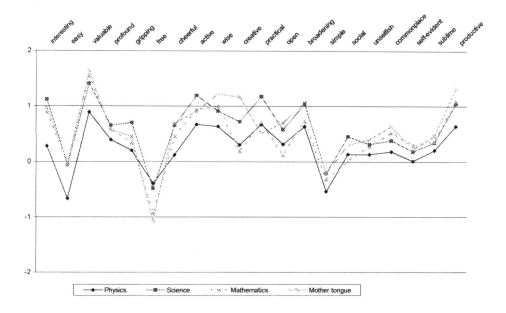

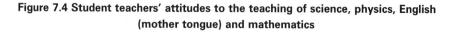

Figure 7.4 Student teachers' attitudes to the teaching of science, physics, English (mother tongue) and mathematics

I once asked experienced teachers (Johnston, 2003) to explore their perception of science education by asking them to identify how it fitted into the constructivist/positivist and traditionalist/post-modernist continua described earlier and shown in Figure 7.3 (Longbottom, 1999). This indicated that teachers had a more creative perception of science education, with recognition of its multi-faceted nature and the importance of scientific learning relevant to everyday life. These findings, however, were in contrast to those of science teachers in previous studies (Lederman and Zeidler 1987) although more akin to the multi-faceted views found to be held by chemistry teachers in Koulaidis and Ogborn's study (1989) and generalist primary teachers (Johnston, Ahtee and Hayes 1998). However, I was unsure whether these views were reflected in the science that is taught in school and so in a further piece of research, student teachers' espoused philosophical views of primary science teaching were compared with their planning and practice.

The student group involved 10 science specialist initial teacher training students at the beginning of their 2nd year of undergraduate work. At the start of a module on the science curriculum, the students were asked to identify their pedagogical views on science education by identifying where they felt science education fitted into the two continua shown in Figure 7.4. Of the 10 students involved, five placed science teaching and learning at the centre of the continua. Four students felt that science teaching and learning was firmly in the constructivist/post-modernist sector and one student felt that it was very slightly in the positivist/traditionalist sector. There followed some teaching on good practice in science teaching and learning and individual planning of science teaching. Finally, student interaction with 30 Year 3 children, while engaged in 'discovery learning approach', was observed. Observations of their practice identified the approaches as falling into four out of five categories, from highly creative guided discovery to highly structured teacher-led imposition of knowledge:

1. Guided discovery and exploration (0 students);
   Children are allowed to explore independently, with guidance from the teacher, by way of appropriate interaction, such as incidental questions (DES, 1967: DfES 2003).
2. Teacher-led exploration (4 students);
   Children are led through an exploration, with almost complete teacher involvement.
3. Structured teacher-led exploration (3 students);
   Children are led through an exploration, with teacher instructions and complete teacher involvement.
4. Structured teacher-led imposition (1 student);
   Children are directly taught knowledge through instruction, questioning and practical activity.
5. Highly structured teacher-led imposition (2 students);
   Children are directly taught knowledge through instruction, questioning and teacher demonstration.

The results for the comparison between the student teachers' espoused views, planning and practice can be seen in Figure 7.5 and show that there is very little correlation between their espoused views, planning and practice. This may indicate a tension between espoused beliefs on the nature of science education and the implicit message within the science national curriculum, which emphasises science as *knowledge consisting of relationships between self-evident variables that are related in regular law-like ways* (Monk and Dillon 2000, p80), in other words, science as empiricism. This is not a new phenomenon, as research has found (Fensham 2001, Taber 2002), the wealth of knowledge on constructivist science teaching has not had a significant effect on the content of science education. However, this tension can only have a negative impact on creative teaching and learning, as new practitioners struggle to come to terms with the ideological rhetoric of creative science education and pragmatic classroom reality.

REFLECTIVE TASK

Compare your planning and practice to the ideas in Figure 7.5 below. Is there a gap between your beliefs about good teaching and learning in science and how you teach?

Student	Views	Planning	Practice
1	Central	Exploratory (C/PM)	Structured teacher-led exploration with a focus on knowledge (T/C)
2	Central	Structured teacher-led (T/P)	Highly structured, teacher-led with a focus on knowledge (T/P)
3	Traditionalist/ Positivist (T/P)	Exploratory (C/PM)	Structured teacher-led exploration with a focus on knowledge (T/C)
4	Central	Structured teacher-led exploratory (T/C)	Teacher-led exploration with a focus on knowledge (T/C)
5	Constructivist/ Post-modernist (C/PM)	Structured exploratory (T/C)	Teacher-led exploration with a focus on knowledge (T/C)
6	Central	Structured teacher-led (T/P)	Highly structured, teacher-led with a focus on knowledge (T/P)
7	Constructivist/ Post-modernist (C/PM)	Exploratory group work with teacher cue cards (T/C)	Teacher-led exploration with a focus on knowledge (T/C)
8	Constructivist/ Post-modernist (C/PM)	Structured teacher-led with some problem-solving (T/P)	Teacher-led exploration with a focus on knowledge (T/C)
9	Constructivist/ Post-modernist (C/PM)	Structured teacher-led (T/P)	Structured teacher-led with a focus on knowledge (T/P)
10	Central	Teacher-led experiment (T/P)	Structured teacher-led exploration with a focus on knowledge (T/C)

Key T/C = Traditionalist/Constructivist   C/PM = Constructivist/Post-modernist
     PM/P = Post-modernist/Positivist   T/P = Traditionalist/Positivist

Figure 7.5 The relationship between the student teachers' views on science education, planning and practice

Problem-solving activities can help learners of all ages develop scientific understandings as well as understandings of the nature of science. One such problem can be to design and make a one-minute timer, a series of energy transfers which take one minute from start to finish. For example, lighting a candle can burn through a thread and release a ramp, down which a ball bearing will roll. This may roll down a maze and then be attracted to a magnet pushing a needle into a balloon which bursts. This variation of a mousetrap game can be undertaken by learners of all ages, as they will apply and build upon their initial knowledge and produce a timer which demonstrates their understanding of different types of energy transfers (light, heat, mechanical, kinetic, magnetic and sound).

Why is creativity in science education important?

While there have been disputes among psychologists as to whether creativity is a characteristic of the highly intelligent (Munn, 1966; Childs, 1986), it is also considered to be a potential in all of us which needs encouragement and motivation to flourish (Medawar, 1969). Creative science education will involve planning for and responding to creative pupil ideas and this has been found (QCA, 2003) to develop curiosity, motivation, self-esteem and academic achievement, as well as having a positive effect on adult life skills. Creative children are more likely to be creative adults, who can solve problems, take risks and be motivated to continue to learn, for as W. B. Yeats identified, 'education is not the filling of a pail but the lighting of a fire'.

REFLECTIVE TASK

Creative science educational experiences have three essential elements; they should be practical, memorable and interactive. The importance of practical exploratory approaches in scientific development is well established and can be seen in many learning models in science (see Renner, 1982; Karplus, 1977; Cosgrove and Osborne, 1985), including the constructivist approach (Scott, 1987), which has become increasingly popular in science education. Practical science will develop important scientific skills and generic cognitive skills such as problem-solving and thinking skills. Scientific thinking skills can be developed by:

- challenging children's ideas, by getting them to test out their hypotheses;
- setting problems for them to solve;
- discussing their ideas and compare with the ideas of others;
- encouraging them to make causal links.

Through practical activities and discussion of ideas (Costello, 2000, p87) children develop thinking in science in the early years (Keogh and Naylor, 2000) as do older children (Jones, 2000; Shayer and Adey, 2002). Through explorations, problem-solving and discussions children begin to explain their ideas, think hypothetically (de Bóo 1999; Osborne *et al.*, 2001) and make causal links between phenomena and their hypothetical ideas. They can also identify their metacognitive processes, that is how they solved problems or the thinking behind their interpretations and hypotheses (Shayer and Adey, 2002; Fisher, 2003).

Consider how thinking skills can be developed within the QCA (2000) schemes of work. How can you add challenge to the activities?

I once asked Key Stage 1 children to explore a collection of toys in a toy box, after reading *Kipper's Toybox* (Inkpen, 1992). They handled the toys and were encouraged to play with them, exploring how they worked. The children were then encouraged to sort the toys according to their properties, putting them into sorting hoops. All the spinning toys were put into one hoop, all the magnetic toys in another, pushing toys in another and jumping toys in another. A magnetic gyroscope which spins on a metal frame with two metal rails, caused a few problems as this was both a spinner and magnetic. One child decided that we could place the gyroscope between the spinning and magnetic hoops, so that it touched both. Another child suggested that we could separate the two parts of the gyroscope and put the spinning part in the spinning hoop and the metal frame in the magnetic hoop (although it was not itself magnetic). A third child suggested an alternative solution, by overlapping the hoops so that there was another section for magnetic spinning toys. This was a good example of children be developing and using their thinking skills to solve simple problems. Further research looking at the skill of observation in children from 4 to 11 years of age (Johnston, 2007) has identified the importance of providing time, space and support for children to enable them to think creatively and solve problems. *Cognitive acceleration,* whole class, group debates or discussions which involve an element of argument are proven to be successful in developing skills and understandings in science and across primary education as well as generic thinking skills (Shayer and Adey, 2002).

Memorable science education supports the development of important motivating attitudes (Johnston, 1996), such as curiosity, which is essential in harnessing children's interest, encouraging them to take risks, make scientific discoveries and construct scientific understandings. Attitudes can usually be observed in some kind of behaviour and the importance of the resulting behaviours is thought to affect development in science (DfEE, 1999; Bricheno *et al.*, 2001). Attitudes can be:

- generic, that is those needed throughout education (co-operation and perseverance);
- scientific, that is those that are important in science education (respect for evidence and tentativeness);
- affective or emotional, (enthusiasm);
- cognitive (curiosity, respect for evidence, thoughtfulness, reflection, tentativeness, questioning);
- social or behavioural (co-operation, collaboration, tolerance, flexibility, independence, perseverance, leadership, responsibility, tenaciousness).

Creative science education can help to develop many of these attitudes, by motivating children to want to explore and discover, encouraging them to work co-operatively and support their cognitive development.

Children need to interact with their environment, their peers and supportive adults in creative science experiences. Creative science learning environments will encourage cognitive development, *encompassing milieus, in which the messages of learning and work are manifest and inviting* (Gardner, 1991: 204). Interacting with others will encourage them to consider the ideas of others and develop thinking skills (Shayer and Adey, 2002). Interaction with supportive adults can challenge ideas and interpretations, with the role of the adult being to facilitate learning rather than impart knowledge, recognising that creative science education is an active rather than a passive experience in which an adult supports children in the development of skills and understandings, which can later be applied in other contexts and everyday life.

Why is it difficult to be a creative science teacher?

Creative science teaching and learning is thought to pose problems particularly regarding time, coverage, control, safety and achievement of learning objectives. In practice, creative science can effectively address all these issues and make learning fun for both practitioner and child.

The science curriculum contains an enormous amount of material and one pedagogical solution is to impart knowledge, as this takes less time than exploration, discovery or investigation. The difficulty of covering the curriculum, together with the understandable fear of a whole class practically exploring and investigating in science, sometimes leads to the type of teaching approaches advocated in literacy and numeracy. This means that some science lessons become whole-class demonstrations which impart knowledge to children en masse. For teachers who lack confidence in science and who are also inexperienced in teaching this approach to science education appears to be an effective way to manage the demands of the curriculum and maintain good levels of behaviour, controlling children's learning and ensuring safety. In fact, such an approach leads to poor quality learning. Effective science learning occurs through teaching approaches which engage and interest children (Hidi and Harackiewicz, 2000), approaches which are practical, developing skills alongside understandings and paying attention to detail rather than coverage, and where practitioners facilitate individual or small-group learning, bearing in mind individual learning abilities and styles (Gardner, 1983).

Science curricula often address ideas and knowledge in a 'fragmented way' (Osborne and Dillon, 2008, p8) and so a recommendation from a report on science education in Europe is that there should be 'more innovative curricula and ways of organising the teaching of science that address the issue of low student motivation' (Osborne and Dillon, 2008, p8). This echoes previous suggestions in education in general (e.g. Reid and Petocz, 2004) that educators need to apply creative ideas more specifically to teaching and learning, or even redefine creativity as many current definitions only loosely apply to education and help in teaching and learning (Mindham, 2005). The very large demands of the science curriculum can be effectively covered by practically focusing on small aspects of conceptual under-standing rather than 'fragmented' knowledge and set in a motivating context which children can relate to. Practical work (explorations, investigations, problem-solving and guided discovery) will support the development of scientific skills (Sc1 of the national curriculum), which cannot be achieved in a non-practical way. The focus on conceptual understanding will help children to apply their understanding in new contexts and support their under-standing in other scientific concepts. Effective and creative science education does take time for children to explore, investigate and discover new ideas. It does involve giving children time and encouragement to support their explorations and discoveries and also support their behaviour. Behaviour is improved by child-centred, creative scientific activities; in fact we can have greater control over behaviour and learning by being less controlling. It is therefore worrying that there are indications from research by the Wellcome Trust, which follows up previous research (Murphy *et al.*, 2005) on assessment at Key Stage 2, that teachers are undertaking less practical work because of behavioural problems and not solely because of assessment demands.

Whole-class directed scientific learning does not allow children to develop their own under-standing, implying that all children need the same experiences and that the practitioner knows exactly what is best for each learner. In fact, children's development is more effective when they are motivated to learn, take ownership over their own learning and work with practitioners to develop knowledge, understanding, skills and attitudes.

Within the primary strategy, creative science education becomes a reality by,

- *Making learning vivid and real, by developing understanding through enquiry, creativity, e-learning and group problem-solving;*

● *Making learning an enjoyable and challenging experience, by stimulating learning through matching teaching to learning styles and preferences;*
● *Enriching the learning experience, by developing learning skills across the curriculum.*

(DfES, 2003: 29)

For many practitioners the problem is how to incorporate the features of effective creative science education, but maintain the rigour and focus on key objectives for development and learning. Scientific concepts, knowledge and skills are static and unchanging, so that creative science activities are almost impossible to deliver. We need to remember that many aspects of science will be new for children and have the potential to inspire them. We can also be creative in our teaching, especially when we become confident ourselves in scientific understanding. Every teacher has the potential for creativity, in the same way that every child has. Too often our creativity in science education is adversely affected by our lack of scientific understanding and we are unable to use our creativity in our teaching.

REFLECTIVE TASK

Do creative children need creative teachers?

If we lack creativity in our teaching, we will structure and control all aspects of learning and restrict any creativity on the part of children. They will be unable to take alternative viewpoints, solve problems and challenge interpretations, and their understandings are likely to be less sophisticated. If we allow children some freedom to explore their own ideas and value their alternative views of the world, then we support creativity and learning (see *Primary Science Review*, 2004, which focused on creativity and science education).

How can you be more creative in your science teaching?

How can we be more creative in our teaching?

Effective, creative science teaching and learning can be best achieved by providing motivating exploratory and investigatory experiences for children. One form of creative science involves structured exploratory discovery learning (Johnston, 2004). Discovery learning (DES, 1967) was popular in the 1960s and 1970s, although over time it was seen to involve children playing without purpose or learning objectives and did not take into account existing conceptual ideas of the world they had developed from birth. This definition has been updated for modern teaching and so an exploratory discovery approach is one where:

● *the child is central to the learning;*
● *children explore and discover things about the world around them, which stem from their own initial curiosity;*
● *children construct their own understandings through exploration and from the experience of discovery, as well as develop important skills and attitudes;*
● *teachers support and encourage children to ensure that their explorations and discoveries are meaningful to them;*
● *teachers utilize knowledge about the children as learners (e.g. Gardner, 1983) and pedagogical theory and practice to provide an excellent learning environment.*

(Johnston, 2004: p21–22).

An example of a creative discovery approach is a potions lesson (after Harry Potter, Rowling, 1997, see Johnston, 2005), which I have carried out with children from Year 2 to Year 6. This begins as a fairly formal lesson with me wearing an academic gown and in role as a Hogwart's supply teacher. During the lesson, the children predict and investigate what will happen if they mix small amounts of substances with water in clear plastic beakers. The substances include unidentified solids (salt, sugar, cornflour, talcum powder, bicarbonate of soda and plaster of Paris) and liquids (white vinegar, detergent, lemonade, cooking oil, lemon juice and colour change bubble bath). Through investigation the children will experience dissolving (salt and sugar), solutions (cornflour, bicarbonate of soda, lemon juice), density (talcum powder, oil and plaster of Paris) and colour change (bubble bath). Later, the lesson becomes more exploratory with children discovering what happens when they mix different substances together in different proportions (vinegar and bicarbonate of soda fizz, plaster of Paris and water produce heat) and they can even write instructions for their potion and identify what effects it will have through an advertisement or jingle. In this way children are developing scientific skills (observation, prediction and hypothesis) and understanding (the way materials change when mixed) through a creative, cross-curricular activity that will motivate them.

Problem-solving is another example of creative science and can vary from the small challenges given to children while they explore or play to specific problems that involve the use of scientific skills and knowledge, sometimes in a technological context. While young children play in the sand, water or discover materials through a potion exploration, the practitioner can challenge them by asking questions.

- What will happen if you add water to the sand?
- How can you make a water spout?
- How can you make the potion change colour/fizz/...?

PRACTICAL TASK PRACTICAL TASK PRACTICAL TASK PRACTICAL TASK PRACTICAL TASK

Design a ball sorter where balls of different sizes and made of different materials (polystyrene balls, marbles, ball bearings, golf balls, table tennis balls, tennis balls) have to be sorted by a machine made out of a large cardboard box and other junk materials.

Criteria for sorting can include size, density, mass, magnetic, etc.

You can also do this activity with children. They are expected to work together in small groups to make accurate, original machines which sort the balls in a number of different ways. At the end of the activity, the machines can be tested and certificates given to groups for originality of design, accuracy of sorting, number of different ways of sorting and group collaboration skills. In this way children are developing skills in designing and making (D&T) as well as planning (Sc1) and knowledge and understanding of forces (Sc4) and materials (Sc3). You can make sure that each group receives a certificate and this can be an added motivational factor.

For younger children, play areas such as a garden centre or bakery (de Bóo, 2004) can lead to scientific learning about plant growth or materials and properties in a cross-curricular way. In these play experiences, children can develop their own understandings at a rate and in a way that is appropriate. Some children will learn best when interacting with other children, while others will be much more solitary in their play but still make good developmental progress.

A SUMMARY OF **KEY POINTS**

> Creativity is not a description that is generally attributed to science.

> Historically, creativity is an essential factor in the scientific discoveries of many famous scientists, such as Darwin, Leonardo da Vinci and Archimedes.

> Science education sits in a difficult position between more creative education and less creative and less flexible science.

> Creative science educational experiences should be practical, memorable and interactive.

> Children need creative teachers to be creative learners.

> Creative science teaching involves challenging and changing approaches and adapting teaching to suit learners.

> The problems of including creative science activities in teaching are time, coverage, control, safety and achievement. However, the benefits in terms of future development outweigh the problems.

MOVING *ON* > > > > > > MOVING *ON* > > > > > > MOVING *ON*

- Try planning and teaching some creative science activities and evaluate their effect on children's learning and behaviour.
- Try working with more experienced and confident science teachers within your school to make the experience more rewarding for you professionally and personally and to help you to understand the scientific concepts underpinning the activities.
- Look for external support from the Association for Science Education, local and national science education conferences and publications and websites (see below for some useful websites).

REFERENCES REFERENCES **REFERENCES** REFERENCES **REFERENCES** REFERENCES

Ahtee, M and Rikkinen, H (1995) Luokanopettajaksi opiskelevien mielikuvia fysiikasta, kemiasta, biologiasta ja maantieteestä, Dimensio (Primary student teachers' perceptions about physics, chemistry, biology and geography), 59, 54–8.

Ahtee, M and Tella, S (1995) Future class teachers' perceptions of their school-time teachers of physics, mathematics and foreign languages, in Tella, S (ed.) *Juuret ja arvot: Etnisyys ja eettisyys – aineen opettaminen monikulttturisessa oppimisympäristössä. (Roots and values: Ethnicity and ethics – Teaching a subject in a multi-cultural learning environment.)* Proceedings of a subject-didactic symposium in Helsinki. Department of Teacher Education, University of Helsinki. Research Report 150, 180–200.

Association for Science Education (1999) *ASE survey on the effect of the National Literacy Strategy on the teaching of science.* Hatfield: ASE.

Beetlestone, F (1998) *Creative children, imaginative teaching.* Buckingham: Open University Press.

Boden, MA (2001) Creativity and knowledge, in Craft, A, Jeffrey, B and Leibling, M (2001) *Creativity in education.* London: Continuum.

Bricheno, P, Johnston, J and Sears, J (2001) Children's attitudes to science, in Sears, J and Sorensen, P (eds) *Issues in the teaching of science.* Abingdon: Routledge.

Childs, D (1986) *Psychology and the teacher,* (4th edition). Chatham: Holt, Rinehart and Winston.

Cosgrove, M and Osborne, R (1985) Lesson frameworks for changing children's ideas, in Osborne, R and Freyberg, P, *Learning in science: the implications of children's learning.* Auckland, New Zealand: Heinemann.

Costello, PJM (2000) *Thinking skills and early childhood education.* London: David Fulton.

Cullingford, C (1996) Changes in primary education, in Cullingford, C (1996) *The politics of primary education.* Buckingham: Open University Press.

Children's Workforce Development Council (2007) *Prospectus of Early Years professional status*. Leeds: CWDC.

de Bono, E (1992) *Serious creativity*. London: HarperCollins.

de Bóo, M (1999) *Enquiring children: challenging teaching*. Buckingham: Open University Press.

de Bóo, M (ed.) (2004) *Early years handbook. Support for practitioners in the Foundation Stage*. Sheffield: The Curriculum Partnership/Geography Association.

Department for Education and Science (1967) *Children and their primary school. A report of the Central Advisory Council for Education (England)*, Vol. 1: Report. London: HMSO.

Department for Education and Employment (1998) *The National Literacy Strategy*. London: DfEE.

Department for Education and Employment (1999) *The National Numeracy Strategy*. London: DfEE.

Department for Education and Employment (1999a) *The National Curriculum: handbook for teachers in England*. London: DfEE/QCA.

Department for Education and Science (2003) *Excellence and enjoyment. A strategy for primary schools*. London: DfES.

Department for Education and Science (2004) *Every Child Matters: change for children*. London: DfES.

Department for Children, Schools and Families (2007) *The children's plan. Building brighter futures*. Norwich: The Stationery Office.

Duffy, B (1998) *Supporting creativity and imagination in the Early Years*. Buckingham: Open University Press.

Fensham, PJ (2001) Science Content as Problematic – Issues for Research, in Behrendt, H, Dahncke, H, Duit, R, Gräber, W, Komorek, M, Kross, A and Reiska, P, *Research in science education – past, present and future*. Dordrecht, NL: Kluwer Academic.

Fisher, R (2003) *Teaching thinking* London: Continuum.

Fraser, B and Tobin, K (1993) Exemplary science and mathematics teachers, in Fraser, B (ed.) *Research implications for science and mathematics teachers*, vol. 1. Perth, WA: National Key Centre for School Science and Mathematics, Curtin University of Technology.

Gardner, H (1983) *Frames of mind: the theory of multiple intelligences*. London: Heinemann.

Gardner, H (1991) *The unschooled mind*. London: Fontana.

Gibson, H (2005) What creativity isn't: the presumptions of instrumental and individual justifications for creativity in education. *British Journal of Educational Studies*, 53:2, 148–67.

Hall, K and Øzerk, K (2008) *Primary curriculum and assessment: England and other countries. Primary review interim report*. Cambridge: Primary Review, University of Cambridge.

Hidi, S and Harackiewicz, JM (2000) Motivating the academically unmotivated: a critical issue for the 21st century. *Review of Educational Research*, 70:2, 151–79.

Inkpen, M (1992) *Kipper's toybox*. London: Hodder.

Johnston, J (1996) *Early explorations in science*. Buckingham: Open University Press.

Johnston, J (2002) The changing face of teaching and learning, in Johnston, J, Chater, M and Bell, D (eds) *Teaching the primary curriculum*. Buckingham: Open University Press.

Johnston, J (2003) 'Teachers' philosophies on science teaching'. Paper presented to the *European Science Educational Research Conference 2003*, University of Utrecht, The Netherlands.

Johnston, J (2004) The value of exploration and discovery. *Primary Science Review* 85, 21–3 Nov/Dec.

Johnston, J (2005) *Early explorations in science*, (2nd edition). Buckingham: Open University Press.

Johnston, J (2007) How does the skill of observation develop in young children? in Venville, G and Dawson, V (2007) *Proceedings of CONASTA 56 and ICASE 2007 World Conference on Science and Technology Education. Sustainable, Responsible, Global*. Perth, Australia: Science Teachers' Association of Western Australia www.worldste2007.asn.au ISBN: 978-0-9803703-0-0.

Johnston, J, Ahtee, M and Hayes, M (1998) Elementary teachers' perceptions of science and science teaching: comparisons between Finland and England, in Kartinen, S (ed.) *Matemaattisten aineiden opetus ja opiminem*. Oulu: Oulun yliopistopaino, 13–30.

Johnston, J and Ahtee, M (2006) What are primary student teachers' attitudes, subject knowledge and pedagogical content knowledge needs in a physics topic? *Teaching and Teacher Education*, 22:4, 1–10.

Johnston J and Gray A (1999) *Enriching early scientific learning*. Buckingham: Open University Press.

Jones, C (2000) The role of language in the learning and teaching of science, in Monk, M and Osborne, J (eds) *Good practice in science teaching. What research has to say*. Buckingham: Open University Press.

Kahn, PH Jr. (1999) *The human relationship with nature*. Cambridge, MA: MIT Press.

Karplus, R (1977) *Science teaching and the development of reasoning.* Berkeley, CA: University of California Press.

Keogh, B and Naylor, S (2000) Assessment in the Early Years, in de Bóo, M (ed.) *Laying the foundations in the Early Years*. Hatfield: ASE.

Koulaidis, V and Ogborn, J (1989) Philosophy of science: an impirical study of teachers' views. *International Journal of Science Education,* 11:2, 173–84.

Lederman, NG and Zeidler, DL (1987) Science teachers' conceptions of the nature of science: do they really influence teaching behaviour? *Science Education*, 71, 721–34.

Longbottom, J (1999) Science education for democracy: dilemmas, decisions, autonomy and anarchy. Paper presented to the *European Science Education Research Association Second International Conference,* Kiel, Germany.

Macdonald, AM (1972) *Chambers twentieth century dictionary*. London: W and R Chambers.

Medawar, PB (1969) *Induction and intuition in scientific thought. Memoirs of the American Philosophical Society. Jayne Lectures 1968.* London: Methuen.

Mindham, C (2005) Creativity and the young child. *Early Years*, 25:1, 81–4.

Monk, M and Dillon, J (2000) The nature of science knowledge, in Monk, M and Osborne, J (eds) *Good practice in science teaching: what research has to say.* Buckingham: Open University Press.

Munn, N (1966) *Psychology* (5th edition). London: Harrap.

Murphy, P, Beggs, J and Russell, T (2005) *Primary horizons: starting out in science*. London: Wellcome Trust.

Ofsted (2003) The education of six-year-olds in England, Denmark and Finland. London: HMI.

Osborne, J, Erduran, S, Simon, S and Monk, M (2001) Enhancing the quality of argument in school science. *School Science Review,* 82:301, 63–70.

Osborne, J and Dillon, J (2008) *Science education in Europe: critical reflections. A report to the Nuffield Foundation*. London: Nuffield Foundation.

Osgood, CE, Suci, GJ and Tannenbaum, PH (1967) *The measurement of meaning*. Chicago, IL: University of Illinois Press.

Prentice, R (2000) Creativity: a reaffirmation of its place in early childhood education. *The Curriculum Journal*, 11:2, 145–58.

Primary Science Review. Creativity and Science Education, 81, Jan/Feb 2004.

Qualifications and Curriculum Authority (2000) A scheme of work for Key Stages 1 and 2 – Science. London: QCA.

Qualifications and Curriculum Authority (2003) *Creativity: Find it! Promote it!* London: QCA/DFEE.

Reid, A and Petocz, P (2004) Learning domains and the process of creativity. *The Australian Educational Researcher*, 31:2, 45–62.

Renner, J (1982) The power of purpose. *Science Education*, 66, 709–16.

Rowling, JK (1997) *Harry Potter and the philosopher's stone*. London: Bloomsbury.

Shayer, M and Adey, P (2002) (eds) *Learning intelligence. Cognitive acceleration across the curriculum from 5 to 15 years.* Buckingham: Open University Press.

Scott, P (1987) *A constructivist view of teaching and learning science.* Leeds: Leeds University Press.

Taber, KS (2002) The constructivist view of learning: how can it inform assessment?, invited presentation to the University of Cambridge Local Examinations Syndicate (UCLES) Research and Evaluation Division (RED), 27 May 2002.

Training and Development Agency (2006) *Qualifying to teach. Professional standards for qualified teacher status and requirements for initial teacher training.* London: TDA.

Useful Websites

Association for Science Education www.ase.org.uk

Science Council www.sciencecouncil.org

Teaching, Thinking and Creativity www.teachingtimeslibrary.co.uk

8
Creative mathematics
Mary Briggs

Chapter objectives

By the end of this chapter you will have:

- **considered whether mathematics is a creative subject;**
- **considered whether creative mathematics is only for the most able;**
- **explored what it means to teach mathematics creatively.**

This chapter addresses the following Professional Standards for the award of QTS:
Q1, Q8, Q10, Q14, Q28, Q29

I am interested in mathematics only as a creative art. (Hardy, 1941)

Introduction: the problem with mathematics

Creativity and mathematics or creative mathematics appears for many to be a contradiction in terms. Mathematics has a reputation for being either right or wrong: where can the creativity be in that? For many people there is no room for discussion as mathematics is seen as a way of proving other areas of study – 'the ultimate truth'. Yet mathematicians discuss the elegance in proofs and the creative patterns in algebra and fractals. The majority of people learning and teaching mathematics don't ever get to study at the level where creativity would appear to really get started. We may feel like the following quote from King that mathematics was to be endured.

> *All of us have endured a certain amount of classroom mathematics. We lasted, not because we believed mathematics worthwhile, nor because, like some collection of prevailing Darwinian creatures, we found the environment favourable. We endured because there was no other choice. Long ago someone had decided for us that mathematics was important...so we were compelled into school classroom fronted with grey chalkboards and spread with hard seats...The room in which we sat was a dark and oppressive chamber and we thought of it then and now as Herman Melville thought of the Encandatas: only in a fallen world could such a place exist.*

(King, 1992, p15)

Our views of mathematics are coloured by the fact that is it often seen as a utilitarian subject. Mathematics taught at school is a basic skill and needed for the real world. Yet how much mathematics do we use in our real lives? Most of us might say we use measures, aspects of number and estimating in our everyday activities. We might see problem-solving as part of mathematics and therefore an aspect we might use in our lives outside education. We may even see problem-solving as creative if there are a number of solutions to a given problem.

Before looking at the issue of creativity within mathematics in detail it would be worth considering your own perspective on this issue. Do you think mathematics is a creative subject? Is creativity situated in specific topics within mathematics or is it possible to see creativity throughout mathematics?

The case for creativity in mathematics

Mathematicians' view of their work is often framed in the use of specific mathematical vocabulary and, therefore, unless we speak mathematically fluently, can appear inaccessible. The following quote from King demonstrates something of that difficulty and a view of mathematics that may be very different to our own.

> *The word 'produce' as used here seems slightly awkward and it would be more natural to replace it with the word 'create' or 'discover'. But I have used the word produce... to describe the work of mathematicians because it is a continuing controversy in mathematical circles as to whether new mathematics is created or discovered... The idea that mathematics, as a physical world seems to exists, independent of human thought and activity is a notion at least as old as the philosophy of Plato... a second view claims that mathematical structures are created and that they have no existence independent of the person that created them. This notion meshes well with the nature of modern pure mathematics.*
>
> (King, 1992, p41)

Society's view of mathematics tends to focus on arithmetic and correct answers to calculations. Mathematics is seen as providing the evidence for other subjects, the proof that things are true if you can prove them mathematically.

The following, about the American poet Robert Frost, is a good parallel with mathematics in that it shows us how a subject or phenomenon is itself a way of looking and serves a wider purpose than the strictly utilitarian. You may know that Frost lived in the farming area of Vermont and was inspired to write poetry through the imagery of the farmers' daily lives.

> *... he understood, as do all true artists, that it is metaphor and symbol, and not plain reality, that is memorable and significant. Mathematicians, like poets, see value in metaphor and analogy. The lines they draw are made, not only of words, but of graceful symbols: summations and integrals, infinities turning on themselves like self-swallowing snakes, and fractals like snowflakes that, as you blink your eye, turn to lunar landscapes. Mathematicians write their poetry with mathematics.*
>
> (King, 1992, p11)

Mathematicians see their subject as having a poetic quality as well as the potential for ambiguity and interpretation.

The challenge to teach mathematics creatively

Mathematics by its nature is often seen as a visual subject with symbols written on a page. Tall *et al*. (2001) suggest that learners need to move towards the abstraction of mathematics to become flexible in their approaches, particularly to calculation, in order to become successful mathematicians. They focus on the child's attention during actions on objects when calculating. Often 5+3 can be seen as an array of objects that children imagine combining to find the total quantity. For some children seeing arithmetic in terms of mental images of objects persists and this prevents them from moving into the higher realms of mathematics. These children rely heavily on counting strategies, which increase the possibility for errors with increasing number size. The higher achievers seem to focus more on the symbolism itself. They utilise known facts and move away from counting strategies more quickly, seeing the relationship between numbers. These skills enable the children to engage more easily with the creative opportunities in mathematics. The ability to visualise in the abstract is a key skill in success in mathematics and not just in relation to number. It is a clear prerequisite skill for success in geometry. Creative activities in mathematics should give learners an opportunity to explore the possibilities, working in ways that motivate and engage their interest.

This means looking beyond the structure of the National Primary Strategy (DfES, 2006) for mathematics three-part lesson structure and differentiation through the use of three levels of tasks, often in the form of worksheets in the main activity phase of the lesson. It also required a shift in thinking about 'personalised learning' from being an entitlement to progressing two levels a year to address children's interests to allow exploration of subjects such as mathematics.

To address this, activities should be used to show how creativity could be enhanced through visual, verbal and kinaesthetic approaches. This links to areas discussed in relation to learning styles, which have gained predominance in recent years. Care is required as children who can flexibly move between learning styles are more successful learners. Children who struggle are often focused on their preferred learning styles alone.

Current definitions of creativity

The DfEE (1999) report on creativity provides a definition, which is broken down into four characteristics. Creative thinking, or behaving creatively, can be seen as imaginative, purposeful, original and of value. If we look at mathematics we can see that thinking mathematically can be purposeful and of value as we can solve problems with mathematical skills and knowledge. There is a considerable debate about whether problem-solving is actually a creative aspect of mathematics and this will be discussed in more detail later. We value calculations and measuring where accuracy is important for safety or economy. The imaginative and original behaviours in mathematics appear at first to be more difficult to access. We might see children creating original methods of solving problems, repeating patterns or creating games.

Young children thinking creatively

Young children are fascinated by words and playing with rhyming, often making up new words. They do this with counting rhymes and counting words. These are areas that we might cite as creative activities within the subject of English or literacy. If you listen to children playing they will invent words for quantities as part of playing with language, language for a specific purpose. Mathematics can be seen as language that we learn to speak. We also learn that precise language can be used to describe situations, events or classify. Two-year-old Alex was overheard trying some of things out as he was talking to his toys. 'Tigger has a tail . . . Alex has no tail.' This small boy was playing with his classification of objects including self, all part of beginning to think mathematically. For his parents this might be a source of celebration but like many small children they choose their own time to explore ideas and for these tired parents this was two o'clock in the morning!

For young children it may be simple connections between the mathematical skills they are learning and the situations they find themselves in. An example of this is a small girl Ellen of about three who was asked by her mother if there were enough drinks for her mother, her brother and herself. Ellen proceeded to count 1, 2 and then instead of saying three she said me and then decided that there were enough drinks for everyone. Ellen was making her own original connections between her counting skills and the need to use one to one correspondence to find out if there were enough drinks for everyone. QCA (2004) describes how you can spot creativity and gives as examples making connections and seeing relationships in mathematics. Ellen is clearly demonstrating a very early start to making connections in order to solve a problem.

Mathematical creativity occurs anywhere young children make connections between what they see and their emerging knowledge of mathematics. I witnessed an example of this when three-year-old Ben was eating his tea of sausage and chips and suddenly he announced, 'I've got a number. It's a number seven.' His chips were stuck together at one end to form the shape of a number seven. The adults sitting at the table chatting about other things when he made the connections for himself did not prompt him to look at his food. He showed by his observations that he was already thinking creatively about mathematics and well on his way to being a confident mathematician.

REFLECTIVE TASK
REFLECTIVE TASK

If you are working with young children you may be able to think of examples similar to those already outlined that will allow you to think about mathematical activity differently from previous interpretation, as creative or evidence of creativity.

Teachers may be misled

Reactions to children's responses are crucial in identifying what is actually happening when children complete a task. Are they demonstrating misconceptions in mathematics or bored so they decide to work creatively with the task given. The result may initially appear to be an incorrect answer. An example would be a child's response to 12 + 23 = giving an answer of 8. Without a discussion with the child it is not possible to interpret exactly what is going on. It may hide a creative playing with numbers rather than a concern.

More able

Wilson and Briggs (2002) looked at more able children's approaches to solving mathematical problems for example:

a and b are whole numbers. What could they be?

$a \div b = 4.125$

One child, Zoe, took time to make sense of the problem from the outset, using her insight to plan a strategic response. She took control of the task, exploited connections and relationships, producing an elegant solution. After thinking for some time, she voiced that she saw the problem as 'See how many times you have to do the 4.125 to make a whole number.' Zoe recognised the relationship:

$$4.125 \times b = a$$

This enabled her to develop the strategy of multiplying 4.125 to make a whole number. But rather than trying numbers randomly, she exploited what she knew about decimals in order to obtain:

$$4.125 \times 2 = 8.25$$
$$8.25 \times 2 = 16.5$$
$$16.5 \times 2 = 33$$

This is an example of a creative approach using the elegance of the mathematics as well as her previous knowledge.

REFLECTIVE TASK

Look out for this kind of example of creative approaches while you are in school. If appropriate discuss examples found with your school-based tutor or mentor in relation to school policies for mathematics and the creative curriculum.

Is creative mathematics only for the most able?

Since the 1980s there has been a developing focus of attention on children who are 'gifted and talented' and this has been linked to numerous additional programmes for these children. One key issue for teachers is how to identify and support these particular learners. Porter (2005) describes some of the difficulties of identification with young children. She suggests that teachers tend to under-identify both the gifted children who appear to engage with activities very slowly and those who are creative and do not conform. At the same time it is possible to over estimate the abilities of children who engage with task readily, cooperate easily and perhaps more tellingly conform to the expectations of adults.

Although Porter's work is focusing on gifted children generally she raises specific issues in relation to mathematics and particularly in relation to children with learning difficulties. We do not associate 'giftedness' with any difficulties; yet Porter (2005) clearly sets out examples of children with a gift in one or more areas of the curriculum but appear to have difficulties in others. This has significant implications for a stance, which allows access to creative mathematics only to the most able. Children with the difficulties Porter describes may well be denied access to the opportunities to be creative in their strongest area. Porter describes the difficulties for teachers to be able to identify these children as more able as their difficulties may mask their true abilities. To avoid this situation access for all to be creative with mathematics would allow children to show their real abilities and offer teachers a different situation in which to accurately assess their potential.

Engaging all learners with the potential for enjoying and therefore seeing the creativity possible within the subject is a key challenge for teachers. Robinson and Koshy (2004) suggest that we look at school mathematics as partitioned into three elements; procedures, application and elegance. They see the way forward for increasing the creativity in mathematics by providing opportunities for children to learn all three elements in order to introduce them to the 'more beautiful aspects of mathematics'.

Briggs (1998) interviewed mathematicians as part of an oral history project focusing on successful mathematicians and their early experiences of mathematics. In these interviews one area explored was when their attention shifted specifically towards mathematics and they showed an early indication of where their interests might lie in the future. All those interviewed identified as their research focus areas of mathematics aimed at those under the age of ten, which is important information for those teaching young children.

This would seem to be backed up by the intentions behind the National Curriculum, which included recommendations for mathematics to be seen as a creative subject. DfES/QCA (1999) states that 'Mathematics is a creative discipline. It can stimulate moments of pleasure and wonder when pupils solve a problem for the first time, discover a more elegant solution to that problem, or suddenly see hidden connections' (p14). These are not recommendations for a few but an entitlement for all children to be able to engage with mathematics as a creative subject and this is where the role of the teacher in facilitating access to this approach to mathematics is paramount.

What does it mean to teach mathematics creatively?

The Primary National Strategy (DfES, 2006) for mathematics, still often described as the 'numeracy hour', began its initial implementation in schools in September 1999. Martin Hughes (1999) describes the strategy as... 'undoubtedly the most prescriptive approach to primary mathematics ever developed in this country' (p4). Has this changed the way we think of teaching mathematics? Definitely. Does it mean that there we see less creativity in teaching mathematics? Possibly.

REFLECTIVE TASK

Can you think of someone who you consider teaches creatively? Does this include their teaching of mathematics? What are the key elements of their teaching that make it creative? Try to list these elements yourself. If appropriate share with your school-based tutor or mentor as part of the development of your teaching and the children's learning.

Comment

These are difficult questions and could suggest that you are looking for continuous evidence of flare and imagination. The issue with this interpretation is that a high level of imaginative teaching can be a clear aspiration but can be hard to sustain across all topics/subjects and may even set unrealistic expectations. This is not to say that this shouldn't be the aim of teaching mathematics. However, we may consider that many people teaching mathematics in the early years and primary age range do not have positive feelings about the subject. These feelings about mathematics are likely to affect approaches to teaching the subject to children.

The National Numeracy Strategy (DfEE, 1999), now part of the Primary National Strategy has made significant changes to approaches to teaching mathematics. The first area of change is the emphasis on numeracy as opposed to mathematics and a clear focus on numeracy skills for everyday life. The second is the structure of the lesson into three clear parts and for some teachers a narrowing of the flexibility in approach and organisation of the lessons that was apparently there before. A conversation with a colleague from a school which had recently been inspected led to a discussion about creative teaching and in which subjects it occurred. (This was a school which had been very successful with its inspection, and many of the lessons had been graded highly.) His perception of the lessons that were graded at the highest levels was where the teachers were taking some risks with the lesson formats and the activities selected. Interestingly the perception was that none of these lessons were within the core curriculum. The power of the inspection in this case was perhaps limiting the creativity among this group of teachers though the discussion extended beyond the inspection period and patterns had begun to emerge. The influence of a structure to the lessons, particularly in mathematics, was apparent for this school. It was felt that somehow, the ability to structure the lessons flexibly had become emblematic of the school's development work on creativity, teaching and learning.

A problem-solving approach

One way of working on enhancing a creative and more open approach of teaching is to offer problems which can be used with children of a wide range of ability and therefore can be used within any class, not a specific class for the most able children. Briggs (2000) argued this particularly in relation to the early years and in response to moving away from the use of worksheets within the main activity phase of numeracy lessons. The focus is much more on what makes good activities. Below is a suggested checklist for deciding what makes a really 'good' task.

PRACTICAL TASK PRACTICAL TASK **PRACTICAL TASK** PRACTICAL TASK **PRACTICAL TASK**

Is my activity:

- accessible to all;
- possible to extend;
- possible to narrow;
- enjoyable?

Does it offer/present:

- a practical starting point;

- opportunities for mathematical discussion;
- a reason for children to record their ideas;
- opportunities for repetition without becoming meaningless both for teachers and children;
- clarity of underlying mathematics?

Think about activities you use in your classroom. How do they compare to this list? Can you find an activity that fits all these criteria? How might you use an activity that fits all these criteria in a mathematics lesson?

If appropriate share with your school-based tutor or mentor as part of the development of your teaching and the children's learning.

Open tasks for children

The teacher can use open task materials in flexible ways that respond to the needs and previous experience of the learners. Organisations like NRICH provide resources which support the most able, but this is within the context of a broad interpretation and view of enrichment, not within a context of provision simply targeting the most able. Good enrichment education is good education for all. Good mathematics education should incorporate an approach that is an enriching and stimulating experience for all children and, some would argue, the teacher, too, in order to stimulate their development in teaching and continue their interest in learning. NRICH suggest that this approach should include content opportunities designed to:

- develop and use problem-solving strategies;
- encourage mathematical thinking;
- include historical cultural contexts;
- offer opportunities for mathematical extension.

Therefore this enrichment is not simply learning facts and demonstrating skills. Mathematical skills and knowledge can be precursors to, and also outcomes of, an enrichment curriculum.

The aim of an enrichment curriculum is to support:

- a problem-solving approach;
- improving pupil attitudes;
- a growing appreciation of mathematics;
- the development of conceptual structures.

(Adapted from Ernest, 2000)

This sounds like a tall order for a teacher and does require the use of a creative approach to planning. It does not mean that teachers must reinvent the wheel but take simple ideas and adapt them for their pupils. Ideas can be adapted from a number of sources, such as old textbooks, puzzle books or notes from old courses. It may appear as though in order to teach mathematics creatively you need to alter your teaching radically and yet the smallest things can change the teaching and learning for the children and make a lesson successful for the learners. Thinking creatively about mathematics teaching is about starting from what you know and adding to it.

Creative mathematics teaching in practice

An example of this was observed in a student teacher's mathematics lesson with a Year 3 class who were working on multiplying by 10. This is an area where there are lots of opportunities for children to acquire misconceptions, the most obvious being that to multiply by 10 just add a zero. This works for whole numbers but doesn't make any difference to the number if over-generalised to decimals. The creativity in this lesson was in the modelling of what happens to numbers when multiplied by 10. The student had set up three large hoops on the floor for the whole class to see marked as hundreds, tens and ones. Children were asked to come out to the front and hold a digit card standing in the tens and ones hoops to make the number 14. Another child was asked to join them but stand initially a little way from the hoops holding a zero or nought. This child became 'naughty nought'.

The student with the children then modelled what happened when the zero was added to the original number pushing (gently) the digits along the hoops to increase their place value. This was completed after they had undertaken discussion about multiplying by 10 and what happened to the numbers with some children clearly spotting a generalisable pattern of adding a zero. The student felt it was important for the children to see and understand what was actually happening to the number. Digital pictures were taken by one of the class to form a display after the lesson to remind children of what had happened to the digits to form a new number after the intervention of 'naughty nought'. This was a creative, simple but effective model for all the children in the class regardless of ability. This approach begins to make links for the children between aspects of mathematics, which is a key finding from the study into effective teachers of numeracy (Askew *et al.*, 1997).

The need to engage children in their learning is a topic of discussion in many countries in relation to mathematics. In Germany, Meissner (2000) describes a project entitled 'We build a village' which concentrated on geometry to further concepts of both plane and 3-dimensional geometry in primary schools. In this module for primary grades (age about 8–10 years) the children worked with about 35 different solids, made of styrofoam, wood, paper-nets, or plastic. The activities for the children were diverse and consisted of: sorting and classifying, folding, drawing, cutting, constructing nets, using plasticine, and building solids and houses with these models. At the end of the module (of about 7 lessons) the children built their own village with a grocery store, a church, a school, houses, as well as a creek, streets and parking areas. This kind of topic approach to teaching and learning is moving back into the primary curriculum with the introduction of the ideas from the Primary Strategy (DfES, 2003) and the subsequent continuing professional development materials. This is enabling teachers to look again at the ways they are constructing the learning to engage children with mathematics and to learn to become creative mathematicians.

Other approaches to being creative with mathematics teaching can be seen in the use of children's current interests to motivate and stimulate curiosity. Briggs *et al.* (2002) are an example of an approach drawing upon a current interest created by the phenomenon of the Harry Potter books. All the activities described in the article are based around the theme of ideas from the wizarding books. The object of the creative approach is to enliven and enrich the mathematics lesson and to offer children a stimulus that they might then go on to develop by themselves. The activities also allow teachers to make connections for the children between aspects of mathematics (Askew *et al.*, 1997).

REFLECTIVE TASK

Think about the interests of the children you teach; can you construct activities that will engage their interest with mathematics and help them to appreciate the creative opportunities within the subject? Find out about the approaches to teaching implemented as a result of the Primary Strategy. What effect has this had on teaching mathematics creatively?

A SUMMARY OF **KEY POINTS**

Cross (2004), now a retired HMI, wrote passionately about the important issues for her in mathematics teaching, which included: How do we engage children in their own learning? How do we engage them with mathematics and encourage them to want to know more? Her article also included a key quotation from the non-statutory guidance written to accompany the first version of the national curriculum in 1989. It states that.

> *Mathematics is not only taught because it is useful. It should be a source of delight and wonder, offering pupils intellectual excitement and an appreciation of its essential creativity* (NCC, 1989).

> Teaching mathematics in this way makes demands on us as teachers, especially if we have not had good experiences of mathematics teaching as learners. This requires us to:

(a) reappraise our preconceptions of mathematics as having no creative potential;

(b) look beyond the current structures for lesson planning in mathematics;

(c) ensure that we develop ways of teaching which encourage problem-solving and open tasks which make use of children's preferred learning styles;

(d) observe children closely so we can identify their interests and their creative use of mathematics not just in mathematics lessons;

(e) study closely the development of children of all abilities in our classes so that we do not fall into the trap of providing creative activities only for the most able or as extension activities for children who finish activities quickly.

MOVING *ON* > > > > > > MOVING *ON* > > > > > > MOVING *ON*

You will find it useful to discuss how teachers in your placement setting/school are developing their approaches to creative teaching and learning of mathematics. If your placement has a teacher with specific responsibility for mathematics and/or the creative curriculum across the school see if you can make a time to talk to this person in more detail about the school's policies and procedures and their role in co-ordinating that approach. Particularly you may want to discuss the following areas.

- Planning for different types of mathematics lessons
- Mathematics across the curriculum
- How records of observations of children are made not just in the early years and how this might be used as a starting point for personalised learning focusing on specific-child interests.

You might also consider:

- What kind of resources could you collect to support a creative approach to teaching mathematics such as stories and games?
- How you can share creative teaching approaches with other students.
- Are there issues for your mathematical subject knowledge to identify, and support creativity in mathematics?

REFERENCES REFERENCES **REFERENCES** REFERENCES REFERENCES REFERENCES

Askew, M, Brown, M, Rhodes, V, Wiliam, D and Johnson, D (1997) *Effective teachers of numeracy: a report of a study carried out for the Teacher Training Agency*. London: King's College, University of London.

Briggs, M (1998) The right baggage?, in Olivier, A and Newstead, K (eds) Proceedings of the 22nd Conference of the International Group for the Psychology of Mathematics Education, Stellenbosch, South Africa. Vol. 2, 152–9.

Briggs, M (2000) Feel free to be *flexible,* Special: *Children*, Hertfordshire: Questions pp1–8.

Briggs, M, Daniell, J, Farncombe, J, Lenton, N, and Stonehouse, A (2002) Wizarding Maths. *Mathematics Teaching*, 180, 23–7.

Cross, K (2004) Engagement and Excitement in Mathematics. *Mathematics Teaching*, 189, 4–6.

Department for Education and Employment (1999) *All our futures: National Advisory Committee for Creativity and Culture in Education Report*. London: DfEE.

DfES (2003) *Excellence and enjoyment: a strategy for primary schools*. Nottingham: DfES.

Ernest, P (2000) Teaching and learning mathematics, in Koshy, V, Ernest, P, and Casey, R *Mathematics for Primary Teachers*. Abingdon: Routledge.

Hardy, GH (1941) *A mathematician's apology*. London: Cambridge University Press.

Hughes, M (1999) The National Numeracy Strategy: are we getting it right? *The Psychology of Education Review*, 23:2, 3–7.

King, J (1992) *The art of mathematics*. New York and London: Plenum Press.

Meissner, H (2000) Creativity in Mathematics Education, in the Proceedings of the Mathematics Education Study Group (MESG), August 7–8, Tokyo, Japan.

National Curriculum Council (1989) *Mathematics: non-statutory guidance*. York: NCC/HMSO.

Ofsted (2003) *Expecting the unexpected*. HMI (www.ofsted.gov.uk)

QCA (2004) *Creativity: Find it! Promote it!* London: QCA Publications.

Porter, L. (2005) *Gifted young children: A guide for teachers and parents* (2nd edition). Buckingham: Open University Press.

Robinson, D and Koshy, V (2004) Creative mathematics: allowing caged birds to fly, in Fisher, R, and Williams, M (eds) *Unlocking creativity: teaching across the curriculum*. London: David Fulton.

Tall, D, Gray, E, Bin Ali, M, Crowley, L, De Marios, P, McGovern, M, Pitta, D, Pinto, M, Thomas, M and Yusof, Y (2001) Symbols and bifurcation between procedural and conceptual thinking. *Canadian Journal of Mathematics and Technology Education*, 1:1, 81–104.

Wilson, K and Briggs, M (2002) Able and gifted: judging by appearances? *Mathematics Teaching*, 180, 34–6.

FURTHER READING FURTHER READING **FURTHER READING** FURTHER READING

Briggs, M and Davis, S (2008) *Mathematics in the early years and primary classroom (creative teaching)*. Abingdon: Routledge.

PART 3:
CREATIVITY IN THE FOUNDATION PRIMARY CURRICULUM

9
Children, creativity and physical education
Sue Chedzoy

Chapter objectives

By the end of this chapter you should have:

- **understood the processes involved in teaching physical education;**
- **developed your own philosophy about the value of physical education and fostering creativity;**
- **recognised what high-quality physical education looks like.**

This chapter addresses the following Professional Standards for the award of QTS:
Q1, Q7, Q8, Q10, Q14, Q18, Q24, Q30

Introduction

The purpose of this chapter is to try to help you to think through your own view of physical education (PE) and to recognise the potential of the subject for enabling children to be creative through movement, either alone or with others. Practical suggestions are made and the creative approach is underpinned with creative theory (Fryer, 1996; Steinberg *et al.*, 1997; Beetlestone, 1998; DfEE, 1999; Craft, 2000; Aires *et al.*, 2004) and good practice in the subject (Schools Council and Assessment Authority (SCAA), 1997; Bailey and Macfadyen, 2000; Hopper *et al.*, 2000; DfES/DCMS, 2005).

The problem with PE

For those of you who remember your lessons in PE as unpleasant experiences on the hockey or rugby fields, being freezing cold and wearing unflattering kit, not being able to vault a horse in the gymnasium while being observed by the rest of the class or struggling around a 1500-metre track, creativity and physical education may not seem to be naturally well-matched. It has to be said that many people have been put off the subject by a few teachers who adopted very didactic teaching styles, favoured the naturally gifted and focused on the activity rather than the child. Some of these teachers were generally insensitive to the individual needs of their pupils and failed to inspire in them a love and appreciation of physical activity.

REFLECTIVE TASK

If you were to write down your views about PE, what would you say?

Some possible answers might include:

- It's about keeping fit and fitness is important for a healthy lifestyle.
- Healthy lifestyles combat illnesses such as heart disease and diabetes.
- It's a range of competitive, creative and challenge-type activities.
- It's only popular with sporty people.
- Everybody can be good at PE.
- It's different from other lessons.

Depending on your own experiences you might emphasise some aspects more than others. When you have completed this exercise turn to Figure 9.1 to see how others have described PE.

Creativity in PE throughout the twentieth century

In the early days of the development of the subject there were hardly any opportunities for pupils to be creative. At the beginning of the twentieth century there was concern that the nation's youth were unfit for joining the armed forces and the government introduced programmes of physical training into elementary schools, based on military drill. In these programmes there was little room for creativity (Board of Education, 1933).

In the 1940s the Ministry of Education took over responsibility for physical education from the Ministry of Health and the subject became more child-centred. Certainly the guidance for primary school teachers in the 1950s (Ministry of Education 1953a and 1953b) recognised the need to relate to children's creative potential within the physical education programme in primary schools. The Plowden Report had an impact on the curriculum which followed and in the early 1970s the government issued a document relating to the physical education curriculum in primary schools named 'Movement' (Department of Education and Science, 1972). This document gave very little specific guidance to teachers on how to foster creativity but it was expected that modern educational dance and gymnastics were taught which encouraged a lot of exploration by children with very little structure.

In the National Curriculum for Physical Education (DES/WO, 1991) the teaching profession was guided towards involving children in the processes of planning, performing and evaluating their ideas and performances. It was intended that the process would underpin what children learn and do in physical education, changing the emphasis from a 'product (activity) based curriculum to a process (learning) based curriculum' (Murdock, 2005). This made more explicit the way in which we should encourage children to be more involved in, for example, composing dances, creating original sequences in gymnastics and water-based activities, working out tactics and strategies in games and athletics activities and creating adventures outdoors. The very nature of the subject is about doing and so performance has always been at the heart of PE, but the concept of pupils planning and evaluating their work and the work of others had never been made so explicit in past guidance for teachers. This

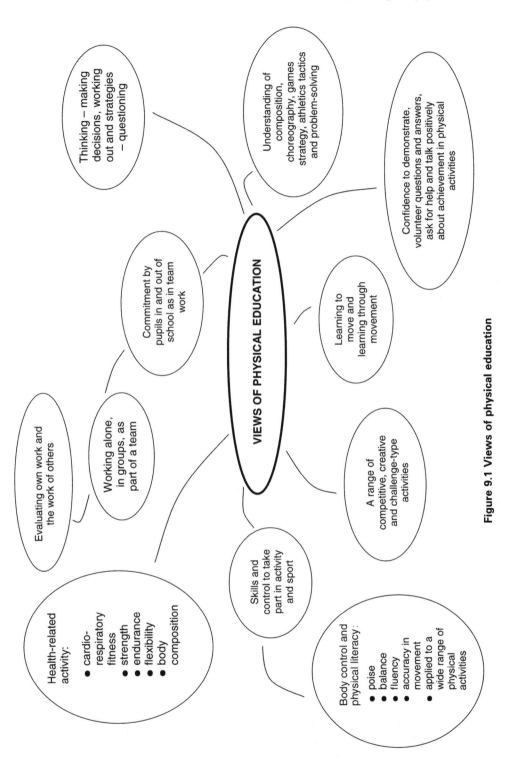

Figure 9.1 Views of physical education

process relates well to the model of learning in other art forms in the primary curriculum such as music, art and drama which involve the processes of composing, making and appreciating.

As Smith (2008) points out, Every Child Matters (ECM) provided an opportunity for teachers to be creative, to reflect on their philosophy for physical education, the curriculum, pedagogy and the whole child's physical education experience in school. (See Smith, 2008 and Council for Subject Associations, 2008) for ideas on the contribution that physical education can make to the ECM agenda to have a significant impact on children's well being.

What does high-quality PE look like today?

When pupils are experiencing high-quality physical education they appear to enjoy the subject, seldom miss physical education lessons, always bring their kit and encourage others to take part. They know and understand what they are trying to achieve and how to go about doing it. They know how to think for different activities, for example composition in gymnastics activities, choreography in dance, games strategy, athletics tactics and problem-solving.

REFLECTIVE TASK

What does this mean in practice?

How can you help children to **think** for different activities?

- What skills do you need to teach them to help them to be able to choreograph a simple dance or gymnastics sequence ?
- What skills do they need to devise a games strategy?
- What skills do they need to be able to adopt a tactical approach to games or athletics?
- What skills do they need to solve problems in outdoor and adventurous activities and other areas of PE?

Children who receive high-quality PE know how to evaluate their own and others' work in a variety of activities. They recognise the contribution that physical education can make to a balanced, healthy, active lifestyle and how success in aspects of the subject might affect their feelings about themselves.

Children who are experiencing high-quality PE have confidence in their ability. They are not afraid to show others what they can do, they volunteer questions and answers, ask for help and talk positively about their achievements, whatever their level of attainment. They explore and experiment with new activities without worrying about failing. Those who are more confident in an aspect of the subject are happy to help others.

REFLECTIVE TASK

In order to be creative in PE children need to be and feel safe, that is both safe in the physical environment and safe to take risks.

- How can you help children to feel safe and secure in their physical space?

- What kind of ethos do you need to develop with your class to enable children to feel confident to explore and experiment in PE?
- How can you help children in your class to value and receive others' efforts and performances in PE with sensitivity? In order to be creative in PE children need to be and feel safe, that is both safe in the physical environment and safe to take risks.

Through high-quality PE children are able to demonstrate improved skills and control, poise and balance. They are able to apply and adapt a wide range of skills and techniques effectively and have developed stamina, suppleness and strength to keep them going. Children experience a range of competitive, creative and challenging activities both individually and as part of a group in high-quality PE programmes. They think about what they are doing and make appropriate decisions for themselves. They work independently and ask questions so that they can organise themselves and make progress. They devise ideas and strategies to help them to improve their performance. Children experiencing a high-quality PE programme show a desire to improve and achieve in relation to their own abilities; they are prepared to take time to practise and refine their performance and welcome the advice of others (DfES, 2004).

Physical education in the National Curriculum (DfEE/QCA, 1999d) requires children to be taught dance, game activities and gymnastics activities every year throughout Key Stages 1 and 2, as well as athletics activities, outdoor adventurous activities and swimming at Key Stage 2. The four strands of the Physical Education National Curriculum include:

- acquiring and developing skills;
- selecting and applying skills and compositional ideas;
- evaluating and improving performance;
- knowledge and understanding of fitness and health.

The Attainment Target for Physical Education contains eight level descriptions with an additional description for exceptional performance. These are central to planning in physical education and, as Gower (2005) reminds us, can be broken down into four aspects: a gradual increase in the complexity of the sequence of movement; an improvement in the demonstrated performance qualities; greater independence in the learning context; and a gradual challenge to the level of cognitive skills required throughout the level descriptions.

PRACTICAL TASK PRACTICAL TASK **PRACTICAL TASK** PRACTICAL TASK **PRACTICAL TASK**

Look at the National Curriculum for Physical Education (DfES/QCA) (1999d).

Look at each of the level descriptions for physical education. Look for the references to planning, performing and evaluating in each of the levels. Choose one of those levels and, using your experience of teaching an aspect of physical education (for example, dance at level 4), describe what you would expect a child to be able to do.

This has implications for the way you help children in their learning in all aspects of PE. You need to give them plenty of opportunities to be creative, to have opportunities to plan for themselves and to help them to develop a language with which to describe their own and others' work so that they are able to evaluate progress against given criteria.

REFLECTIVE TASK
REFLECTIVE TASK

- What kind of environment do you think you need to foster in your classroom to enable children to be creative in PE?
- How can you help children to feel free to explore and experiment in the different aspects of PE?
- What knowledge, skills and understanding do children need as tools for creativity in this subject?
- How can you encourage other children in your class to value the originality of opinion, response to a task or different interpretation to a given task?

All aspects of the National Curriculum for Physical Education lend themselves to developing and celebrating children's creativity. You as a teacher have the key to opening this up. First of all you need to value the subject and feel reasonably confident in your own subject knowledge. You do not need to feel that you are an expert in all areas of activity but you do need to feel secure in setting up a safe physical environment (see AfPF, 2008) and have a basic understanding about how children learn in and through physical education. You also need to help children to develop the vocabulary in movement so that they are able to use their skills to form their individual movement patterns.

PRACTICAL TASK PRACTICAL TASK PRACTICAL TASK PRACTICAL TASK PRACTICAL TASK

Select one of the areas in the National Curriculum for Physical Education. Design a work card to give to a group of children to help them to devise an original dance, game, gymnastics, athletic, swimming or outdoor and adventurous activity.

- What space will be available to them?
- What equipment will be available to them?
- How long will the activity need to last?
- What guidance will be required with regard to safety?
- Are there any cross-curricular links you would like the children to include?
- How can the activity be linked in some way to previous work to enable the children to use previously acquired skills?

Creativity in athletic activities

Athletic activities in the primary school involve running, jumping and throwing activities. At this stage of children's development it is important that they have success in these activities so that they feel good about themselves and recognise that, with practice, they are all capable of improving their performance. It is important that children are given time and plenty of opportunity to explore and experiment with different actions related to athletics, and that there is a fine balance between cooperative and competitive activity within the programme.

During the warm-ups for athletic activities children can experiment with different ways of running and can work alone, in pairs or small groups to make up and create their own running activities (Bray, 1992). Examples might include: asking the children to devise a warm-up in a grid which involves running in different directions: forwards, backwards, to the left, to the right and diagonally; creating a maze to run through, around or over using hoops, bean bags, skipping ropes or low hurdles. Ask children to work in small groups and go on a journey in a single file: the first person in the line chooses the way of running, i.e. small steps, cross steps, large strides, variety of way and the rest of the group follow. The leader decides on the route, and on a signal the person at the back jogs to the front and creates the running pattern and pathway.

An example of larger-scale planning in athletics activities was described by Hornsby (1991) where children in Year 2 in a first school were set the problem-solving exercise of planning the Sports Day for the whole school. The children selected the activities, gave them names, created their own record sheets, wrote and sent the invitations, planned and prepared the refreshments, and had a wonderful time learning across the curriculum (Chedzoy, 2000).

Creativity in dance activities

Dance as a performing art seems to be the most obvious area of activity in the Physical Education National Curriculum to contribute to children's creativity and I am sure that if you have studied dance in your initial training you are aware of the potential for developing children's creativity through the activity. Dance provides opportunities for artistic and aesthetic education, and experiences in which children can develop emotionally and learn to express moods and ideas symbolically. Dance can also help children to develop rhythmic and musical sensitivity and a knowledge and understanding of the art form. Dance education can also contribute to children's understanding of traditional dance forms from different times and places.

In dance you will encourage children to compose dances by exploring and improvising, making decisions and solving problems . Give them opportunities to share their ideas with others through practical demonstration or discussion. This will help them to shape and refine movement phrases to form dances. Through performance children will develop physical skill and a repertoire of actions to travel, turn, jump and perform gestures to perform a set dance, express an idea, tell a story or communicate a mood. You need to give children time and opportunity to view dances, to appreciate their meaning, actions and qualitative and spatial features (Chedzoy, 1996).

There is such a wide range of stimuli for developing dance. These include other curriculum areas such as music, history, geography and art. Starting points for developing dance could be poems, stories, photographs, paintings, posters with different colours, text shapes and contrasts. Television adverts or film clips containing professional dance works may also be used to inspire children to create their own dances.

Even when teaching folk dancing you can encourage children to adopt a creative approach. For example, teach the children some basic moves and figures such as do-si-do, arches, right-hand, left-hand star, promenade, and ask them to compose their own circle or line dance in small groups using some of these figures involving meeting and parting.

Creativity in games activities

A high-quality games programme in the primary school will enable children to become confident and competent in a variety of invasion games, net/wall games and striking and fielding games.

Some people feel that all games teaching needs to be governed by the rules and regulations of the major game, or even their mini-versions such as high-five netball, uni-hoc, five-a-side football, pop lacrosse, tag rugby or short tennis. If you watch children playing games in the park or on the playground you will often see that they make up their own structures and rules – jumpers for goals and boundaries and carefully negotiated rules to help the game flow. Rules that are negotiated and agreed by the group are more likely to be adhered to by children – which for you as a teacher makes things easier with regard to organisation. All governing bodies of sport advocate small-sided games for children of primary school age and if you are able to rely on children in your class playing games to their own rules you do not have to referee or umpire to help keep order in the group.

You might also consider adopting a creative approach to helping children understand the principles involved in the tactics and strategies of games. For example, ask children to work in pairs to make up a game involving aiming at a target.

All ball games require the accurate sending of a ball/shuttlecock into space or to a goal or target. Focusing on this skill in an innovative way can be fun and also helps the children to understand the basic principles of play. Ask the children to select their own target from a range of equipment. The targets could be markings on the ground, wall or fences, such as circles, faces, animal shapes or rocket shapes, or children could draw their own targets with playground chalk. Posts, trees, skittles and hoops also make suitable targets. Ask the children to choose their own equipment to send to the target. This could be a small or large ball, a bean bag, a rubber quoit, or a unihoc stick and ball. Ask the children to decide on their own area of play and agree on any rules before play begins. Will there be a method of scoring? If so, how will the score be recorded?

At the end of the session ask the children to show and share their ideas with others. Ask the children to evaluate their games. Ask questions such as: Is it easier to hit a target when you are close or far away? Is it easier to hit a big target or a small target? Is it easier to hit a target with a small ball or a big ball? Ask the children to give their game a name and ask them to write it up using the computer so it can be played by others at a later date (Chedzoy, 2000).

Any basic skills which you have taught the children can be used to help them to be creative in devising their own version of practices and small-sided games. Visit www.ncaction.org.uk/creativity/whatis.htm to see an example of this approach with a Year 8 class: 'Like hockey but different'. The same principles apply to games in the primary school and you might be surprised how competent children are at creating their own games, demonstrating the tactics and techniques required for understanding and playing invasion, striking/fielding and net games.

Creativity in gymnastics activities

Gymnastics activities is an area of the curriculum which can be a worry to newly qualified teachers with all the inherent concerns about safety and progression. Once you have more experience you will be comforted by the fact that children are in fact your best resource in this area of the curriculum. Their responses to your challenges will be rich and varied and if you can 'capture the moment' with good observational skills and ask children to show others in the class their movements you will enable children to increase their 'movement vocabulary' so that they have more ideas with which to create longer and more complex sequences. The most popular form of gymnastics taught in primary schools is educational or informal gymnastics (Reynolds, 2000). This approach is also sometimes described as curriculum gymnastics (Williams, 1997). In this form of gymnastics the pupil works at his/her own level within a framework set by the teacher. This is rather different from formal gymnastics in which the child has to perform stylised vaults and other prescribed gymnastic agilities. There are many good books to guide you through a progressive programme of curriculum gymnastics activities (Underwood, 1991; Benn and Benn, 1992; Williams, 1997; Devon LEA, 2002).

Creativity is at the heart of curriculum gymnastics. You are asking children to find different ways of travelling, jumping, balancing, turning, swinging, hanging, climbing and transferring weight from one area of the body to another. If you create a climate of mutual trust and encourage children to sensitively evaluate their own and others' work they will enjoy creating their own original pieces of work. It is an area of the curriculum which should be accessible to all, regardless of physical shape or athletic ability. In assessing children's ability in this area of activity, as in other areas of the physical education curriculum, credit should be given for the child's ability to compose sequences and appreciate the aesthetic qualities of performance as well as for the performance itself.

Creativity in outdoor and adventurous activities

The primary focus of teaching Outdoor and Adventurous Activities is to teach problem-solving skills, to focus on process, to learn to co-operate and to learn from group mistakes while participating. In a significant majority of Outdoor and Adventurous Activities, the skills, knowledge and understanding are almost immaterial to the primary focus, and do not significantly feature even as a secondary focus.

(Martin, 2000)

Outdoor and adventurous activities are defined as problem-solving activities which can be planned in and around the school environment, using existing facilities and taught to the whole class by their class teacher. This is opposed to outdoor pursuits and outdoor education which tend to need specialist facilities and specialist tuition.

No two solutions to problems set for children will be identical as children will need to co-operate with others, make decisions and work together to test themselves in a variety of situations, and the outcomes will always vary accordingly. Different forms of orienteering such as cross-country, score orienteering and line orienteering contain elements of navigation, decision-making and physical activity. (McNeill *et al.*, 1987; McNeill *et al.*, 1992; Chedzoy, 2000). Trails such as obstacle trails and string trails can present children with the challenge of making connections and seeing relationships. You can be imaginative in stimulating children's interest in their surroundings by taking photographs of features in the school and school grounds such as flowers, trees, shrubs, walls, murals and pond life and then backing these onto a firm fabric, giving each a number and setting up a trail for the children to follow. Another way of organising a trail is to create a texture trail, then give the children a base map, a wax crayon and a large sheet of paper with clues for the texture children should look for at given locations. Children then chase off to find them and make a rubbing of the texture, for example bark, brickwork, leaf or netting. You could encourage children to create their own texture trails.

Creativity in swimming

Try not to always think of swimming in the primary school as only teaching children in straight lines to learn and refine the prescribed swimming strokes. Of course you will wish children to develop water confidence and efficiency in moving through the water and to be able to fulfil the requirements of the National Curriculum for Physical Education which, by the end of Key Stage 2, requires them be able to swim at least 25 metres and have a good knowledge and understanding of safe practice in and around water. However, children can have a great deal of fun and develop confidence in the water if you can think of interesting ways to help them to be creative in these lessons. In fact it's worth remembering that most activities which can be planned, performed and evaluated on land can also be enjoyed in the water. This can make things easier for you as a teacher as you can help your children to transfer some of the ideas developed in the hall or on the field to be further explored in the water!

For children who are not confident in the water these activities will need to take place in shallow water in which children are able to move with their flotation aids.

Use music – this might be over a sound system in a public pool or a suitably insulated deck if used pool-side, or use percussion to stimulate the movement. Ask the children to travel with big steps, little steps, high knees, forwards, backwards and sideways. Their way of travelling is planned by them and they can choose the arm actions to go with their stepping pattern. Ask the children to think about different still shapes and perform them – wide, narrow, twisted, curled. Ask the children to think of characters – how would they move in the water? Find different ways of turning, spinning and rolling around in the water.

For stronger swimmers ask them to create different swimming patterns joining front and back swimming strokes with a turn, spin or roll. Ask the children to make gestures in small groups to create Mexican waves (i.e. one performs a simple action which is repeated by the rest of the group one after the other). Make patterns with the water, sprinkling, swishing, splashing (not at each other!) and whirling using different body parts, i.e. fingers, toes, elbows or knees. Suggest that the children make up their own patterns, for example picking up water in their hands and letting it fall through their fingers making patterns at different levels. Ask partners to share and join patterns together. You can ask the children to work in small groups together making circle patterns just as you might do in a folk dance so that the children compose their own patterns, for example holding hands, travelling four steps to the right, followed by four steps to the left, walking together into the middle and lifting hands high to repeat. The task you might set them could be to 'make up a pattern together' which involves everybody working in unison (all doing the same thing at the same time) which involves travelling (stepping, marching, swimming) meeting and parting.

A SUMMARY OF **KEY POINTS**

Physical education's development as a subject.

> **Understand the processes involved in teaching physical education today so that you can enable children to plan, perform and evaluate across the range of activities in the physical education curriculum.**

Your views about physical education.

> Have a clearly defined philosophy about the value of Physical Education and recognise the potential for fostering creativity across the whole of the physical education curriculum at Key Stages 1 and 2 (see J. Lavin (ed.), 2008).

Recognise what high-quality physical education looks like.

> Be able facilitate creativity by helping children to think for and through different activities.

> Help children to develop skills of evaluation and a language with which they can evaluate their own and others' work.

Create a safe environment in which children feel free and confident to take risks, explore and experiment and to create innovative and original episodes in and through movement.

> This requires you to pay particular attention to the physical space and facilities.

> It also requires you to foster a climate of mutual respect where all children feel free to share and demonstrate their work without fear of failure or ridicule.

MOVING *ON* > > > > > > MOVING *ON* > > > > > > MOVING *ON*

Never forget, your children are your best resource, always give them time and opportunity to develop and share their ideas with others. Take care to value each and every contribution in the creative process and encourage your children to do the same. Plan well, look ahead, seek advice and remember, a rich and stimulating physical education programme will lay the foundations for active healthy lifestyles. Every child deserves the chance to achieve their full potential (Lavin, 2008) and you can make a difference.

REFERENCES REFERENCES **REFERENCES** REFERENCES **REFERENCES** REFERENCES

Aires, J, Wright, J, Williams, L and Adkins, R (2004) The performing arts, in Jones, R and Wyse, D (eds), *Creativity in the primary curriculum.* London: David Fulton.

The Association for Physical Education (AfPE) (2008) *Safe practice in physical education and school sport.* London: AfPE.

Bailey, R and Macfadyen, T (eds) (2000) *Teaching physical education 5–11.* London: Continuum.

Beetlestone, F (1998) *Creative children, imaginative teaching.* Buckingham: Open University Press.

Benn, T and Benn, B (1992) *Primary gymnastics – a multi-activities approach.* Cambridge: Cambridge University Press.

Board of Education (1933) *Syllabus of physical training for schools.* London: HMSO.

Bray, S (1992) *Fitness fun.* Crediton: Southgate Publishers.

Chedzoy, S (1996) *Physical education for teachers and coordinators at Key Stages 1 and 2.* London: David Fulton.

Chedzoy, S (2000) *Physical education in the school grounds.* Crediton: Southgate Publishers.

Council for Subject Associations (CfSA) *Primary subjects: making every child matter.* Physical Education and Dance. CfSA.

Craft, A (2000) *Creativity across the primary curriculum: framing and developing practice.* Abingdon: RoutledgeFalmer.

Department for Education and Employment (DfEE) (1999a) *All our futures: creativity, culture and education.* The National Advisory Committee's Report on Creative and Cultural Education. London: HMSO.

Department for Education and Employment/Qualifications and Curriculum Authority (DfEE/QCA) (1999d) *Physical education: the National Curriculum for England.* London: HMSO.

Department of Education and Science (DES) (1972) *Movement – physical education in the primary years.* London: HMSO.

Department of Education and Science/Welsh Office (DES/WO) (1991) *Physical education for ages 5 to 16: proposals of the Secretary of State for Education and Science and the Secretary of State for Wales*. London: HMSO.

Department for Education and Skills/Department for Culture, Media and Sport (DfES/DCMS) (2004) *Learning through physical education and sport: a guide to the school sport and club links strategy*. London: DfES.

Devon Local Education Authority (LEA) (2002) *A Devon approach to physical education: curriculum gymnastics*. Devon: Devon Curriculum Advice.

Fryer, M (1996) *Creative teaching and learning*. London: Paul Chapman Publishing.

Gardner, H (1983) *Frames of mind: the theory of multiple intelligences*. London: Heinemann.

Gower, K (2005) Planning in PE, in Capel, S (ed.), *Learning to teach physical education in the secondary school*. Abingdon: RoutledgeFalmer.

Hopper, B, Grey, J and Maude, T (2000) *Teaching physical education in the primary school*. Abingdon: RoutledgeFalmer.

Lavin, J (ed.) (2008) *Creative approaches to physical education: helping children to achieve their true potential*. Abingdon: Routledge.

Martin, B (2000) Teaching outdoor and adventurous activities, in Bailey, R and Macfadyen, T (eds) *Teaching physical education 5–11*. London: Continuum.

McNeill, C, Marland, J and Palmer, F (1992) *Orienteering in the National Curriculum: a practical guide*. London: Harveys.

McNeill, C, Ramsden, J and Renfrew, T (1987) *Teaching orienteering*. London: Harveys.

Mead, G (1934) *Mind, self, and society*, ed. Morris, CW. Chicago, IL: University of Chicago.

Ministry of Education (1953a) *Planning the programme: physical education in the primary school*. London: HMSO.

Ministry of Education (1953b) *Moving and growing: physical education in the primary school*. London: HMSO.

Murdock, E (2005) NCPE 2000 – where are we so far?, in Capel, S (ed.) *Learning to teach physical education in the secondary school*. Abingdon: RoutledgeFalmer.

Reynolds, T (2000) Teaching gymnastics, in Bailey, R and Macfadyen, T (eds) *Teaching physical education 5–11*. London: Continuum.

Schools Council and Assessment Authority (SCAA) (1997) *Expectations in physical education at Key Stages 1 and 2*. London: SCAA.

Smith, P (2008) Creativity matters, in Lavin, J, *Creative approaches to physical education: helping children to achieve their true potential*. Abingdon: Routledge.

Steinberg, H, Sykes, E, Moss, T, Lowery, S, Leboutillier, N and Dewey, A (1997) Exercise enhances creativity independently of mood. *British Journal of Sports Medicine,* 31, 2405.

Underwood, M (1991) *Agile*. Cheltenham: Nelson.

Williams, A (1997) *National Curriculum gymnastics*. London: Hodder & Stoughton.

Wilson, A (1996) *How far from here Is home?* Exeter: Stride Publications.

Useful website

Qualifications and Curriculum Authority (QCA) (2005b) www.ncaction.org.uk/creativity/whatis.htm

10
Creative and imaginative primary art and design
Paul Key

Chapter objectives

By the end of this chapter you should have:

- **explored how to develop as an artist-teacher;**
- **developed a greater understanding of the creative process;**
- **understood how to take your own positive steps to developing a *curious classroom*.**

This chapter addresses the following Professional Standards for the award of QTS:
Q1, Q2, Q7, Q10, Q14

Introduction

The purpose of this chapter is to encourage you to think about yourself as a creative and imaginative teacher of art and design. In addition we will consider how this approach to teaching will contribute to children's experiences in art and design, making them more meaningful and purposeful, as well as inventive and imaginative. The intention is to help you see art and design in more ambitious ways, in flexible ways, and in trusting ways. To think about primary art and design in these ways may well demand a leap of faith, but they could help improve the way art and design is taught. In doing so art and design can be the exciting and rewarding subject it has the potential to be, for teachers and for pupils.

This creative approach to teaching and learning is set in the context of the National Curriculum 2000 (DfEE/QCA, 1999), the National Advisory Committee on Creative and Cultural Education (NACCCE, 1999) model of creativity, and the Primary Strategy, Excellence and Enjoyment (DfES, 2003).

Being creative and imaginative

The NACCCE (1999) publication *All Our Futures: Creativity, Culture and Education* appeared during a period of government-led drives to raise standards in mathematics and English, following the introduction of the Primary Numeracy and Literacy Strategies (DfEE, 1999; DfEE, 1998). Although the initial impact of the NACCCE report was restricted by the emphasis on numeracy and literacy it has since become a significant reference for those wishing to stimulate fresh ways of thinking about primary education.

In this important document creativity is considered as a mode for learning, which involves 'Imaginative activity fashioned so as to produce outcomes that are both original and of value' (NACCCE, 1999, p29).

Using **Imagination** involves:	Being **Original** can be:
Alternative outcomes	Individual: in relation to previous work
The unconventional	Relative: in relation to a peer group
Non-routine	Historic: it can be uniquely original
Generating originality	
Combining existing ideas	
Re-interpreting	
Making analogous relationships	
Pursuing **Purposes** involves:	Judging **Value** involves:
Being actively engaged	An evaluative mode of thought
Applied imagination	Judgement and analysis
Being deliberate	Individuals and groups
Solving a problem	Trying out ideas
Changing from initial intentions	Critical thinking
	Immediate response or longer periods of reflection

Figure 10.1 Creative activity

The document continues to describe how it sees the relationship between Imagination, Purpose, Originality and Value, in both *generative* and *evaluative* terms. It goes on to suggest that 'helping young children to understand and manage this interaction between generative and evaluative thinking is a pivotal task of creative education' (NACCCE, 1999, p31).

The relationship between making (generative) and evaluation (evaluative) is a process echoed consistently in curriculum models for art and design, including the National Curriculum Council, Arts in Schools Project (NCC, 1990) and the current National Curriculum 2000 (DfEE/QCA, 1999). To promote these ways of thinking and working, it is useful for teachers to be mindful of the complexity of the process. The relationship between making and evaluation does not necessarily follow a neat linear path, there will be notable periods of engagement: of *focus*, *withdrawal*, and *breakthrough* (NACCCE, 1999). In addition the timescale can be stretched and drawn out, or alternatively things can happen quickly and suddenly.

Steers (Preface in Meager, 2006) suggests a further useful summary of the creative process, involving four interlinked phases.

- **Preparation** – in which the problem or question is defined, reformulated and redefined.
- **Generation** – moving beyond habitual pathways of thinking.
- **Incubation** – conscious planning and subconscious scanning of the of the problem or idea often following a period of relaxed attention.
- **Verification** – where ideas are analysed, clustered and evaluated, followed by detailed planning and implementation.

Figure 10.2 Phases of the creative process

With a developed sense of the creative process it is possible to envisage a teacher, a curriculum and pupils working in a productive and evaluative way. We can picture an atmosphere of *playful and purposeful experimentation*. We can imagine periods of focus, withdrawal and breakthrough. We can envisage flexibility and focus. Equally we can see some of the tensions which will exist in terms of assessment or accountability, in monitoring and in progression. However, to work in a creative, playful and purposeful way and to encourage pupils to do the same, we need to do things a little differently. To make this shift it is helpful to consider existing practices in primary school art and design.

REFLECTIVE TASK

Refer to Figure 10.1 the NACCCE model of creativity and Figure 10.2 opposite:

Have you observed any art and design lessons which have elements of the NACCCE model of creativity, or periods of preparation, generation, incubation and verification?

Did you observe time and space for pupils to *focus, withdraw* and *breakthrough*?

Could you identify a sense of *playful and purposeful experimentation*?

Do you consider there to be barriers to individual, original and purposeful art and design activities?

What opportunities can you think of to encourage individual, original and purposeful art and design activities?

Primary school art and design: establishing a rationale

The National Curriculum 2000 (1999) details a positive approach to primary art and design education, involving exploration, investigation and making, review, revision, and development. It states: 'Teaching should ensure that investigating and making includes exploring and developing ideas and evaluating and developing work' (DfEE/QCA, 1999, p120).

This encouraging statement is then extended through the programme of study and includes: the adaptation of personal ideas through imaginative processes of investigation, development and exploration, evaluation and review. The National Curriculum suggests that this fairly open, process-led approach to learning in art and design be supported by knowledge and understanding in three areas.

1. The visual elements: line, colour, tone, pattern, shape, space and form, and how these can be combined and organised for different purposes.
2. Materials and processes: drawing, painting, printmaking, collage, digital media, textiles, and sculpture, and how these can be matched to ideas and intentions.
3. Artists, craftspeople and designers working in different times and cultures, in a variety of genres, styles and traditions.

It also implies that children will develop practical skills, skills of looking and seeing and skills related to discussion.

(DfEE/QCA, 1999, p120)

However, despite the positive aspects of the National Curriculum, in practice emphasis is often placed on what can be taught, rather than on what can or might be learnt (Steers,

2003). Consequently planning and teaching are implemented in fairly predictable ways. Unfortunately, these narrow interpretations can result in:

- an emphasis on particular examples of art;
- an emphasis on the visual elements (line, colour, tone, pattern, shape, space and form), which become isolated from meaning or purpose;
- little consideration of presentation or audience;
- limited exploration of personal themes;
- limited exploration of drawing to invent, explore or imagine, as evident in children's *self-initiated* imagery (Adams, 2003; Anning and Ring, 2004) to explore and develop personal themes.

Despite its inclusion in the National Curriculum, art and design is often considered and presented as a marginalised subject (Prentice, 1999). Consequently art and design in primary schools continues to revise and reposition itself in terms of its aims, values or possibilities. It has done so for the best part of a century, through theory, through practice, through publications, through exhibitions, and through the tireless energy of individual advocates. This has led to a number of well-documented *rationales* for art and design education, as it jostles with other marginalised subjects, for limited time, status and value in a busy school curriculum.

There are rationales which emphasise the subject, rationales which emphasise the individual, others which emphasise society, and the cultural significance of art. There are rationales which champion expression, others which venture for social change through the democratic process of education, and in our case art and design education, and others which promote the development of skill and technique. For the purpose of this chapter we don't need to rehearse these extensively, although further study will reveal the varied and interesting history of art and design education (Efland, 1990; Macdonald, 2004; Thistlewood, 1992).

This evolving and developing history reflects a process of change and renewal which is claimed by some to be the very lifeblood of art and design education (Steers, 2003), to be encouraged and not suppressed. Art and design educators are certainly grateful there has been no national strategy for art and design or indeed for creativity. However, the apparent need to revise the rationale for art can be seen as either a consequence of the need for change, or in some way the *symptom* of continued change. That is to say *change* becomes the orthodoxy for a subject that claims to avoid orthodoxy in its quest for difference and originality.

Either way, the picture can appear confused, and perhaps understandably school-based practice becomes informed by a number of 'bits' taken from alternative rationales. In places practice is coherent and well conceived, and the results are interesting and varied, but at other times progress in art and design is hampered by poorly conceived rationales.

In his examination of the influences on primary art and design teaching Prentice (1999) suggests that existing practice is often based on the poorly defined concepts: of skill acquisition, of innate ability, of giftedness, of self expression, of freedom, of creativity, of originality, and of child art. A particular consequence of these ideas is the notion of the teacher, and the interventions they choose to make or choose to resist. The teachers, the choices they make, and the actions they take, are particularly relevant in this chapter as we move towards considering their creative and imaginative roles.

To guide your thoughts about teaching, curriculum and pupils, a clearer rationale built on workable principles will be helpful.

Adapted from Steers and Swift (1999) 'A manifesto for art in schools', itself based on principles of difference, plurality, and independent thought, good practice in primary art and design is identified where:

- Teachers and pupils are encouraged to be confident in exploring personal lines of enquiry, and creative action and thought
- Art is seen as a relevant and meaningful activity for and by pupils
- The curriculum has greater range and diversity
- Classrooms encourage choice and self-directed activity

Figure 10.3 Principles to guide practice

These principles can then be used to inform a potential rationale which recognises art and design as:

> *a powerful way of generating and exploring new ideas and feelings, and giving them visual form, and in the process, making personally significant meaning. It is the way in which this meaning-making comes about through engagement in practical work and through informed personal responses to diverse works of art that is central to learning in art.*

(Prentice, 1999, p150)

A challenge for all teachers of creative primary art and design is to help children produce *personally significant meaning,* through the manipulation of ideas, tools, materials, and visual qualities. The making of personally significant art work can be enhanced in an environment which encourages *self-direction, choice and diversity*, and in turn the environment can be established in a climate of *flexibility, ambition and trust.*

REFLECTIVE TASK

Have you seen or experienced different rationales of art and design in the primary school, some of which reflect skill acquisition, innate ability, self-expression, or creativity and child art?

Look at school policy statements for art and design. Can you identify a rationale of art and design education which they appear to advocate?

Which rationales do you feel an affinity with?

Can you identify principles in the policy statements which echo the principles above (Figure 10.3)?

PRACTICAL TASK PRACTICAL TASK PRACTICAL TASK PRACTICAL TASK PRACTICAL TASK

Write down four principles which you intend to keep in mind when teaching art and design in the primary school. Look at your principles; which areas are perhaps more complicated than you first thought? For example, how will you provide opportunities of choice and when will you prevent choice? What are the implications for you in managing this in the classroom?

The teacher, the curriculum and pupils: establishing and maintaining professional discretion

The recent period of primary education, following the 1988 Education Reform Act, has been characterised in many ways by 'national strategies' and regimes of accountability and testing. With much of the focus placed on improvement in literacy and mathematics, as well as general school improvement, it is of little surprise that work in art and design has tended to be marginalised and limited. As Eisner (2003) suggests, when attention is drawn to schools 'the tendency is to tighten up . . . to mandate, to measure and to manage' (2003, p375). The loss of *professional discretion* (Eisner, 2003) in such a climate has the potential to reduce curriculum material to rather mundane activities, and methods of teaching to *delivery and efficiency.*

As you develop your professional identity, informed by peers, experience, reading, research, practice, beliefs and values, you will begin to feel confident about how you see yourself as a teacher. It is important that teachers maintain this identity and that it is robust enough to withstand particular trends. When we believe in things we tend to approach them 'wholeheartedly' (Dewey, 1933), and in education the benefits can be enormous. We are able to work in creative, imaginative and purposeful ways.

There are many examples of currrent practice, which have not been bound by particular constraints, which have gone out on a limb, which are wholehearted, show what can be achieved: activities in galleries, Big Draw events, the Artworks programme 1999–2004, Room 13 in Scotland, Nigel Meager's Creative and Cultural projects in South Wales, the HEARTS project, the START publication, and the work of energetic school-based individuals. Their achievements are in a large part due to an awareness of the possibilities of art and design for children's learning, a strong rationale, and also a willingness to challenge existing practice and to reconsider the role of those involved.

To begin to understand how primary art can be taught in similarly creative and imaginative ways, and how learning in art can be wrapped in a creative and imaginative approach, with a sense of curiosity, we need to look closely at teachers, at the curriculum and at pupils. We will look at these in turn and while doing so consider them in relation to three key themes: *flexibility*, *ambition* and *trust*.

Flexibility: this is a key feature not only of artistic practice but of imaginative and creative teaching.

Ambition: ambitious projects in school, some of which are recognised nationally as examples of good practice (Artworks), are certainly ambitious in their scope, their scale and their challenge.

Trust: this is a key feature of any classroom that hopes to encourage creative art and design. It implies a positive approach to children, to their ideas, to materials and to ourselves as teachers. It's a way of approaching risk-taking, a feature of art and design, that recognises the stakes of taking risks as being relatively low.

The primary art and design teacher

From your experiences of schools and teaching you will be aware that it takes considerable time to become the teacher you would like to be. Becoming a teacher of art and design is no different and we can learn from both current and past practice. Herbert Read, Marion Richardson and Viktor Lowenfeld, all influential voices in the development of art and design teaching, and in particular 'child-centred' art education, offer insight into their visions of the art and design teacher.

Through the publication *Creative and Mental Growth*, first published in 1947 and now reprinted in its eighth edition, Viktor Lowenfeld influenced, and continues to influence, the ways in which we think about children and their art, and consequently how we approach teaching. Much of his writing focuses on the significance, the development and the meaning of children's creative art activities. Lowenfeld presents a view of children's art activity as being spontaneous and personal, and inevitably he questions how teachers can encourage and preserve such creative expression.

In particular Lowenfeld identifies a possible tension between adult conceptions of art and the art of children encountered in the classroom:

> *From the discrepancy between adult taste and the way in which a child expresses himself arise most of the difficulties that prevent children from using art as a true means of self-expression.*
>
> (Lowenfeld, 1982, p8)

To avoid the pitfalls of such discrepancy, and to allow opportunities for self-expression, and in turn to develop rounded individuals, Lowenfeld presents a clear role for the teacher:

> *If it were possible for children to develop without any interference from the outside world, no special stimulation for their creative work would be necessary. Every child would use his deeply rooted creative impulses without inhibition, confident in his own means of expression. Whenever we hear children say 'I can't draw' we can be sure that some kind of interference has occurred in their lives.*
>
> (Lowenfeld, 1982, p8)

This famous quotation tells us a great deal about Lowenfeld's art and design education and his teacher. In Lowenfeld's view, we might have had our potential for creative expression taught out of us through teacher intervention (interference). This may sound very odd in an initial teacher education setting where interventions need to be clear, making appropriate use of modelling, demonstration, instruction, questioning, or directing. Lowenfeld advocates a very different role for the teacher. His vision of the teacher is one who allows creativity to *unfold*. There may be truth in this vision, but it remains at times a poorly conceptualised idea (Prentice,1999) of primary school art and design teaching. As a result, teachers often assume that to help the *unfolding* they should adopt a non-interventionist approach, with little or no consideration of alternative methods. You may find a middle ground between the *all* or *nothing* approaches a useful alternative.

Writing in 1948 and reflecting on her early days in teaching Marion Richardson echoes this non-interventionist approach and gives a flavour of her view of children, art and education:

> *I began to see that this thing we had stumbled on...was art not drawing; something as distinct and special and precious as love itself, and as natural. I could free it, but I could not teach it; and my whole purpose was now directed to this end, as I set out to learn with and from the children.*

> (1948, p13)

Marion Richardson extended her interest in children and art throughout her education career, and can be regarded as one of the most influential figures in the promotion of 'child art'. It's possibly reassuring that someone of such distinction is unsure of exactly how to teach. As she suggests, she is willing to learn from children, demonstrating qualities of trust and flexibility.

Herbert Read is a similarly influential figure. From his detailed exploration of art and education, *Education Through Art*, published in 1942, his ideas about the teacher still resonate today. As with Lowenfeld and Richardson, Read is also interpreted as identifying the teacher in a mainly supportive role. In Read's conception of art education he presents three distinct activities: self-expression, observation and appreciation. For these to make sense to the pupil he sees a role for the teacher, to bring together the possibility of *spontaneous activity* with the *social activity of appreciation*. 'Generally speaking...self-expression cannot be taught...the role of the teacher is that of the attendant, the guide, inspirer, psychic midwife' (Read, 1958, p209). However he adds that there is scope for training and direct teaching, to improve skills of observation. As for appreciation, he says:

> *This can undoubtedly be developed by teaching (but only by the age of adolescence)...Until then the real problem is to preserve the original intensity of the child's reactions to the sensuous qualities of experience – to colours, surfaces, shapes and rhythms. These are apt to be so infallibly right that the teacher can only stand over them in a kind of protective awe.*

> (Read, 1958, p209)

These visions of teaching may be very difficult to imagine, let alone embrace. Citing your teaching strategies on a lesson plan as *psychic midwifery* could well attract some close attention. However, considering Lowenfeld, Richardson and Read, not only helps us to see their legacy but also to consider alternatives. We are seeking a model for a teacher that fits our principles, our rationale, our version of creativity and our aim of flexibility, ambition and trust. The *artist teacher* appears to be such a model.

REFLECTIVE TASK
BEELECLIAE IVSK

Have you experienced a teacher who may fit with the examples identified by Lowenfeld, Richardson or Read?

If you can draw, do you put it down to not being taught, as Lowenfeld implies?

If you can't draw, do you put it down to being taught, as Lowenfeld implies?

Can you see a place for a teacher who takes this distanced supporting role in schools today?

Can you identify the challenges they would face to their teaching approach?

The artist teacher

A model for our emergent creative teacher is that of the artist–teacher, or to rephrase this slightly, one who sees teaching as an art. The *artist–teacher* model advocates an approach to teaching which echoes that of the artist.

Eisner (1985) suggests both teaching and art as:

A source of aesthetic experience
Being dependent on the perception and control of qualities
Heuristic or adventitious activity
Seeking emergent ends

(Eisner, 1985, p177)

Figure 10.4 The artist–teacher

This conception is very useful as we identify a teacher who recognises the limitations of Read and Lowenfeld, but also sees the restrictions of orthodoxies of teaching present in many primary schools. The *artist–teacher* would not only work in the ways described by Eisner but they would fit our model of flexibility, ambition and trust, and also in our principled rationale for art and design education.

What does the flexible teacher do?

Adapted from Dewey (1938, *Experience and Education*) Eisner (2002) recognises the importance of *flexible purposing*, and sees it in the context of 'improvisational intelligence' (Eisner, 2002, p77). In these situations pupils and teachers are encouraged to shift direction, to change their aims during the course of work, where ends are not set, and means to achieve them are constantly revised. These changing and evolving ends are encouraged through 'conversations' with work. This requires a *conversational* approach involving teachers, pupils and the evolving work.

Our flexible teacher enters a conversation with work, with ideas and with pupils: this should be at the heart of all good art teaching. The conversation requires our teacher to be involved in careful *listening.* This may seem odd, in the context of visual art, but where the teacher *listens* to pupil ideas and to the way materials are being used and shaped, a conversational exchange begins to emerge. This conversation needs to be set in a relationship of reciprocity: between pupils, teachers, ideas and materials. Dewey (1933) can help us further as we think about ourselves as teachers entering a conversation, and with it a sense of reflection. As with other notions of reflective practice and certainly embedded in flexible purposing is the idea of 'suspending ideas' and being 'open-minded' (Dewey, 1933; Schon, 1987). Our willingness to put things on hold, to follow personal themes, to let work develop in unpredictable ways is dependent on our established principles (Figure 10.3).

What does the ambitious teacher do?

The ambitious teacher needs to be flexible, and they need to be trusting. If we are ambitious in terms of scale, scope and challenge, we can remain curious, continue to ask questions. We can begin to open up ideas with children, we can be more ambitious:

- What will happen if...?
- What might happen when...?
- I wonder what this might look like?
- How could these things be combined?

Equally, the ambitious teacher can see beyond the usual constraints of time or space. That is not to say these constraints don't exist but to realise that positive alternatives exist. The National Curriculum 2000 *Breadth of Study* (1999, p121) advocates work that is produced collaboratively and on a variety of scales. Unfortunately the majority of work produced in schools is limited in scope by the confines of a timetable, and by space; more curious and adventurous teachers attempt to see beyond and around these limitations.

What does the trusting teacher do?

The trusting teacher is flexible and ambitious. To encourage work that is purposeful and inventive, meaningful and original, pupils must have the freedom to work in flexible and inventive ways. As we have noted this may well involve an element of risk, but the suggestion is that in the calculation of risk, trust plays an important role.

We need to trust our instincts, trust our feelings, trust pupils and trust their ideas. This means some sessions may be long, others short. Rather than an hour every Wednesday, ideas could be worked on continuously in sketchbooks for 15-minute spells each day over a week or fortnight. This could encourage more personal and meaningful responses.

Seeing yourself as an artist–teacher

If you've never considered yourself as an artist–teacher you may find this concept slightly unusual and tricky to take on board. However, as we continue to emerge as teachers, through a combination of theory and practice Atkinson (2002) suggests that 'each different pathway of teaching and learning is structured by its respective values' (p151).

Although the constraints of external agencies and particular regimes of control (OFSTED, TDA, QCA) may not encourage a reflection on our pathways, or the values that structure them, this chapter is very much centred on the potential we have to: 1. recognise ourselves, pupils, the curriculum and the classrooms we inhabit, and 2. bring about change. That is to say, we can establish our evolving identities not only in line with the standards set by others but by what we believe to be right. If you believe in the idea of creativity and imagination as being liberating and worthwhile, you will need to be alert to your current values, and to those which are sympathetic with creative and imaginative activity, those of the artist–teacher, and create space for it in your week. As Eisner (2003) suggests, by doing this we maintain our *professional discretion.*

In developing an identity as a teacher, there will be times when the *pathway* is less clear, is contradictory or compromised. Being aware of ourselves in a *pathway* of possibilities, ranging from the didactic to the heuristic (Figure 10.5), is the first step to bringing about change.

REFLECTIVE TASK
REFLECTIVE TASK

Look at Figure 10.5, Addison and Burgess' (2000) *Didactic/Heuristic continuum.* You will notice a continuum, or pathway, of teaching and learning approaches and possibilities.

Where would you position yourself on this scale, and where would you like to position yourself?

Consider the idea of 'professional discretion' and the action you can take to maintain your own sense of identity.

Use the continuum as a way of considering the roles of teachers in any art and design lessons you are able to observe.

Centred	Learning	Teaching	Characteristics	Pupil	Teacher	Justification	Drawbacks
Teacher	Passive	Didactic	Instruction Information Demonstration Closed procedures and structures	Depend-ent Memoris-er Imitator	Expert Provider	Outcomes are certain Introduces techniques Conditions pupils to observe, listen and record Confirms the teacher as expert	Can be authoritarian Single perspective Can alienate Pupils may become dependent Results in conformity and normative outcomes Knowledge may be lost unless reinforced using other methods
	Respons-ive and activity-based	Directed	Rehearsing and initiating activities Response to given stimuli Working to exemplars Conditioned/determined structures Probable findings already known by teacher	Respond-er	Trainer Director Resourcer	Provides common experience of NC art and design Enables: Continuity and progression Identification of pupils not on task Ease of assessment Efficient transfer of skills Activity: individual/pair/group	Knowledge is given/fixed Determined by teacher's experience: often privileging making Neglects: Prior knowledge Individual needs
	Active and experien-tial	Negotiated	Discussion/debate Collaborative work Purposeful investigation Critical evaluation Multi-faceted and flexible structures Interaction Reflexivity	Contrib-utor Interactor	Facilitator Motivator Guide Negotiator Supporter	Provides: Intelligent making Critical thinking Learning as social activity, art as social practice Mutual trust Learner as teacher/teacher as learner Enables pupils to: Communicate ideas Evaluate their own and others' work Negotiate their own learning Cross boundaries	Time-consuming Difficult to co-ordinate and resource Difficult to monitor and assess Teacher requires breadth of knowledge Teacher needs to be ready to relinquish control

(Continued)

| | | Heuristic | Empower-ing and liberating | Meeting needs Answering hypotheses Experiment-ation Unknown findings Discovery Problem-solving Investigation | Research-er Self-motivator Inventor Discover-er | Coordinat-or Recipro-cator | Encourages: The application of knowledge to practical contexts Pupils as planners Divergent thinking Risk-taking | Pupils need to be ready to take on initiatives Difficult to resource Only works with self-motivation Teacher may feel insecure Teacher needs to acknowledge self as learner |
| Pupil | Open | | Dependent Redundant | Self-determined structures, motivated by pupil interest Exploration | Agent Director | Attendant Technician | Appropriate for highly-motivated highly-resourceful learners | Can be chaotic, unfocused Lacks boundaries Can invite stereotypical responses, and/ or a rejection of learning |

Figure 10.5 Addison and Burgess' Didactic/Heuristic continuum

The primary art and design curriculum

Where the interpretation of the National Curriculum is positive, interesting work has been developed. However, there is a 'gulf between the most and least successful schools' (QCA, 2005). Prentice (1999) offers useful suggestions to extend work beyond the visual elements, by including issue-based work, including 'enquiry into personal identities, family relation-ships, the immediate locality or distant places' (1999, p161). He suggests materials and processes can be extended through 'combining and recombining a range of materials' (1999, p161). And he tackles the difficult area of extending the range and use of artists, craftspeople and designers to included more contemporary practice.

In your emerging role as a creative and inventive teacher of art and design it is hoped you will be able to approach the National Curriculum 2000 (DfEE/QCA, 1999) in an *extended and positive* way, seeing potential where there may otherwise have been resistance.

The flexible curriculum

To match our principles (Figure 10.3) and thoughts on creativity we need to adopt appro-priate planning approaches, approaches which encourage and allow for periods of preparation, generation, incubation and verification (Steers, 2006). Unfortunately, we have been conditioned into curriculum planning utilising a particular type of learning outcome or objective. These are specific and un-ambiguous; they refer to skills, knowledge or under-standing, and in many ways indicate what can be taught. Barrett (1979) describes these as 'behavioural objectives'. Behavioural in that there is an identifiable change in 'behaviour' following an experience or teaching input: a child will be able to sort, will be able to identify, will know the name of, will be able to mix, will know how many. 'In art these objectives are relevant in the processes used to develop certain skills which help pupils to reach personal solutions' (Barrett, 1979, p36).

This appears very neat. But as we all know life isn't neat and 'students learn both more and less than they are taught' (Eisner, 2002, p70). In isolation, behavioural objectives are inappropriate for our flexible curriculum. However, Eisner (1985) is helpful; he details a type of objective which encourages enquiry: an 'expressive objective':

> *An* expressive objective *describes an educational encounter: it identifies a situation in which children are to work, a problem with which to cope, a task in which they are to engage... With an expressive objective what is required is not homogeneity of response among students but diversity. In the expressive context the teacher hopes to provide a situation in which meanings become personalised and in which children produce products, both theoretical and qualitative, which are as diverse as themselves.*
>
> (Eisner in Barrett, 1979, p37)

Planning and preparing work which encourages diversity and personal responses will benefit from the 'expressive' objectives described by Eisner. The flexible curriculum or series of lessons, or indeed individual lessons, will then be in a position to foster ambition and trust.

The flexible, ambitious and trusting curriculum

To gain a sense of what the flexible, ambitious and trusting curriculum might look like, or entail, the following examples are from the Higher Education, the Arts and Schools (HEARTS) project at the University of Winchester. First established in 2003, with co-funders including Esmee Fairbairn Foundation and Paul Hamlyn Foundation, the HEARTS project is a national project involving 11 initial teacher education providers. It aims to extend and develop the role of the arts in primary initial teacher education and training.

At the University of Winchester the HEARTS project offered an opportunity to explore a number of interesting practice-based initiatives, including the use of vocabulary to develop children's art work and the idea of students as artist–teachers. In particular students were encouraged to plan in open and flexible ways, working from pupil-led ideas, and to consider their emerging professional identities.

The work produced by children during the project included sketchbook-based enquiry, sound and movement performances, montage work, three-dimensional studies and story telling. It is a clear testament to the pupils' commitment to learning in and about art and design. It serves as a reminder of what primary art and design might look and feel like. Not only does the work have a sense of purpose and energy, it illustrates what pupils will engage with if entrusted with a sense of ownership.

Importantly, the project highlighted how easily strategies for teaching other curriculum areas can dominate thinking in terms of pedagogy. We were able to remember that alternative teaching methodologies do exist, and do work. And, that a more heuristic pedagogy can foster conversation that is pupil- and work-centred, rather than teacher-dominated, and an outcome for children that is meaningful and purposeful.

Flexible, ambitious and trusting pupils

For pupils to be flexible and ambitious, for them to be curious, playful and inventive, we need to present ourselves and the curriculum in a particular way, so that pupils are trusting of others. From that position pupils will be able to trust their own diverse thoughts and playful experimentation. However, this remains a real challenge. It is perhaps the biggest of

HEARTS project: Supporting Creative Art & Design

TEACHERS	PUPILS	CURRICULUM
Supportive	Personal	Negotiated
Imaginative	Curious	Choice
Heuristic	Meaningful	Challenge
Reflective	Playful	Flexibility

In the examples shown we can see primary school children exploring a range of personal and at times significant imagery, initiated by children. They have used a range of materials and explored a number of themes. In all cases the supporting role of the teacher while important was one of encouragement and co-operation. Resources were made available which the children managed and explored themselves. Pupil ideas were valued and given time to germinate, short regular sessions and longer more sustained sessions, including

- exploring repetition with recurring motifs;
- embellishment and experiment using masking and resist methods;
- montage used to explore scale and size with humorous consequences;
- storytelling with action drawings;
- collecting, storing and documenting, walks and journeys explored with simple journals.

In all cases the work is exploratory, sometimes in the early stages of preparation or incubation, but embedded in a context of **FLEXIBILITY**, **TRUST** and **AMBITION**.

IMAGINATIVE	ORIGINAL	PURPOSEFUL	VALUABLE
Preparation	Generation	Incubation	Verification
FOCUS	WITHDRAWAL	BREAKTHROUGH	

Figure 10.6 HEARTS project

Creative Art & Design Process

all the challenges presented: to encourage pupils to believe you and believe in themselves. This requires a teacher and a curriculum that marries intention with action.

CASE STUDY
HEARTS project

Consider the case of Clare, a final year student, who was given an opportunity to learn and teach in a very open way, as part of the HEARTS project, where we endeavoured to match intention with action. There was one overall aim for the project: to teach the arts in interesting and inventive ways. Clare was not bound by the constraints of the National Curriculum or the normal assessment regimes for herself as an undergraduate teacher. Her commentary reveals the move from uncertainty and limited trust, a period of being 'tricked', towards trust, confidence and curiosity. Clare describes her own background as 'non-arts'.

There have been various points during the project when I have been very sceptical and cautious, particularly at the start. I found it very difficult to understand how Paul and Jay (tutors) could expect us to know what was expected or what the module was about when they confessed or led us to believe that they didn't know themselves. In retrospect, although this was quite scary to start with, I would say it has proved quite effective and the 'not quite telling us everything' or 'trickery' aspect seems to have been a running theme of the project, with the people running the workshops also seducing us into doing things. I found this particularly interesting as I would honestly say that if they had told us what we would have achieved at the end of each session then I wouldn't have believed I could do it. The same would probably have happened if Paul and Jay had explained what they wanted too clearly.

The most enjoyable part for me was the school-based sessions. I found it very beneficial to see what we had learnt in action and to see the response we received from the children. I was still finding it hard to come up with original ideas, and at several points wanted to retreat to the safety net of the National Curriculum and behavioural objectives. However, I was managing to be a little more creative though, and if a member of the group suggested something I was often able to run with the idea and spiral from their idea. It is only since spending time in school away from the project that I have noticed a change in my thinking which has surprised me. During the preliminary visits to my final school placement, I have been able to watch art lessons and I was extremely surprised at how frustrated I became at the lack of investigation, play, exploration and expression and how desperately I wanted to take over the lesson; to make it more fun and thought-provoking for the children and to give ownership back to them. I found myself sitting with a group of children talking to them about what they were doing while experiencing this whirlwind of ideas running through my head of what could be altered or developed and all the exciting things that could come out of the quite boring, mundane task that they were doing. I suddenly stopped myself and realised how weird that was and wondered where it had come from especially as I wasn't consciously trying to think of ideas.

I think the most surprising thing about that was that I didn't realise quite how much I had taken away from the project.

A SUMMARY OF **KEY POINTS**

Clare's account reveals not only an aware and reflective teacher, but a developing artist–teacher. We can hear her identity evolve, and with it her sense of trust. She begins to trust her teachers, her pupils and, importantly, herself.

This account is indicative of the trusting pupil we are interested in encouraging. In addition it reveals that the *pathway* towards trust echoes the creative process itself. That is, there is a period of focus, withdrawal and breakthrough.

If Clare's account becomes your account, and an account of pupils you work with, then you will be taking positive steps for yourself, the curriculum, and pupils to be flexible, ambitious and trusting. And the work you have conversations with is likely to be meaningful and purposeful, inventive and imaginative. You will be some way towards developing a *curious classroom*.

MOVING *ON* > > > > > > MOVING *ON* > > > > > > MOVING *ON*

This chapter has presented a number of ideas which in themselves are ambitious. It is hoped that some of the material will filter through into your practice, might influence how you teach your next art lesson, or perhaps your lessons in your second teaching post, or beyond. It is completely understandable that at times situations demand that we teach in more contained and teacher-led ways; in ways where outcomes are more predictable and manageable. However, as you gain confidence in yourself, subject material and children, you could well be looking for a more creative approach, where you can learn from and with the children in your classroom.

One of the ways you can maintain *freshness* in your thoughts about art and education, in children and schooling, is to keep in touch with the arts:

- watch films;
- read novels;
- write poetry;
- play an instrument;
- form a band;
- go to a festival;
- dance;
- go to galleries;
- look up at buildings;
- take photographs;
- pay attention to sculpture;
- draw;
- paint;
- sew.

REFERENCES REFERENCES **REFERENCES** REFERENCES **REFERENCES** REFERENCES

Adams, E (2003) *Power drawing*. Drawing Power, The Campaign for Drawing.

Adams, E (2003) *Start drawing*. Drawing Power, The Campaign for Drawing.

Addison, N and Burgess, L (2000) *Learning in art*, in Addison, N and Burgess, L *Learning to teach art and design in the secondary school*. Abingdon: RoutledgeFalmer.

Anning, A and Ring, K (2004) *Making sense of children's drawings*. Maidenhead: Open University Press.

Atkinson, D (2002) *Art in education: identity and practice*. London: Kluwer.

Barrett, M (1979) *Art education: a strategy for course design*. London: Heinemann.

Dewey, J (1933) *How we think*. Boston, MA: Heath and Company.

Dewey, J (1938) *Experience and education.* New York: Macmillan.

Department for Education and Employment (1998) *The National Literacy Strategy: framework for teaching.* London: HMSO.

Department for Education and Employment (1999) *The National Numeracy Strategy.* London: HMSO.

Department for Education and Employment/Qualifications and Curriculum Authority (1999) *The National Curriculum.* London: HMSO.

Department for Education and Employment (2003) *Excellence and enjoyment: A strategy for primary schools.* London: HMSO.

Efland, A (1990) *A history of art education*: *intellectual and social currents in teaching the visual arts.* New York: Teachers College Press.

Eisner, EW (1985) *The educational imagination*: *on the design and evaluation of school programs.* London: Macmillan.

Eisner, EW (2002) *The arts and the creation of mind.* Yale, CT: Yale University Press.

Eisner, EW (2003) Artistry in education. *Scandinavian Journal of Educational Research*, 47:3, 373–84.

Lowenfeld, V and Brittain, WL (1982) *Creative and mental growth.* New York: Macmillan.

Macdonald, S (2004) *The history and philosophy of art education.* Cambridge: Lutterworth Press.

Meager, N (2006) *Creativity and culture art projects for primary schools.* Corsham: NSEAD.

NACCCE (1999) *All our futures: creativity, culture and education.* Report from the National Advisory Committee on Creative and Cultural Education, to the Secretaries of State for Education and Employment, and Culture, Media and Sport, DfEE.

National Curriculum Council (NCC) (1990) *The arts 5–16: practice and innovation.* Harlow: Oliver and Boyd.

Prentice, R (1999) Art: Visual Thinking, in Riley, J and Prentice, R (eds) *The curriculum for 7–11 year olds.* London: Paul Chapman Publishing.

Qualifications and Curriculum Authority (2005) *Art and design subject report.* http://www.qca.org.uk/11457.html

Read, H (1958) *Education through art.* London: Faber.

Richardson, M (1948) *Art and the child.* London: University of London Press.

Schon, D (1987) *Educating the reflective practitioner.* San Francisco, CA: Jossey-Bass.

Steers, J (2003) Art and design in the UK: the theory gap, in Addison, N and Burgess, L (eds) *Issues in art and design teaching.* Abingdon: RoutledgeFalmer.

Steers, J (2006) Preface, in Meager, N *Creativity and culture: art projects for primary schools.* Corsham: NSEAD.

Steers, J and Swift, J (1999) A manifesto for art in schools. *The Journal of Art & Design Education*, 18(1), 7–14. Oxford: Blackwell.

Thistlewood, D (1992) *Histories of art and design education – Cole to Coldstream.* Corsham: Longman/NSEAD.

Useful websites

Artworks – the Artworks programme 1999–2004 can be accessed at www.artworks.org.uk

START – the magazine for primary and pre-school teachers of art, craft and design. Information is available at www.nsead.org/publications

HEARTS – Higher Education, the Arts and Schools can be accessed at www.hearts.uk.com

11
Creativity in the music curriculum
Sarah Hennessy

Chapter objectives

By the end of this chapter you should have:

- **developed confidence in your own ability to use your imagination and your children's ability;**
- **explored how to structure activities;**
- **understood the need to see yourself and your children as artists.**

This chapter addresses the following Professional Standards for the award of QTS:
Q1, Q14, Q25, Q25(d)

Introduction

In this chapter I offer a rationale for music in the primary curriculum as a source and resource for creativity. It is well understood that many primary teachers, in training and with experience, are anxious about their abilities to teach music. This has much to do with the perception that teaching music requires advanced skills in singing, playing an instrument and reading notation. Using and strengthening the natural abilities to make music that we all have is much more important and while I do not believe that one can learn to teach music through merely reading about it, I do believe that teachers should give some time to reflecting on what informs practice and what can support better practice. That being said, nothing can replace learning through practical musical enagagement with friends, colleagues and children. This is where confidence and understanding for teaching are nourished.

Confident teachers are much more likely to use their imagination, take risks and be responsive to their pupils. Confidence develops through sustained engagement with both musical thinking and music activity. In this way we come to understand and appreciate the nature of music-making and learning in music. David Elliott (1995) refers to this view of learning as *praxial,* that is, not only learning through doing but also music-making which is located in a social and cultural context. Music is a human activity, something we do intentionally, thoughtfully and in response to how we live.

Creativity in music learning

Not everything we learn in music demands creativity. There are skills we may want to master (such as playing a rhythm on a drum accurately and fluently), or knowledge we want to acquire (such as the source or origins of a particular piece of music). These need practice and study; but the motivation to learn these things should derive from the desire to try something new, develop a new idea, find a particular sound – in the pursuit of making music. And, even when mastering a skill, the activities or context for the practice can be given more meaning by the teacher's imagination and their ability to enable children to find their own solutions.

Creativity in music learning is not an afterthought, something we think about if there's time or as an occasional break from 'work'. Creativity is an essential component of effective learning when the purpose of learning is to enable learners to act and think independently, to grow and change and ultimately to make an original and valuable contribution. Music in schools has not always reflected this view wholeheartedly for a number of reasons:

1. The National Curriculum in England was conceived in such a way as to promote a compartmentalised view of the primary curriculum with a focus on individual subjects, which appeared to discourage integration across subjects around themes or topics. This meant that timetables often became increasingly rigid, making it difficult to consider innovative or flexible approaches to learning.
2. An emphasis on Literacy and Numeracy (with their attendant Strategies) has reduced teachers' energies and motivation towards the rest of the curriculum.
3. There may be a tension in teachers' minds between the notion of work (individual, product oriented, knowledge acquisition, useful, systematic) and the pleasurable, 'non-academic' image of music (and the arts in general). Music may be seen as a luxury that, when the pressure is on, becomes expendable.
4. Creativity in music is inevitably noisy. Noisiness may be viewed as a negative condition in school: a quiet environment suggests studiousness, discipline, calmness, whereas noise means lack of control. Teachers may find it difficult to reconcile this in the context of music-making – and especially when encouraging exploration and experimentation with sound – a necessary element of creative music-making.
5. Musical creativity may be believed to be found only in adult musicians.

A recent reassertion of the importance of integrated and enjoyable approaches to teaching and learning brings hope that the worst effects of recent policies may be healed by a renewed acknowledgement of the central importance of creativity in education (DfES, 2004).

There have also been, in the last few years, three major government-funded initiatives directly focused on improving music education at Key Stage 2. It is too soon to say how effective they will be in their aims but there is already evidence that participation and activity have increased, and class teachers are being given more opportunities to learn from specialist colleagues. The initiatives are as follows.

- KS2 whole class instrumental and vocal tuition (often called Wider Opportunities) – funding provides all schools with tuition for one year group for one year. This may be provided by LA music services or other music tutors who work alongside classteachers to introduce the learning of instruments to one chosen year group. The idea is to stimulate interest which will continue beyond the 'free' year and encourage more children to take up specialist instrumental or vocal learning. The approach to teaching whole classes encompasses the National Curriculum programme of study for music so that listening, composing and improvising are also developed.
- Sing Up is a 3-year project aimed at improving singing in primary schools (see www.singup.org).
- Find Your Talent is the newest initiative and, at the time of writing, in its pilot stage. The aim is to increase experience and learning in all the arts for all primary age children through the normal timetable as well as extended provision. For music this might involve opportunities to hear live music, working with a musician in partnership, expanding the range of activity offered in the normal timetable or in extended provision.

The renewed focus on developing performance skills through singing and learning an instrument may shift the focus away from creative music-making and also relies on good working relationships and partnerships between specialist tutors and class teachers. Good practice in music teaching should always aspire to an integration of listening, composing and performing – and it is creativity which motivates and gives meaning to music learning of all kinds.

Some readers might be surprised at the idea that music learning is not necessarily concerned with creativity – surely the arts are synonymous with creativity? They certainly encompass creative thinking, inventiveness, innovation, novelty, risk-taking, problem-solving, speculation and meaning-making. But of course they also involve skill training, acquisition of knowledge about the art form, and analytical and critical thinking. Perhaps music in formal education, more than other art forms, has been rather imprisoned by these latter concerns to the neglect of the creative aspects. Composing is seen as the preserve of a chosen few with exceptional talent, and the opportunities for creative music-making, more broadly defined, often struggle to be acknowledged in the other musical activities of performing and listening.

REFLECTIVE TASK

Consider your own experience, as a child, of learning music in and out of school.

Are your memories positive or negative?

When I ask this of my students their memories are often coloured by a mixture of strong emotions:

- the 'buzz' of being part of a performance event, of joining in and achieving something; or
- the fear of failure, the misery of rejection, or the drudgery and guilt surrounding practice.

The 'buzz' is what we should all have the opportunity to experience; negative experiences are almost always the result of a teacher's judgement or teaching habits.

Do you recall making up your own music, or working creatively in a music class?

Among generalist student teachers positive responses to this last question are rare – there is sometimes the memory of playing instruments or adding sounds to a story or drama. The impression gained is of intermittent opportunities – if they existed at all.

What is creative music-making?

A note to the reader
When I refer to 'musicians' I mean anyone who makes music, however simple or tentative.

When I refer to the music-making behaviours of young children these are often very close to the behaviours of novice musicians of any age. Experience through listening and making; and interactions with others will all contribute to development – whether you are a five-year-old or a 25-year-old.

Musical creativity can be viewed as both a product and a process in which the musician/music-maker expresses and communicates their ideas and feelings through:

- interpreting, adapting or arranging the music of others in a new way;
- joining in with a new part;

- improvising;
- composing;
- making imaginative/unexpected connections with other media such as language, movement or visual images;
- combining with, or finding musical ideas in poetry, dance, or art works.

We need to consider the differences between child and adult musicians – if we carry in our heads a perception of the latter then children's achievements will often seem inadequate and insubstantial. We need to learn to listen to what children's music *is* (Glover, 2000), not what is missing (not quite in tune, not in time, lacking in structure). It is easy to be critical when musical ability is based on a strict and unforgiving mastery of technical skills: if you can't sing in tune – mime; if you can't keep time – stay quiet.

Frameworks for activities should allow children even at the very earliest stages of their development to use their musical imaginations and be creative. The originality, risk-taking and novelty will be relative to their experience and ability rather than relative to all possible music. As a teacher you may well hear these kinds of musical ideas many, many times in your classroom but what you are listening for is something that is new for that child or group at that moment (consider the idea of 'small c creativity' as discussed by Craft (1999)).

All music-making has the potential to be creative. Creative activities, in which children make their own choices or decisions, add something to or adapt a given idea, all involve creative musical thinking:

- contributing to or giving their own interpretation of a song;
- making an arrangement of a given piece of music (adding accompaniment and deciding how the piece is to be performed);
- inventing a short melodic pattern and developing it into a sequence or a complete piece;
- composing a backing track for a rap;
- improvising a rhythm in the gaps between another given rhythm;
- choosing sounds to represent the sound of waves on a beach, and deciding how to begin and end the 'sound picture'.

Teaching for creativity

There needs to be a distinction between creative teaching in music and teaching for creative music-making. The former can exist without the latter but the latter is unlikely to result without the former

Creative teaching involves finding imaginative, unusual, surprising, adventurous approaches to putting across concepts and knowledge, or to making skill building enjoyable and motivating. Children may learn more effectively and engage more fully with the lesson as a result, but there may be no creative opportunities for them in the experience. Learning to read notation using colours, puppets or funny faces is still about learning to read notation. Singing a song about the Vikings may be fun but may not make a musically imaginative or challenging contribution. However, asking the children to compose their own song (music as well as words) or composing music in response to a Norse myth will. Teaching for creativity requires a kind of 'letting go' on the part of the teacher, and providing a safe space in which the children can find challenge and new insights about music and about themselves.

There is not the space here to discuss in detail the role of music in supporting and enriching creative activities in the rest of the curriculum. Suffice it to say that bringing music and music-making into humanities, other arts, core subjects and physical education not only feeds the imagination and understanding, but also puts music in its proper context of being an integral part of the cultural and social world in which children learn. This is not to suggest that music should be artificially inserted into non-music topics. But where there are obvious links the opportunities should be exploited, not least to increase children's involvement with music!

The focus of the rest of this chapter will be on creative processes and activities within music learning.

Teaching songs

The song repertoire used in primary schools should encompass a wide range of styles and traditions. Popular music (as opposed to classical/high art music) in all traditions is created to be infinitely flexible and adaptable, learned aurally through joining in and in a social setting. Each time a song is sung it will change according to the abilities and feelings of the singers and the context in which it is sung.

When teaching a song, consider the opportunities for children to create their own interpretation. The material that exists (the words, the melody and the accompaniment when there is one) is only part of the music. Making decisions about how to sing the song (expressive elements: speed, dynamics, liveliness, calmness, etc.), how to arrange the song (solos, everyone together, how to begin, how many repeats and how to vary each repeat, etc.) and what to add in the way of accompaniment are all musical choices to be made and experimented with. In this way children learn about the many ways musical material can be changed to give different meaning. Of course instrumental music can also be explored in these ways.

ACTIVITY 1

Suggested sequence of activities for teaching a song

- Sing it through to give a sense of the whole. Ask children to listen out for anything they notice: repetitions, interesting words, surprises.
- Is the song a gentle, calming song or does it make you want to move (is it a work song or a going to sleep song, a story song or a love song, a funny/comic song or a protest song, a song for a single singer or a group)? Thinking about the meaning and context for the song will help in deciding how to sing it (i.e. how to interpret it in performance).
- Learn the chorus first. Children can invent their own pattern of movement (dance sequence, makaton, or just expressive gestures) to accompany it. From these the class choose movement patterns that they like (appropriate and manageable) and everyone practises – what happens if not everyone can manage it? Can the children solve the problem? Possible solutions include:
  – simplify;
  – break into sections for different groups to perform in sequence;
  – practise;
  – differentiate so that some perform a more complex version of the pattern.

- The possibilities for different ways of singing encourage 'possibility thinking' (what if we sing it faster, change the dynamics, vary the numbers singing together?).
- There are choices to be made to achieve a satisfying 'fit' of form and content. Some ideas may feel quite awkward and uncomfortable.
- Older children might divide into groups to perform their own version of the same song to each other.
- There may be a performance recorded on CD (song books often include this) – how does that performance compare?

Skill building

Introductory skill-based activities are now a very familiar part of the music lesson. They give group focus, and introduce and establish the skills needed for listening and music-making. They are often devised as circle games: inventing and passing sounds; following the leader in making body sounds; echoing and sequencing clapped or sung patterns; keeping the pulse collectively and feeling silent beats; accompanying simple songs with actions and so on. In some ways these 'games' are disguised 'drills' – for children to practise in an enjoyable way. What will enable such games to become creative activities for the children is to invite them to make the 'game' their own – to invent variations, add new elements, play independently of the teacher as leader. Such activities should have a strong connection to the main activity of the lesson, so that , for instance, the rhythm patterns used in an echo game are used as the basis for improvising, or accompanying a song, or are listened out for in a listening piece.

Listening

On the face of it, listening may appear to be unrelated to a focus on creative music-making; but listening is crucial in developing skills, knowledge and understanding in the music-making process as well as listening as audience. Our musical imagination is engaged through repeated listenings; and thinking and talking about how music makes us feel, and about what's going on in the music. Listening and responding to music through movement and dance, painting, drawing or writing gives meaning and makes connections between different forms of expression and imagery. A multi-sensory approach feeds the imagination and expands possibilities for our own ideas. Attentive listening while creating music will develop the ability to change and refine ideas, to get closer to what we imagine. Listening to a piece of music can provide the starting point for children's creative work, or a moment during the process to listen how another composer has responded to the same idea. Giving time to listening to the music made in class (through live or recorded performances) affirms the value of children's work and encourages critical reflection.

Improvising

Improvising and composing are considered distinct activities but in the musical behaviours of young children and the inexperienced they overlap and merge. Improvising can be seen as a form of musical play (Hennessy, 1998): spontaneous, of the moment, not fully worked out before it is sounded, a kind of musical doodling. It may not be intended to be communicated to anyone else: 'the musical stream that results may be highly-structured or more exploratory' (Glover, 2000). It is, however, inevitably based on what the performer can do at that moment – and so arises out of prior learning or experience. Often the design and layout of an instrument will dictate the gestures or patterns which result. It is not something that appears out of thin air even though it may appear to do so. Improvising at a more developed stage involves knowledge, skills and practice in order to create within a given musical frame or style – this is what jazz musicians do, for example. If musicians are encouraged to play with ideas, and play by ear (without notation), to not worry about every note sounding perfect and to play and sing along with others, they are more likely to develop the confidence to improvise. Songs and musical frameworks for instrumental work which include little gaps or sections within them for improvising are a 'safe' place for children to develop their improvising abilities in this direction. The Orff approach (see Buchanan *et al.*, 1996; Goodkin, 1997) promotes this way of working – starting from simple accessible ideas and providing supportive musical frameworks within which everyone can participate at their own level.

Composing

Composing involves a putting together of ideas – something planned and worked out. A composition is developed in stages with alterations, edits and revisions. In the hands of younger children the revision process may be barely touched upon – the inexperienced are more likely to accept the first idea which appears and stick to it. This will be compounded by lack of time in lessons and the teacher's degree of understanding of how to mediate the process of revision. Encouraging development and revisions requires careful handling – to gauge when enough is enough or when the musicians are keen (or willing) to stay with it. Knowledge of individual children, and their capacity for focus and critical thinking will inform the teacher's decision to encourage a group to work further with a piece or agree that, for now, it is ready to be performed, recorded and more or less 'fixed'.

Group compositions are more likely to have a discernible shape and structure where you can hear (and see) how the piece has been put together. You may have asked for a particular structural feature to be used (repetitions, ostinato, ABA, canon, verse/chorus) but even when you don't, children, especially when working with others, will come up with a structure which organises who plays what when. Also children, especially when working in groups, may often impose a linear 'narrative' form on their work in the absence of a given structure. Musical structures involve repetition (exact or with variations), question and answer, contrast and silence. Finding ways of encouraging children to work with these elements will lead to more developed and musical outcomes and greater musical understanding. Jo Glover provides an in-depth explanation and discussion of the different ways in which children compose. She encourages us to understand children's music as a musical world quite distinct from adult music, and also argues for self-initiated composing (2000).

A note on notations

Many view musicianship as synonymous with being able to read and write conventional notation (i.e. dots on the stave), despite the fact that the vast majority of music-makers in the world do not use notations of any kind. Especially for young children in primary school, notation should always follow practical and aural engagement, not precede it. Notations of all kinds can and should, on occasion, be used to support and illuminate aspects of music learning. Paintings, sculptures and graphic art can all combine with music to offer starting points or structures for composing, responses to music or ways of analysing music. Inviting children to create their own notations will develop their understanding of the possibilities and limitations inherent in representing music in this way.

The creative process

As you can see there are different ways in which we can work creatively in music and which do not necessarily result in a completely new 'composition'. It is helpful to think of creativity in music as a process through which many different outcomes may emerge. In this process we can identify a number of phases or stages which are sequential and cumulative, but also cyclical, that is earlier stages may be revisited through the process. These stages are in many ways common to all creative processes whether in music or other disciplines. The particular aspect of the process in music which we need to acknowledge is *time.* As with dance and drama, experiencing music takes place in and through time. This temporal quality dictates much of the way we engage with music both in teaching and learning, and the process of creating in music should be framed by this understanding.

I have borrowed a model developed by Wallas (1926) and adapted it to provide a frame for how to recognise and plan for children's engagement with the creative process. Wallas identifies four phases which he names:

- preparation;
- incubation;
- illumination;
- verification.

Preparation

In the classroom this initial stage almost always commences with a 'commission' – a task instigated by the teacher as part of a unit of work. However, it could also arise from children's ideas and motives.

The preparation stage will encompass:

- the stimulus (e.g. pattern of movement, poem, a visit to a wood, a visual image, an instrument or an existing piece of music) through which the structural or expressive framework is agreed – or given;
- the assembling of resources;
- initial focusing activity (listening game, exercise, song, conversation) exploring the elements which link the stimulus to musical ideas;
- establishing the mode of working (whole-class, groups, pairs) and providing some ground rules (scope of the piece and time available for working on it).

If the composition is to be based on small-group work, the teacher may also use this phase in a quite directed way in order to take the class through a model of the suggested way of working – the kinds of decisions they will need to make, and a chance to try out and listen to how the basic ideas can be worked on.

In the teacher's planning there needs to be careful thought given to how much freedom or constraint is permitted (Burnard and Younker, 2002). Too much freedom can be as difficult as too little and the balance between them varies according to the experience and dispositions of the children.

There is a tendency to believe that creativity must be entirely free, open and unfettered – the teacher's role is to 'light the blue touch paper' and stand back. The teacher, in this view, just provides the initial stimulus, the resources, the space and the time – she has no function once the children are working other than to ensure that they stay on task and arrive at a product in the time available.

Fortunately this idea has been largely discredited and it is recognised that children learn more effectively when their experience is mediated by 'knowledgeable others' (Hennessy, 1998). This clearly supports the notion of creativity as a social phenomenon.

REFLECTIVE TASK

If you were asked to compose a piece of music – anything you liked and for any purpose you chose – how would you feel? How would you approach the task?

You would have to make every decision from scratch and in effect decide on your own constraints (rules): how long, what structure, mood, melodic content, etc. If you have composed before you may feel undaunted by this and enjoy the freedom. If you have never composed or done very little, you might find this quite paralysing – even if you play an instrument or sing quite confidently.

Would this be easier alone or with others?

On the other hand composing a piece in which you can only use three notes on a recorder might feel much less threatening and more achievable. At the same time, for an experienced composer, limitations can be challenging and exciting.

It is evident that in creative activity we need both freedom and constraints – freedom to experiment, invent, find our own ideas; and constraints to support, challenge and give focus.

Incubation – exploring and experimenting

This is the phase which creates the most difficulties in the classroom context. It is likely to be noisy and therefore difficult to provide good conditions and difficult to gauge how long different groups or individuals need. Incubation might mean quite solitary thinking or a period of exploring, experimenting and the musical equivalent of doodling (noodling) with others. The teacher's role in this phase requires skills of facilitation and guidance rather than direct instruction. Children need to explore, experiment and improvise with the materials and ideas provided. Because of noise there has to be more management than perhaps seems appropriate – and more than one might need for other creative activities such as poetry, drama, or visual art, for instance. Turn-taking, listening to each other, short periods of free play, whole-class involvement with opportunities for individual suggestions to be tried and tested, all need planning (many publications offer ideas on how to achieve this).

If you are able to use time flexibly you might consider planning for small groups to explore and experiment at different times through the week – if there is an adjacent space available. If this phase is stretched over several days in this way children may want to record their ideas for recall (i.e. audio recording or finding a way to notate).

If using electronic keyboards or computer software children can use headphones – and save or record their ideas.

Illumination – choosing and organising

This is the phase in which decisions are made about what to work with and what to discard. Once choices are made the process of organising and refining takes place. As mentioned earlier young children may arrive at this stage very quickly – choosing the first idea they come up with. As they develop their understanding and skills they will become more discerning and more confident to discard or revise ideas. The teacher's role is to encourage and nurture this awareness through listening, sensitive questioning, suggestions for development, even challenging their decisions – in fact, scaffolding their learning (Hennessy, 1998).

Verification – rehearsing, performing and evaluating

Once the piece is composed (organised, assembled, fully fashioned) there comes the phase of 'fixing'. Rehearsal may still involve changes but essentially this is the stage prior to performing. In the classroom this is likely to be an event in which the composition is performed 'live' to others (the rest of the class, another class, at an assembly) or recorded and played back.

Traditionally the final product is viewed as the end of the process and the achievement should be celebrated. The accumulated experience will resonate in various ways and there should be time, after the event, for the children to evaluate their work and what they feel they learned. Articulating their reflections through writing, drawing or talking should help in developing a sense of ownership and independence.

We can see and hear what children can do in their acoustic compositions – no one is likely to compose something they cannot play themselves as most composing arises out of personal trial and error, so there is likely to be a close link between performing ability, musical understanding and the kinds of compositions children produce.

It is often suggested that there is no 'right' and 'wrong' in creative music-making – however, there is fitness and unfitness, appropriateness and inappropriateness. These are in many ways subjective terms but they are inevitably informed by common cultural experiences and ideas about balance, the relationships between certain patterns and gestures in sound and what they signify in terms of feelings, movements, natural phenomena, etc. For instance, there are very recognisable and common musical representations of different intensities of rain. Young children will tend to find simple and literal responses to events or moods in a story – often fairly predictable. As they become more experienced and exposed to more and more possibilities they will challenge themselves and be challenged to move away from clichés and experiment with more novel ideas.

The contexts for musical creativity

Children are steeped in music from the moment they are born (and before) (Young, 2003) – in contemporary Britain it is impossible to avoid regular, daily contact and immersion in music. By the time children enter school they are likely to have acquired a well-developed repertoire of music through TV, radio, background music in shops and, hopefully, songs and bits of music encountered in play and social settings. In this way children learn to recognise how music is structured, to respond to rhythms, to predict the shape of a tune, to separate the familiar from the unfamiliar. They learn to move and dance to music and to recognise its mood. They adopt and adapt music within their play activity: babbling, cooing, chanting, singing, using objects as instruments and dancing. They are already musically experienced. This is part of enculturation – as we learn language, ways of behaving and ways of inter-acting in the family and social groups, we also absorb musical behaviours.

When children enter school we need to recognise and build on this knowledge and experi-ence. Children will already be immersed in the music of their home culture and its relationship to what is offered in school can affirm or deny their own emerging musical self. A valuable and authentic way for teachers to learn about their children's musical lives is not only to invite them to create and share their own music in the classroom, but also to listen in on how children use music in their play.

Creative music-making will:

- reinforce and help to develop their musical ideas;
- increase and strengthen their abilities in controlling sound (technique);
- encourage social interactions through and around music;
- give meaning to their music learning.

School is only one of many places where music learning for children happens and one might argue that 'school' music is a genre all its own – made up of an exclusive repertoire never heard outside of school (unless to invoke 'school'). What primary schools can provide is a structured, safe and sociable setting for music-making. They can foster musical interactions so that children can then take their music-making into other settings: at home, with friends, at after-school clubs and community-based activities.

Creative activity carries a certain momentum which can depend on many factors:

- the relevance and imaginative potential of the initial stimulus and purpose of the task;
- an appropriate balance between constraint and freedom within the task;
- children having some real control over musical decisions – feeling that the music is theirs;
- the quality of the resources and environment in which the children are working;
- the successful match between the demand of the task and the abilities of the children; and
- responsive and encouraging teachers.

ACTIVITY 2

Atmospheric winds
The purpose of the lesson is to explore the contrast between long and short sounds; to develop skills in controlling long and short sounds, vocally and on wind instruments, and to create a composition which exploits the sound qualities they have explored.

Preparation
- Play an introductory 'game' to establish group focus for listening and vocal control, and to think about and invent long sounds and short sounds.
- Pass a vocal sound round the circle on the end of your finger – a steady horizontal movement, but wiggly or stabbing action will change the sound. First everyone reproduces the same then each invents their own. Different physical movement triggers a 'matching' vocal response and vice versa.
- Listen to a piece of music made up entirely of sustained sound and move to it (e.g. an excerpt from *Atmosphere* by Ligeti).

- In the circle listen to the music again and ask the group what they hear, how it makes them feel or what they imagine.
- Ask them to make long continuous sounds with their mouths or voices (humming, blowing, quiet singing on a single note, whistling) – contrast with very short sounds. Ask individual children to find gestures for conducting the class performing these two contrasting sounds.

Incubation

- Introduce lots of cardboard and plastic tubes of different lengths and diameters and ask children to find different ways of sounding them (blowing across the opening, blowing into the tube, tapping it on the ground). If there are children who play blown instruments (recorder, penny whistle, flute, trumpet, etc.) they can include these (as part of the overall texture or perhaps a specific contrasting section). This could lead to an exploration of pitched notes and how they sound in different combinations (do some tubes produce the same note? Do some notes sound comfortable together? Why? Can you alter the sound of your tube and control the way you play it – quietly, gradually getting louder?...and so on).
- Conduct (and let the children conduct) everyone playing short sounds and long sounds – altogether, in small groups, solos, combinations of short and long, only long high sounds, only short low sounds and so on.

Illumination

- Create a whole-class piece based on these sounds and patterns – considering repetitions and contrast. Don't forget silence! (Children decide on the content and structure, and fix this by showing the sequence visually – how?: graphics, streamers/ribbons and unifix blocks, ... do different colours show different 'colours' of sound?)

NB Blowing is quite tiring and might make children dizzy so you could add a contrasting section based on percussive sounds made with their soundmakers – maybe free impro-visation (represented in the score by a scribble!).

Verification

- Once the piece is constructed and the score is fixed, the piece should be rehearsed to ensure everyone knows what they are doing and gets a feel for the overall sound and structure. Invite individual children to sit out and listen – to give feedback on balance, quality, etc. Record or perform to others. It could be combined with dance or become the atmospheric music for a drama.

Creating a musical environment

- For individual explorations and musical play for young children, a sound corner works well: devise an area of the classroom where instruments are available, perhaps at certain times of the day or week, e.g. a few chime bars, a xylophone with a variety of beaters, two or three different sized drums (see Hennessy, 1998, for detailed guidelines), or headphones plugged into a keyboard and an audio recorder for children to record their stories and songs.
- Build up the best possible range and quality of instruments for the classroom. This will take time, but resist buying cheap as the sound will be disappointing.
- Use poems and stories which have sound content or which evoke movement or atmospheres which can stimulate music-making.
- Exploit the musicality of speech and enjoy the sounds and rhythms of words.
- Look for opportunities to include music in other areas of the curriculum – not only as support for learning

in that area but also to further musical aims.

- Include music for listening wherever possible – to feed the imagination, and enrich sensory experience.
- Invite parents or colleagues who play instruments to play to the children.
- Involve secondary school pupils in performing and helping with music-making.
- Exploit opportunities for involving community and professional musicians in special projects or ongoing support.

A SUMMARY OF **KEY POINTS**

> **Teaching for creativity involves taking risks and being confident in your ability to use the imagination of your pupils, allowing the power and responsibility to shift between you and the children. It requires everyone to engage in the process, however limited their contribution might be: this includes the teacher.**

> **The music teacher's role is often one of managing the activity, asking questions, capturing interesting ideas and ensuring that all the children are able to participate at an appropriate level. It may also be necessary to arbitrate among different ideas (or where little is forthcoming, offer some) and suggest some structure.**

> **It is impossible to produce simple formulae for success as so much depends on the particular children you are working with, your knowledge of them and your own musical interests and enthusiasms. Creative activities you plan may not work, or work beautifully sometimes and not at other times.**

> **Teachers need to see themselves as artists alongside their pupils so that they can enter the musical world of children and thus come to understand how to nurture and support their explorations and discoveries.**

MOVING *ON* > > > **>** **>** **>** MOVING *ON* > > > **>** **>** **>** MOVING *ON*

Supporting children's musical creativity requires you to be open-eared and open-minded about all kinds of music. It also requires a certain attitude of mind towards processes and possibilities. To teach creatively for creativity in music:

- try to see music as activity rather than fixed material that children must learn to master;
- look for musical possibilities in words, gestures, and everyday sounds; and find imaginative connections and stimuli in stories, poems, pictures and patterns;
- look for opportunities to collaborate with colleagues in developing imaginative connections between different curriculum areas;
- if you have musical interests pursue them for your own pleasure and learning but also look for opportunities to challenge yourself with new ways to make music.

REFERENCES REFERENCES **REFERENCES** REFERENCES **REFERENCES** REFERENCES

Buchanan, K, Chadwick, S and Dacey, L (1996) *Music connections: practical music for all primary class teachers, Key Stages 1 and 2*. London: Cramer Music.

Burnard, P and Younker, BA (2002) Mapping pathways: fostering creativity in composition. *Music Education Research*, 4:2, 245–62.

Department for Education and Skills (DfES) (2004b) *Excellence and enjoyment: a strategy for primary schools*. London: DfES.

Elliott, DJ (1995) *Music matters*. New York: Oxford University Press.

Glover, J (2000) *Children composing 4–14*. Abingdon: RoutledgeFalmer.

Goodkin, D (1997) *A rhyme in time: rhythm, speech activities and improvisation for the classroom*. Miami, FL: Warner Bros Publications.

Hennessy, S (1998a) *Coordinating music across the primary school*. Abingdon: Falmer Press.

Hennessy, S (1998b) Teaching composing in the primary curriculum, in Littledyke, M and Huxford, L (eds) *Teaching the primary curriculum for constructive learning*. London: David Fulton.

Young, S (2003) *Music with the under-fours*. Abingdon: RoutledgeFalmer.

Wallas, B (1926) *The art of thought*. New York: Harcourt Brace & World.

Teaching materials (a selection)

MacGregor, H (1995/6) *Listening to music, elements 5+*. London: A & C Black.

MacGregor, H (1995/6) *Listening to music, elements 7+*. London: A & C Black.

MacGregor, H (1995/6) *Listening to music, history*. London: A & C Black.

MacGregor, H and Gargrave, B (2004) *Let's go shoolie-shoo*. London: A & C Black.

MacGregor, H and Gargrave, B (2002) *Let's go zudie-o*. London: A & C Black.

Music express (2003) London: A & C Black.

Orff-Schulwerk American Edition (1977–82) *Music for children*, vols 1 and 2. Schott.

Richards, C (1995) *Listen to this (KS1)*. Saydisc.

Richards, C (1995) *Listen to this (KS2)*. Saydisc.

Song books

Birkenshaw-Fleming L (1990) *Come on, everybody, let's sing*. New York: Holt, Rinehart & Winston.

Clark, V (2002) *High, low, dolly, pepper*. London: A & C Black.

East, H (1989) *Singing sack*. London: A & C Black.

Gadsby, D and Harrop, B (1982) *Flying a round*. London: A & C Black.

Sanderson, A (1995) *Banana splits*. London: A & C Black.

Stannard, K (2004) *Junior voiceworks* series. Oxford: Oxford University Press.

Thompson, D and Winfield, S (1991) *Junkanoo*. Harlow: Longman.

Thompson, D and Winfield, S (1991) *Whoopsy diddledy dandy dee*. Harlow: Longman.

Websites

www.bbc.co.uk – ideas for teachers, information and links to other sites.

www.creativepartnerships.org.uk – Arts Council initiative creating arts projects between schools and artists.

www.gridclub.com – teaching materials.

ictadvice.org.uk – BECTA site.

www.mtrs.co.uk – ideas.

www.ncaction.org.uk – advice on assessment and case studies.

www.o-music.tv.

www.orff.org.uk – Orff Society holds courses for teachers in creative approaches to music teaching and learning.

www.standards.dfee.gov.uk/schemes/music – schemes of work for music devised by QCA.

www.youthmusic.org.uk – major source of funding for out-of-school music-making.

12
What has creativity got to do with citizenship education?
Hilary Claire and Richard Woolley

Chapter objectives

By the end of this chapter you should have:

- **understood how creativity is fundamental to citizenship;**
- **explored how empowering citizenship education can be for children and teachers;**
- **developed your ideas of cross-curricular approach of citizenship education.**

This chapter addresses the following Professional Stgandards for the award of QTS:
Q2, Q6, Q10, Q15

Introduction

This chapter will raise some questions about citizenship education to help you think about:

- the importance, for the future of our society, of creative people with vision;
- values in citizenship education;
- qualities and characteristics of people who can think creatively about citizenship issues;
- the creative teacher of citizenship;
- the creative curriculum in citizenship.

This chapter will not concentrate on explaining citizenship education, but on exploring the conditions and possibilities in the curriculum for creative responses to citizenship education. If you are unsure about its concepts and remit, look at Part 1 of *Teaching Citizenship in Primary Schools* (Claire, 2004).

The global context of citizenship education

In the last 15 years there have been arresting examples of citizens confronting their history and creatively developing new systems of governance to promote social justice – Northern Ireland, nations which were part of the former USSR, South Africa. Historically, there are many examples of people dissatisfied with existing systems who determined to develop democracy and citizenship in new ways – Ancient Athens, England at the time of the Civil War, the Glorious Revolution and throughout the nineteenth century, America and France at the end of the eighteenth century, the Russian Revolution. Now, international conflict, global warming and other environmental hazards challenge the future of our children. Recently, Nelson Mandela appealed to the rich world to take on its responsibility to the poor in Africa and elsewhere.

In all these circumstances – historical and contemporary – people have to think with vision – not just pragmatically – about the nature of society and people's relationship to government and each other, locally and globally. The Robinson Report (NACCCE, 1999) was unequivocal, claiming that Britain's economic prosperity and social cohesion depended on unlocking the potential of every young person and enabling them to face an uncertain and demanding future (1999, pp6–7). We have every reason to believe that as the twenty-first century rolls on, creative as well as pragmatic and principled thinking about social, economic and political problems and solutions will be essential. When children are asked about their future, they tell us clearly that they fear war, racism, crime, and environmental meltdown (Hicks and Holden, 1995; Holden, 2005).

Creativity, citizenship and children's education

The Aims, Visions and Purposes statement at the beginning of the National Curriculum document acknowledges that children's education should encourage wider visions of a future society, not just fit them for the status quo. Sometimes encapsulated in the terms 'minimalist' and 'maximalist', there is a continuum in citizenship education: at one pole, a conservative desire to maintain the status quo, at the other, a conviction that citizenship education (CE) is about moving us along the road towards social justice; (see Claire, 2001, pp1–2). The former concentrates on knowing about public systems and obedience to the law; the latter envisions and is prepared to work for wider ideals.

But even the conservatives, who would like to keep things as they are, are forced to deal with changing, often unexpected, circumstances. The old ideas don't always work; old dogs must learn new tricks; creative solutions become essential.

So, creativity becomes fundamental to citizenship, whether at the radical or the conservative end of the continuum, or at points in between. Participative, active citizens of all political persuasions will need the ability to construe problems and consider creative solutions. Conformist/conventional thinking and attitudes will not lead to solutions in a changing world.

Creativity, democracy and values

CE is imbued with values – as has been recognised from its inception in the curriculum. Government bodies have tried with little success to establish a set of common values that everyone should live by and ended up with lists that offend nobody and still leave us with controversies. Because CE is about the ways we organise society and live alongside one another, it is imperative that principles of human rights and social justice are the yardstick for systems and proposed changes. Still, the detail will always be contentious. When we ask children to consider creative solutions to social issues we must make sure that they constantly measure them against values which we debate in terms of principles and consequences. When we ask them to judge other people's creative proposals they must also refer to values.

This is because creativity can be the handmaid of evil as well as benign change. People are capable of creative problem-setting and creative solutions, but creativity does not automatically ensure justice. No doubt, gas chambers were perceived by Nazis as 'creative'. In South Africa in the early 1950s, the Nationalist Government came up with the 'creative' solution of apartheid, to solve what they had defined as the 'problem' of diverse groups living alongside one another. For the next forty years appalling injustice was perpetrated to carry out the so-called creative solution. Contrast a very different creative solution to economic and political problems: the New Deal in 1930s America. Following Keynesian economic theory which turned classical economics on its head, Roosevelt tackled poverty by providing work through government programmes.

Democracy requires citizens who can:

- analyse and synthesise ideas and information from a variety of sources;
- evaluate the ways problems are defined and the possible consequences of proposed solutions;
- resist brainwashing by powerful – even hegemonic – arguments.

They will need to be independent and capable of principled, creative lateral thought and imagination. They need the education and value systems to reject arguments such as those perpetrated by Nazis, white supremacists or fundamentalists, and realise that the problem itself has been wrongly defined. There are arguments that people who allow themselves to be led by the nose by their leaders have experienced an education which encouraged conformity and obedience, and punished any questioning of authority figures (Adorno, 1950). We are not advocating anarchy in the classroom: order is fundamental to successful teaching. However, we believe that being open-minded to alternative perspectives grows with the experience of creative debate and opportunities to come up with your own creative solutions to issues.

REFLECTIVE TASK

We are suggesting that citizenship is linked to creativity through the following requirements for a free democratic society:

- creative thinking about problems and solutions in society;
- independent minds governed by principled moral thinking and capable of resisting pressure to conform;
- the presence of an opposition which critiques the status quo and offers alternative programmes and goals.

Any critique which can't offer alternatives will be negative, limited and backwards looking:

- envisioning alternatives – whether radical or conservative – requires thinking outside the box, perceiving possibilities and being psychologically prepared to take risks and face challenges.

Using Figure 12.1 opposite, consider how many of the concepts, skills and personal characteristics already influence or affect your own professional practice. Which ones feel comfortable or natural to you, and which present a greater challenge?

What is citizenship education about anyway?

The thoughts shown in Figure 12.1 opposite and developed by a group of practising teachers and teacher educators may help you with an overview of its concepts.

Figure 12.1 Citizenship education

The diagram shows that citizenship education comprises a number of concepts, skills and personal characteristics.

PRACTICAL TASK PRACTICAL TASK PRACTICAL TASK PRACTICAL TASK PRACTICAL TASK

In Table 12.1 on page 152 we have started to develop the concepts in Figure 12.1 under headings with examples. Try to complete this table, adding any other examples that you think should have been included.

In what respects can citizenship education be creative?

In Figure 12.1 and your completed version of Table 12.1 there are two possible ways to consider creativity. One relates to the approaches (pedagogy) you adopt to help children understand concepts or acquire particular gobbets of knowledge. The other relates to the possibilities you provide for children to think creatively themselves about issues and possible solutions. Both require *creative teaching* but the intentions will be different. Curriculum and pedagogy which encourage children's creativity are empowering and liberatory for children; it will be part of your professional intention to develop *their* vision, hopes and dreams. It will be your investment in the future of the planet.

Table 12.1 Development of CE concepts

Knowledge and understanding	Skills	Attitudes/personal characteristics
Human rights and children's rights	Investigation – research, critical thinking	Commitment to human rights and social justice Concern for people beyond own circle at local, national and/or international levels
Ideas about possible futures	Creative thought	?
Knowing about political systems/democracy	Knowing how to participate effectively; make your voice heard	?
Knowing about community organisations and issues	?	Values and concern about society; developing empathy and respect
Knowing about different roles and responsibilities	Knowing how to approach people in different roles and how to exercise responsibility oneself	Willingness to take responsibility and take on different roles
Identity/multiple identities, of self and others	?	?

What sort of person is capable of thinking creatively about issues in society and their own role?

Self-esteem and identity development – links with creativity and citizenship

In the National Curriculum guidelines for primary schools, Personal, Social and Health Education (PSHE) and Citizenship Education are yoked together. Though PSHE may appear to be about personal qualities, they are essential to CE because pupils will grow into and hopefully influence the *social world*. High self-esteem and identity development are central to citizenship: to respect others' identity, understand their situation and grant them 'worth', even if they are very different from you, you must first respect yourself and your own worth, and feel confident about your own identity. George Mead (1934) explained how judgements and responses from 'significant others' contribute to identity development and self-esteem. Peers and teachers in school as well as parents/carers and community members are critically significant for young children.

More recently, Jeffrey (2004) explained, using his own research, that we develop our identity and our capabilities in a social world: the very experience of creative learning in a creative context, contributes to positive self-esteem and social identity – all the more when a young learners' group experience is enjoyable, active, social and emotionally engaging. Indeed, the NACCCE Report (1999) emphasised two justifications for creative approaches in education:

to address the kind of future we want for the human race, but also because creative teaching and learning can promote children's self-esteem. It follows that we need to consider the environment and ethos that children will experience and how these can help them develop a strong sense of their own worth and identity, alongside an appreciation of others.

Citizenship, creativity and taking risks

Much theoretical writing about creativity emphasises the centrality of taking risks in one's thinking and planning. If your 'big new idea' goes against conventional thinking, you may not dare voice it for fear of an incredulous reception or jeering. Risk-taking is not just a physical thing like bungee jumping, though you may get an adrenalin rush as you prepare to argue a minority position. It's psychologically and emotionally charged: you are exposed and on your own. Even if you have a metaphorical map, it will be incomplete, warn of precipices or have blank bits. Think about the women who campaigned to be allowed to enter higher education – or any other campaign which went against the status quo. They had to be courageous, not just have persuasive arguments. We need to remember of course that something well-tried and familiar for adults may not be so for young children. This applies to the risk-taking they may feel if we ask them to work in unfamiliar ways, or to think for themselves – without the water wings of the worksheets, the familiar textbooks. For some children, something as ordinary as working in a group where you have to take a role or expose your views to others will be highly risky. So along with high self-esteem, children who are asked to think creatively and unconventionally about the social world need courage – and they need the conditions which nurture their courage and do not undermine it.

Given how important their social world is to children, preparing the ground for taking risks in the ways they think about problems and solutions is essential. Do remember that taking risks with thinking is a greater challenge for some children than for others; this applies to children in Year 6 as well as those in the Foundation Stage. So you will want to consider a psychologically supportive environment which encourages children to think outside the box without fear of ridicule. Perhaps it means working with trusted friends and having the solidarity of a group to back your ideas. Perhaps it means working through role play or games, or with puppets, or some other distancing technique, which allows them to play safely with new ideas.

Rules, playing and creativity

Margaret Boden (2001) emphasises that the psychological ability to work without clear rules or to change the rules is an oft-ignored aspect of creativity. It follows that the classroom ethos we establish must encourage and not punish children for critiquing the rules and, where appropriate, changing them. Beyond that, the capacity to play with ideas – even play with rules – encourages creative thinking. So you might encourage your pupils to envisage a 'what if' world – where animals are in charge; where children are really adults' equals, where there are no adults, where the cars all vanish overnight. Some 'playing with ideas' will be seriously related to real events – suppose you were part of the unpredicted devastation wreaked by a tsunami, a cyclone or a drought which turned you from a wealthy farmer to a refugee. The 'imaginings' that such work invites are part of encouraging the kind of empathy as well as creativity children will need later, as concerned and proactive global citizens.

REFLECTIVE TASK

- Children who have a strong sense of identity, self-worth and self-confidence can make choices for themselves, discuss and advocate what they would like to see happen – and why; listen carefully to alternative points of view, and be prepared to change their minds.

- We lay the foundations for concepts, skills and knowledge which will develop as the child matures towards adulthood. This means in practice that from the nursery and throughout primary school we consider confidence and identity building as children learn both to listen to and 'hear' others' positions and express their own ideas with confidence and without undue criticism.

- Thinking unconventionally and creatively can mean playing with ideas, imagining, letting go of rules and taking risks. Reducing the social and psychological risks will facilitate creative thinking.

Consider a lesson you led recently. Using the three bullet points above, identify how you supported children, how you encouraged independence and what strategies you used to develop positive interaction and mutual appreciation and understanding.

The school curriculum, creativity and citizenship

Creative CE is about looking at our social world with critical eyes, identifying what we would like to improve, and then developing realistic, appropriate ideas and plans.

'Mirrors and windows...roots and wings'

Someone has said that we need mirrors to reflect our world, and windows opening out to wider horizons and possibilities; roots so that we know who we are and feel strongly connected, and wings so that we can fly, fantasise, hope and dream. These seem perfect metaphors for creative CE. You must start with the mirrors and roots, so that you are not misinformed, alienated, apathetic and disengaged. To change things you need to understand what you are dealing with in terms of economic, historical, social and political realities. But without the windows and the wings there can be no visions of the future. The notion of 'teaching for tomorrow' (Hicks and Holden, 1995) is best exemplified through the work of development education associations, the global citizenship movement and World Studies Trust (see Hicks, 2003). Their active pedagogy is admirably suited to work in citizenship. Much of their focus has been on global connections, particularly using geography as the vehicle. A range of useful resources are available from Oxfam (www.oxfam.org.uk/education) and Teachers in Development Education (www.tidec.org). However, the principles of 'teaching for tomorrow' apply across the curriculum and connect at all points with CE.

Teachers and curriculum

So far, we have considered some of the personal qualities which may be important for creative thinking generally and CE specifically. Within the child's experience in school, starting with the youngest, there are some other necessary conditions for nurturing qualities and attitudes of creative citizenship.

1. Creative, democratic and empowering teachers who:
- are committed to developing creative citizens for the future;

- create a classroom climate in which children experience democracy first-hand;
- see possibilities for developing children's ability to engage with the present and the future;
- know how to develop an ethos of collaboration and trust – both essential because of the risks and dynamics of thinking creatively;
- know how to set up opportunities for creative thinking about society – whether 'blue skies' thinking, or pragmatic.

2. A creative curriculum which:
- enriches children's knowledge about society through biographies, stories and situations which challenge and stimulate their understandings of possible actions and ways of life in the world;
- develops qualities and capabilities of empathy, creative problem-setting and problem-solving;
- develops and encourages higher-order thinking skills.

The creative teacher

Having your own vision about creative teaching

We have said that CE can be either at the minimalist or the maximalist end of a continuum. Creativity in your classroom will depend on your philosophy of education and interpretation of your own role. People with a highly instrumental and minimalist view of CE are unlikely to want to encourage creativity or open-ended situations in which children pose problems about society and try to tackle them. But we do need to consider that we are preparing young children for the rapidly changing twenty-first century.

Being able to take risks as a teacher

Many experienced teachers know that it is possible to crush children's creativity into ready-made moulds where they parrot the expected answers and do what they have to do to get good marks or teacher approval or stay out of trouble. Moving children on from this conformist, uncreative approach to their own learning may have to start with the teacher her/himself being prepared to take some risks. In *Teaching Citizenship in Primary Schools* there is an account of a teacher called Paula who, faced with discipline problems in her Year 6 class, responded empathetically and creatively to the children – and simultaneously found solutions to their and her difficulties (see Claire, 2004, pp87–9). An important message from Paula's story was that she had to take a number of risks herself. She had to break free from a repressive school system which did not give children space to bring their concerns to teachers' attention; she had to take a risk that listening to children's perspective on some difficult issues might open 'Pandora's box', as she put it herself. Basically, she had to be prepared to trust herself and the children sufficiently to set something new moving without knowing quite where it would go. This is a really important message to those of you who hope to encourage children's creative response to citizenship issues. It's not just yourself you'll have to trust, your own good sense, judgement, ability to create and manage a much more open classroom – but you'll have to trust the children.

Managing a collaborative and trusting classroom

To get 'there' from 'here' will be quite easy if the school ethos already ensures that children work collaboratively, take responsibility seriously and know how to manage themselves in situations where they have considerable autonomy. For others, the very opposite may be the case. You will need to set yourself and the children small achievable goals towards ition, responsibility and autonomy on the journey towards a more distant ging creative responses to citizenship issues. You'll need to make your bjectives' as clear as you would the day's plans for literacy. You'll need to gies you know for positive behaviour management, clear boundary setting, t how they're doing and the progress you hope for (e.g. listening to each vith people who are not part of their clique, actively participating, etc.). You'll go for group reward systems, intrinsic motivation and collaboration, not individual competition and extrinsic rewards. You'll avoid damaging criticism. Your 'further goal' will be about working together towards solutions to societal problems – because they think it's worthwhile, not because they'll get a gold star.

Your goal of building greater trust between children shouldn't be confined to Circle Time. Use games and PE. Think about puppets, role play, pair and small-group work on stories, design, art and maths as possible opportunities for children to learn to talk more openly, listen and work together in trusting respectful ways.

Creative teaching – perceiving opportunities

Your vision of your role as a teacher and how you encourage learning and your intention to build greater trust and autonomy may mean some quite creative curriculum innovations. You'll need to look for opportunities and plan to implement them.

Boden (2001) explores the relationship between knowledge and creativity and points out that creative thinking develops from what we already know, not in a vacuum. We transform what we already know by changing some of the rules; we think more creatively through engaging with other people's ideas – maybe through reading or through collaborative planning or conversation. CE is privileged, because you can use any other subject you choose to further its aims – and combine them in any ways you think will work. So you might get children to consider how they would like to improve an area of wasteland near their school (which would certainly be a citizenship topic) and your work could include some design and technology, science, art, letter writing, making a PowerPoint presentation and role play. You might use a painting in a museum to reflect on emblematic, cultural representations of power, celebration or religious difference (for example, André Fougeron's *American Civilisation* which is in Tate Modern – in the centre a man worships a car, surrounded by images of war and poverty – or the *Delhi Durbar* painting in the Bristol Museum of Empire and Commonwealth History (see Harnett *et al.*, (2005)). This will be the starting point for children to think about their own values, the people with power in their own society and how it is expressed.

Or you might start with the traditional Indian art of puppet-making to help children think about deforestation (Growney, 2005). Growney taught a primary class about puppet-makers substituting papier mâché for wood through a cross-curricular project in global citizenship, involving picture books like *The People Who Hugged Trees*, making puppets, perspective, talking about the different people involved in forestry, and work on sustainable development.

It's important to give yourself permission to think outside the box and to know that after the rather repressive years when the National Curriculum was first introduced, creative cross-curricularity is encouraged in a variety of recent official documents, whose very titles hint at their agenda: for example, the Primary National Strategy: *Excellence and Enjoyment*(DfES, 2003) and *All Our Futures: Creativity, Culture and Education* (DfEE, 1999a).

REFLECTIVE TASK

REFLECTIVE TASK

Reflect on some work that you have recently done with children. Could you have introduced a citizenship theme, for example about rights and responsibilities, identity, understanding other people's perspectives, what we might do when people feel excluded or bullied? Perhaps you asked children to write poems, or explore themes in a text – could this have gone in other directions? One Year 4 teacher helped her children to develop and role-play alternative non-violent endings to *Romeo and Juliet* – which is about peaceful conflict resolution in CE. In Table 12.2 a grid has been started – try to add some examples from your own curriculum knowledge and work.

Table 12.2 Introducing CE themes

Existing curriculum work	Creative extension	CE concepts, etc.
Learning about Anne Frank in history	Discussion and research about current examples of 'race hatred' and discrimination on religious grounds. Decisions about what the class can do to make its views known	Human rights; racism, courage of people who defied Nazis and hid the the Franks – challenging discrimination; considering socially just solutions to problems
Reading *Charlotte's Web* in English	Setting up a debate about how we treat farm animals; whether we should eat meat	Values; tolerance of diversity
Data handling using stats to create bar graphs and pie charts	Using statistics from web about the different languages people speak in Britain (or local area if multi-cultural); finding out from council the age spread in the borough and graphing these	Discussing the composition ethnically and in age terms of our society. Considering what these mean for schools or wider community – school support, translation services, services for elderly and children
Measure	Finding out whether you could get round the school easily if you were in a wheelchair	*??*
??	*??*	*??*

The creative curriculum – beyond instrumentalism

Inspiring children and enriching their knowledge base

You can support children's creative thinking about their own and others' identity, human rights, possible futures, their potential power and their relationships through introducing them to a range of analytic tools and concepts that move them beyond their current experiences and understandings. This is Vygotsky's zone of proximal development in practice – building into the unknown with scaffolding. It's fundamental to a wider vision of education, beyond instrumentalism. For citizenship it may mean helping children think about their world in terms of such concepts as the following:

- *The individual's relationship to society*, e.g. how far aspects of a competitive, individualistic, materialist society create difficulties between individuals, communities and internationally, and how far such characteristics promote dynamism and progress. You could use a story like *The Selfish Giant* to help children grasp these difficult ideas, going beyond the story itself, to talk about contemporary, real issues, and where we need to share and work collaboratively in society.
- *Gender relationships*, e.g. how far conventional ideas about roles, rights and responsibilities get skewed into oppressive power plays and how far they serve stability. (Perhaps Anthony Browne's *Piggybook* could stimulate such thinking?)
- *Self-expression and instrumentalism*, e.g. what is the point of artistic endeavours whether personal or communal – should the government spend money on free art galleries and sculptures in public places?
- *Should the wealthy 'north' take responsibility for the poverty and instability in some parts of the 'south'* (less developed countries)? Are we 'our brother's keeper'? A story from the Bible could be the starting point.
- *Is war always justified?* Perhaps start with songs about soldiers like The Dixie Chicks' *Travellin' Soldier* which was banned at the time of the 2004 Iraq War, Bruce Springsteen's *Youngstown* or John Lennon's *Imagine*.

You're unlikely to use the abstract words but stories, poetry, music and art are important ways to open children's minds to critiquing their own society and possibilities for progress. Remember that everyone needs ideas to bounce off – even the most creative people stand on the shoulders of the giants who came before them. It's also about progression in learning – you offer images, stories and ideas which young children may not comprehend in depth but which will form the basis for their conceptualisation of possibilities in the future. You can also explore the affective domain – considering how emotions and empathy help us to understand and respond to a range of issues.

Here are some more ideas:

- *Using a poem* – some examples

> *White Comedy*
>
> I waz whitemailed
> By a white witch,
> Wid white magic
> An' white lies,
> Branded by a white sheep
> I slaved as a whitesmith
> Near a white spot
> Where I suffered whitewater fever.
> Whitelisted as a whiteleg
> I waz in de white book
> As a master of white art,
> It waz like white death.
>
> Benjamin Zephaniah, from 'Propa Propaganda'

Vegan Steven

There was a young vegan
Called Steven,
Who just would not kill for no reason,
This kid would not eat
No cheese or no meat
And he hated the foxhunting season

Benjamin Zephaniah in *A Little Book of Vegan Poems*
(www.benjaminzephaniah.com/rhymin.html#british)

Some say that Peace is calm and relaxing
And some say it takes your problems away.
Some say it makes your heart glow
And some say it is utter madness.

Does it look like a jigsaw muddled up?
Or does it look like an angel?
Does it stick with you all the way?
Or does it wave goodbye?

Katherine, aged 11 cited in Adams, Hyde and Woolley (2008, p74)

- *a story* – Anthony Browne: *Willy and Hugh* (all about bullying, friendship, the power of gangs) or *Piggybook* (a mum refuses to do the housework and her children and husband find out just what women's work entails); Mary Hoffman: *Amazing Grace* (possible futures, breaking the stereotypes);
- *a role play* – between a group who'd like to stop parents taking their kids to school in individual cars, and those who support it (individual rights *vs* environmental pollution and traffic);
- diamond-ranking with an artist and musician included with the doctor, teacher, childminder (see Claire, 2004, pp11–12; Clough and Holden, 2002, pp55–7);
- *art* – such as Figure 12.2 from Southern Africa, showing people working communally and Figure 12.3 from nineteenth-century Venice, a world turned upside down – 'what would it be like if we lived there...?';
- *philosophy for children* – text (could be from a newspaper), a cartoon, a photo or painting act as stimuli for children's own questions (see Claire, 2004, Chapter 3 for more on philosophy for children).

Children can't be expected to think creatively about an environment with beautiful innovative buildings or inspiring landscapes if they've never seen any – even in pictures. So perhaps bring in pictures of Gaudi's architecture in Barcelona, or Corbusier's estates on the outskirts of Paris, which in their time were supposed to offer a brave new world to working people – but have not fulfilled this vision.

Some more ideas for stimulating creative thinking about citizenship concepts

Historical and current examples

For opportunities to learn about values and issues starting with people and groups who wanted to change things:

Figure 12.2 – 'Scrumbling for water' – lithograph showing 'Crossroads' squatter camp outside Cape Town, South Africa, by Patrick Holo, 1994 (artist unknown, original in author's possession)

Figure 12.3 'Il mondo alla rovescia' – 'The world turned upside down' (artist unknown, original print in author's possession)

- Martin Luther King, Mahatma Gandhi, Nelson Mandela, Maya Angelou, Eglantine Jebb (who founded the Save the Children Fund) – all concerned with social justice and human rights.
- People concerned with the environment and uses and abuses of science and technology, e.g. Rachel Carson, a progenitor of the environmental movement; Arundhati Roy who campaigns in India; Greenpeace; WWF.
- People concerned with the effects of war and conflict, e.g. Save the Children Fund, UNICEF, Amnesty, Anne Frank Educational Trust, Holocaust Trust, Red Cross, Médecins sans Frontières.

Starting with fiction

Much children's fiction is about 'quest' and challenge, difficult choices, fighting the dragons and the giants or confronting evil, and personal qualities – courage, vision. From Philip Pullman, Anne Fine or Lemony Snicket to feminist and traditional fairy tales, myths and legends, there are opportunities to get children thinking about their values, concerns and their own willingness to become engaged. Frank Zipes (1987) and Bob Dixon (1977) have explored the power of traditional fairy stories and children's fiction to socialise girls and boys into conventional and conservative discourses. More recently, Bronwyn Davies has used feminist versions of familiar stories to get primary children thinking about gender and power (Davies, 2003). Familiar children's material has been used by a serious academic to get people thinking about how they make choices, and what the consequences of alternative choices might have been. For instance, was the Little Mermaid wise to accept the appalling conditions of life on earth or should she have stayed beneath the sea with her sisters? What did Humpty think he was doing sitting on a wall with such a fragile shell and so little mobility? (Dowie, 1999, 2005) The important thing for teachers is to consider how pupils can engage with dominant discourses and critiques, moving from the metaphorical and fictional to today's real world. What are 'our dragons'? What qualities do we need to slay them? What choices should we carefully think through?

Linking with art and music

Certain artists represent reality or challenge the status quo, so that we see the world differently. Some theorists believe that without exposure to critical art we are 'dumbed down' into passivity and political apathy (Adorno, 1991). To harness this material for creative CE means being prepared to include the political and social content of art and music, not just concentrate on form. Beyond the examples illustrated above, think about Picasso's *Guernica*, Dubuffet's drawings of wartime Paris or poster art from round the world. These resources are intended to do more than extend children's cultural base. After the discussion, children should themselves try and use art, photography or posters to interpret contemporary issues.

Drama techniques

Role play, simulations and other drama techniques might well be your most powerful vehicles for creative work in CE: they can liberate creativity, allowing children to play with new ideas and new personae in safe contexts, to imagine and consider 'what if?'.

Preparing for local study in the primary history curriculum, some of my own students worked with newspaper cuttings about various historical campaigns, which included keeping a hospital open, stopping nuclear waste going through the borough, a *Rock Against Racism* concert in the late 1970s, the dustmen's strike and a march of unemployed workers in the 1920s.

They quickly appreciated the opportunity to use cross-curricular approaches to explore historical issues about rights, responsibilities and advocacy and take this into contemporary concerns. So, their plans included using the photos and articles to set up freeze-frames, with children taking different positions which were then animated, the class writing letters to the press, holding a debate, making a simulated TV programme and learning some of the songs from the old campaigns. They would follow through by identifying a contemporary concern and planning a campaign themselves, learning about the range of possible ways to make your voice heard: making banners, designing leaflets and holding meetings.

A SUMMARY OF **KEY POINTS**

In this short chapter it has only been possible to skim the surface of a huge subject, but we hope that creative teachers will use these ideas as a springboard, and in turn empower their pupils to think and plan creatively for their own future. Toss a pebble into a pool – watch the ripples spread. The surprises and the rewards are great when you become a creative teacher, so that CE for your pupils is creative, liberating and empowering.

> Creativity is fundamental to citizenship. Participative, active citizens of all political persuasions will need the ability to construe problems and consider creative solutions. They will need to be independent, and capable of principled, lateral thought and imagination; they will also need to be able to realise when 'problems' have been wrongly defined. Creativity does not automatically ensure justice.

> Central to citizenship education are high self-esteem and development of identity. To respect others' identity, understand their situation and grant them 'worth', you must first respect yourself and your own worth, and feel confident about your own identity.

> Remember that taking risks with children and working with them to explore and change perceptions are greater challenges for some children than for others; this applies to pupils in Year 6 as much as those in the Foundation Stage.

> Try to conceptualise citizenship education as a journey towards a more distant goal of encouraging creative responses to wider societal issues. Set yourself and the children small achievable goals towards greater collaboration, responsibility and autonomy on this journey. Make your 'responsibility objectives' as clear as you would the day's plans for literacy.

> Citizenship education is privileged, because you can use any other subject you choose to further its aims – and combine them in any ways you think will work. Your goal of building greater trust between children shouldn't be confined to circle time.

MOVING *ON* > > > > > > MOVING *ON* > > > > > > MOVING *ON*

- You may feel that some of the issues that children will raise will be controversial, and feel understandably nervous about this. Choose an issue that is particularly prominent in the news media at the present time. Create a mind map of questions which you anticipate children might ask. What is your own response to each question? Which questions might you find it difficult to address and what strategies could you use to avoid being defensive and to help children to work towards their own solutions/attitudes? An exploration of a range of issues including war and peace, climate change, democracy and sustainable development can be found in *The Challenge of Teaching Controversial Issues* (Claire and Holden (eds), 2007).
- Using Oxfam's *Education for Global Citizenship: a guide for schools* (available to download at http://www.oxfam.org.uk/education/gc/), consider the range of citizenship-related skills that can be integrated into your teaching. Develop your lesson-planning format to include an area to include citizenship skills which will run alongside other curriculum areas. Explore the effectiveness of including such cross-curricular links as part of your daily or weekly evaluations.

- Choose one of the strategies outlined in this chapter (e.g. using poetry, freeze frame, photographs or artists' work) and develop an activity to undertake with a group of children to explore ideas about possible futures. How might the people be feeling in the situation that is portrayed? How does the situation or issue make the children feel? How would the children wish to change the situation presented? What possible alternatives can they think of?

REFERENCES REFERENCES **REFERENCES** REFERENCES REFERENCES REFERENCES

Adams, K, Hyde, B and Woolley, R (2008) *The spiritual dimension of childhood*. London: Jessica Kingsley Publishers.

Adorno, TW (1950) *The authoritarian personality*. New York: Harper & Bros.

Adorno, TW (1991) *The culture industry: selected essays on mass culture*. Abingdon: Routledge.

Boden, MA (2001) Creativity and knowledge, in Craft, A. Jeffrey, B and Leibling, M (eds) *Creativity in education*. London: Continuum.

Claire, H (2001) *Not aliens: primary school children and the PSHE/citizenship curriculum*. Stoke-on-Trent: Trentham Books.

Claire, H (ed.) (2004) *Teaching citizenship in primary schools*. Exeter: Learning Matters.

Claire, H and Holden, C (2007) *The challenge of teaching controversial issues*. Stoke-on-Trent: Trentham Books.

Davies, B (2003) Working with primary school children to deconstruct gender, in Skelton, C and Francis, B (eds) *Boys and girls in the primary classroom*. Buckingham: Open University Press.

Department for Education and Employment (DfEE) (1999a) *All our futures: creativity, culture and education*. The National Advisory Committee's Report on Creative and Cultural Education. London: HMSO.

Department for Education and Skills (DfES) (2003) *Excellence and enjoyment*. London: HMSO.

Dixon, B (1977) *Catching them young with political ideas*. London: Pluto Press.

Dowie, J (2005) *The mermaid and the Bayesian* (in circulation). Available by sending an e-mail with subject 'Send Mermaid' to jack.dowie@lshtm.ac.uk

Growney, C (2005) *Primary design and technology and citizenship*. See website: www.citizemLinfo/pdf/commarticles/Cathy_Growney.pdf

Harnett, P *et al*. (2005) My 'self' and the wider world: Interpreting the British Empire and Commonwealth Museum. See website: www.citized.info/pdfycommarticles/Penelope-Harnett.pdf

Hicks, D (2003) Thirty years of global education: a reminder of key principles and precedents. *Educational Review*, 55:3, 265–75.

Hicks, D and Holden, C (1995) *Visions of the future: why we need to teach for tomorrow*. Stoke-on-Trent: Trentham Books.

Holden, C (2005) The citizenship challenge: educating children about the real world and real issues, in Ross, A (ed.) *Teaching citizenship*. London: CiCe, University of North London.

Jeffrey, B (2004a) *End of award report: creative learning and student perspectives* (CLASP) *project*, submitted to ESRC, November.

Jeffrey, B (2004b) Meaningful creative learning: learners' perspectives. Paper given at the ECER conference, Crete. See website: opencreativity.open.ac.uk/pdf/ECER04-CL+Meaningfulness.pdf

Mead, G (1934) *Mind, self, and society*, Morris, CW (ed.). Chicago, IL: University of Chicago.

National Advisory Committee on Creative and Cultural Education (NACCCE) (1999) *All our futures: creativity, culture and education* (The Robinson Report). London: DfEE.

Zipes, F (1996) *Creative Storytelling: Building Communities, Changing Lives*. Abingdon: Routledge.

Zipes, J (ed.) (1987) *Don't bet on the prince: contemporary feminist fairy tales in North America and England*. New York: Routledge.

13
Creativity in primary design and technology
Dan Davies and Alan Howe

Chapter objectives

- **To argue for the importance of design and technology to children's creative development.**
- **To suggest creative starting points for design and technology activity.**
- **To introduce the notion of social creativity.**

This chapter addresses the following Professional Standards for the award of QTS:
Q1, Q7, Q10, Q14

Introduction

Design and technology (D&T) can claim to be at the heart of any curriculum that seeks to develop children's creativity, and was originally conceived as such. In the original proposals for the subject in the National Curriculum, the Design and Technology Working Group (1988) suggested that it involves:

> The development of design and technology capability to operate effectively and *creatively* in the made world. (para 1.2, our italics)

PRACTICAL TASK PRACTICAL TASK PRACTICAL TASK PRACTICAL TASK **PRACTICAL TASK**

In the current National Curriculum (NC), an 'Importance of...' statement for each subject is included prior to the programmes of study. How many of these statements refer to creativity?

You will have discovered that all but two of the introductory 'importance of' statements for subjects in the current National Curriculum (DfEE, 1999c) claim to contribute to children's creativity, yet design and technology is the only one to mention it twice! What makes D&T such a creative subject?

Well, firstly, if we take the oft-quoted definition from the highly influential report *All Our Futures* (NACCCE, 1999): 'imaginative activity fashioned so as to *produce outcomes* that are both original and of value' (our italics), we can see that the emphasis upon *production* is central to D&T activities. D&T is a hands-on activity in which children make real, tangible objects. It is, however, also 'minds-on', involving a balance between doing and thinking, action and reflection. The act of designing inevitably involves imagining something that does not yet exist. At its best, D&T offers children open-ended tasks which do not have a prescribed 'right answer' and involve an element of choice (of shape, colour, materials, function, etc.) so that their outcomes will all be original. Evaluation is also central to the 'minds-on' dimension of D&T; children need to learn to appraise others' designs as well as their own.

Secondly, Koestler's (1964) definition of creativity as 'the ability to make connections between previously unconnected ideas' seems to describe well the sorts of ways in which designers think (e.g. linking clockwork and radio, or cyclones and vacuum cleaners). D&T can provide children with opportunities to bring together ideas from different areas of the curriculum (e.g. knowledge about materials, electricity or nutrition from science, understanding of 3D shapes and measurement from maths, people's different needs and lifestyles from geography). D&T draws particularly on children's 'visual literacy' – their abilities to 'read' colour and form, patterns and symbols, and to reassemble these elements into aesthetically pleasing outcomes. It shares this with art and design, and can perhaps claim to represent a third major form of representation, alongside words and numbers.

Thirdly, accounts of creative *processes* also seem to echo those that designers or children might undertake in the course of a D&T project. For example, Dust (1999) suggests that at least four phases of creativity are commonly identified, to which we have added imaginary examples from the development of the Dyson vacuum cleaner:

1. *Preparation* – investigating the problem and gathering data (e.g. trying out many vacuum cleaners to measure their loss of suction as the bag fills up);
2. *Incubation* – usually an unconscious/subconscious phase (e.g. going away and thinking about something else, perhaps observing tornadoes or water flowing down plugholes);
3. *Illumination/revelation* – the insight, the moment of creation (e.g. if we could make two 'mini-tornadoes', one inside the other, it would suck air into a vacuum cleaner powerfully);
4. *Verification/reframing* – the 'testing', usually through communicating the outcome to peers or 'gatekeepers' in the 'field' or domain (e.g. making hundreds of models and prototypes, taking them round trade fairs, showing them to manufacturers).

If we consider these against the processes identified in the National Curriculum Programme of Study (PoS) for D&T (Table 13.1) we can see striking correspondences. You will notice that the steps in the process do not occur in the same order, but we need to remember that in both cases they 'do not generally occur in a tidy linear path: they often overlap and the process can be entered and left at any stage' (NGfL Scotland, 2003). There is also no equivalent of 'incubation' in D&T as prescribed by the National Curriculum, although there seems to be a recognition by teachers that children should be given more time to think and discuss ideas during the school day.

The fourth reason why D&T and creativity go together is concerned with thinking skills. One of the 'creative thinking skills' identified in the National Curriculum is 'problem-solving'. Problem-solving is a thinking skill that has received much attention over the years, and the strategies to solve practical problems have long been promoted in D&T (see, for example, Roden, 1999). The extent to which it is generic or transferable is debatable (if you can solve mathematical problems, it does not necessarily mean you can solve design problems), but its importance in D&T is profound. Design problems tend to be 'wicked', that is they are not clearly defined like mathematical problems and involve many factors such as materials, technology and human lifestyles. This sometimes makes them not look like problems at all: 'design and make sandwiches for a picnic' sounds more like an opportunity for trying out new combinations of fillings. Playing around with ideas, another characteristic of creative

Table 13.1. Correspondence between models of creative and D&T processes.

Dust's (1999) synthesis of creative processes	D&T National Curricuum Programme of Study
Preparation	4. Knowledge and understanding of materials and components
	3. Evaluating processes and products
Incubation	
Illumination/revelation	1. Developing, planning and communicating ideas
Verification/reframing	2. Working with tools, equipment, materials and components to make quality products
	3. Evaluating processes and products

D&T, is a problem-solving activity, although within a low-stress, relatively unstructured framework. We don't necessarily need to set children artificial 'problems' (for example, 'build a tower to support a marble') but we do need to support them in developing strategies that will help them think through problems in the midst of designing and making. For a food technologist, designing a sandwich that will stick together, taste pleasant and not make the bread too soggy presents a whole range of challenging problems – it's no picnic!

Creativity and values in D&T

Before we look in detail at classroom practice we need to consider why we want children to be creative in D&T and how we will know if they have been. This involves applying value judgements – what is your response to a child who has creatively combined materials to make an innovative weapon? If we analyse further the NC 'Importance of D&T' statement it becomes clear that design and technology is a 'future-oriented' subject in that children are being asked to imagine how things might be different and better. David Orr (1993, p16) claims that:

> Students in the [twenty-first century] will need to know how to create a civilisation that runs on sunlight, conserves energy, preserves biodiversity, protects soils and forests, develops sustainable local economies and restores the damage inflicted on the earth. In order to achieve such ecological education we need to transform our schools and universities.

> (Orr, 1993, p16)

Orr is applying his values, which are associated with education for sustainable development, to identify problems that, in his opinion, require creative solutions. We don't often ask children to think very far into the future – what could we design to improve people's lives in ten, twenty years' time? Perhaps in order to engage children's creativity we need to be setting more 'blue-sky' design projects, inviting children to project themselves forward in time.

REFLECTIVE TASK

REFLECTIVE TASK

Hicks and Holden (1995) report on a survey of children's visions of the future. They found that while half the children at age 7 thought about their own personal futures often, less than a quarter reflected on the future for their local area. Encouragingly, 41 per cent claimed to think about the future of the world often, with a further third considering it 'sometimes'. While the majority considered that their own futures would improve, they were less optimistic about other people and the planet as a whole. Eleven-year-olds in particular were worried about increasing pollution, poverty and wars:

> Their choice for preferred futures indicates that many would like a future based on greater environmental awareness, and their action as individuals reinforces this as an area of concern. (Hicks and Holden, 1995, p78)

In your experience, are children encouraged to think about 'a better future' during D&T lessons?

The findings of Hicks and Holden will not surprise any teacher who has discussed global issues with his or her class. The problem lies (as with all of us) in the differences between what children say and what they do. At a mundane level, their apparently wasteful use of resources in a design and technology project (cutting a circle out of the middle of a piece of card for example) may frustrate us. Often it is that they have not made the connections between the big ideas of environmentalism (e.g. deforestation) and their individual choices (how much paper to use).

So a further dimension of decision-making for children can be to introduce *eco-choice* points in a project in which they are given the relevant environmental information to make sustainable decisions. Batheaston Primary School has used its international links to obtain recycling data from different European Countries, and has compared the rates of decomposition of different materials by burying them. They have used the information to design class gardens, which grow food for the school canteen to reduce food miles. Children are also involved in the design of animal boxes and a weather station in the school grounds, together with a Mediterranean garden, withy dome, bark trail, sand pit, fossil wall and range of limestone rocks from a local mine (www.batheastonprimary.co.uk). Children have worked with sculptor Edwina Bridgeman on a number of installations, as part of the 5x5x5 = creativity project (www.5x5x5creativity.org.uk).

PRACTICAL TASK PRACTICAL TASK **PRACTICAL TASK** PRACTICAL TASK **PRACTICAL TASK**

How could common classroom design-and-make assignments such as fairground rides, coats or fruit salads be adapted to engage children with values consistent with sustainable development?

Starting points for creativity in D&T

Through looking at what experienced teachers do in the classroom (Howe *et al.,* 2001), we have identified three ways that teachers provide motivational and inspirational starting points for D&T activities that support the development of children's creativity. These are:

- building on children's interests;
- identifying real opportunities;
- using relevant contexts.

For example, in a reception class making wheeled vehicles, we observed how the class teacher used the *children's interests* to identify a context for learning:

> *[The children] had lots of experience of working with a variety of construction kits on a small scale. There was a class 'craze' for making ever more elaborate wheeled vehicles. Katherine, the class teacher, wanted to capitalise and build on this enthusiasm. This led to her making formative assessments about what the children were able to do, their language development, their knowledge and understanding of the world and their interests. She had also identified a need to give the children opportunities to work on a larger scale and to develop the skills of cutting and joining wood... To begin the project, Katherine discussed with the class their recently made wheeled models, and introduced a new word – 'axle'. She showed them how an axle could be used to link pairs of wheels and allow them to turn. Some children were able to make freehand labelled drawings of vehicles whilst others used the models as designs for the next stage... The children discovered how PVA glue and elastic bands might be used to join pieces of wood through this activity. At times they became engrossed in this to such an extent [Figure 13.1] that they lost a sense of time and place – they were 'in the flow...'.*

(Howe *et al.*, 2001, pp22–3)

Figure 13.1 Developing wheeled vehicles from children's initial interest

Csikszentmilhalyi (1997, 2002) coined the phrase 'in the flow' to describe the most productive and fulfilling phases of the creative process, a state he characterises by intense concentration, absorption, pleasure and lack of awareness of time passing. By providing children with *real opportunities* their sense of engagement with the task can carry them into this state. For example, at Bromley Heath Infants School in South Gloucestershire, D&T co-ordinator Sarah Stillie chose to take advantage of the new housing development being built locally to provide children with the opportunity of observing structures at various stages of completion, and consider ways in which the development would impact upon the local community. She was also anxious to provide children with a sense of the social setting within which homes are bought and sold, so set up an estate agency in the classroom role-play area, complete with ICT-generated advertisements, index files, property descriptions and key tags. When children came to undertake the design-and-make assignment (DMA) she wanted them to be able to consider the particular needs of individuals, so set up a 'fantasy' scenario in which children would design for story characters. They were to group the resulting models in a housing development ('Fairytale land') which considered issues of access, space and traffic.

A classroom role-play area is also an example of a *relevant context*. In other examples we have seen, contexts were provided through the use of story or by referring to needs within the school – to help someone, to put on an assembly or to redesign a library. Relevant contexts are particularly important in helping young children to design for others, because without significant scaffolding many find it very difficult to think beyond their own needs and wants. For example, the children in the autumn of Year 1 at St Philip's Primary School, Bath, carried out a DMA to make a sandwich that they would like to eat. The starting point was, therefore, a discussion about their own preferences. Their teacher had judged that it would be too demanding for them to think of the needs of others while, at the same time, meeting the requirements to plan before making and remembering safe and hygienic practices. Later in the year, when the children were more secure with the notion of designing and making, she 'scaffolded' their transition from egocentricity to awareness of the perspectives of *others* during work on playgrounds. The class went to look at a playground as the starting point for thinking about the equipment different age groups would like and where a playground should be sited so as not to offend residents.

REFLECTIVE TASK

Are the teachers above teaching for creativity, teaching creatively, or both?

Helping children to generate creative ideas

Having 'good ideas' is fundamental to creativity; it is an obvious point to make, yet do we actually teach children in a way that develops their ability to think creatively? A study of 5,000 pupils undertaken at the University of Cambridge (2008) found that many sometimes struggled to develop original ideas, a situation they described as 'design fixation'. By 'good' ideas we refer here not only to inventing new products but also to considering new ways of looking at things and doing things. It is important to note that we are using the 'ideas' in the plural here. We want children to be able to come up with a *number* of possibilities, *then* evaluate their potential before proceeding. This is related to a measure of creativity – 'ideational fluency' – in common usage in the USA. We want to avoid situations where children say 'I can't think of anything!' or on the other hand proceed with the first idea that occurred to them. This is not to say that every time children do D&T they should come up with three ideas and chose the 'best' one. That would be too formulaic. We do believe children should have the opportunity to think before proceeding.

The D&T curriculum provides a framework for allowing children time to think by suggesting they should investigate and evaluate 'a range of familiar products' (DfEE, 1999c, p93). Although the processes of D&T can occur in any order and begin at any point (see Table 13.1) we believe there is a strong case for beginning with *evaluation*. D&T and evaluation have a 'special relationship', and it is difficult to think of a great innovation in design that has come about without a keen awareness of what has been done before. We need not worry that by exposing children to existing products they will simply 'copy' them – some degree of transformation is inevitable in the process of making an idea their own. The key to making an investigation and evaluation activity (IEA) a spur to generative thought is the teacher's choice of a range of different design solutions around a common theme, and the 'scaffolding' of children's ability to 'interrogate' these objects (Figure 13.2).

Figure 13.2 'Interrogating' a collection of musical instruments to provide design ideas

For example, we can use questioning which focuses children's attention on key aspects of the objects being evaluated. This needs to begin with questions that encourage closer observation and initial investigation, such as:

- What shapes can you see?
- What materials have been used?
- How many pieces have been used in construction?
- What does it feel/taste/smell like?

Next, we can ask children to consider the human factors behind the design of the product being evaluated, and to think about future developments as this may provide a springboard for their own ideas:

- Who do you think this product was designed for? How can you tell?
- Describe how they would use it – can you imagine any difficulties they might have?
- Could you improve upon the product, and if so, how?
- How would you redesign it for a different user (perhaps for a child, an elderly person, an astronaut, a fictional character)?

So, through evaluation of the made world, children's ideas can be sparked and their creativity enhanced. Handled in the wrong way, however, looking at what already exists can be an inhibitor to creative thought. Such a situation could arise if the children see only one or two alternatives, if they think the teacher values one solution above others, or if one product seems perfectly suited to the specifications set for the children's design-and-make assignment.

A set of techniques developed by Robert Eberle (1997) and known by the acronym SCAMPER can be usefully applied to D&T contexts to enable children to see existing artefacts or products in a new way and so aid 'ideational fluency':

Substitute:	What if we substituted one material with another in this bag or vehicle?
Combine:	What if we combine the ideas from these two pupils or groups?
Adapt:	What if we adapt this idea to be more environmentally friendly?
Modify:	What if we magnify this shape to make something much bigger? (e.g. a cup becomes a house). What if we 'magnify' this aerial photo to make a fabric design?
Put to other uses:	What if we use this bag as a hat or that hat as a bag?
Eliminate:	What if we remove as much material as possible from this design?
Reverse:	What if we turn this inside-out or upside-down?

(Eberle, R, 1997)

Another common way of supporting idea generation is *brainstorming* or *blue-sky thinking*. Essentially this is an uninterrupted process during which a teacher might invite immediate responses to a given scenario, e.g. a 'wolf-proof house' for the three little pigs. Children throw any words or ideas that occur to them into the 'pot' for recording on a large sheet of paper or interactive whiteboard. The ground rules are to avoid evaluating the ideas immediately, and certainly not to laugh at them! Such a flow of ideas in response to a problem or scenario can be enhanced if the thinkers work in small groups initially to allow a chance for discussion. The discussion may start from a very open-ended question – 'what winds you up?' – or completing the statement – 'we really must do something about...' Another technique is for ideas to be written or drawn on paper aeroplanes – this literally allows ideas to be 'tossed around' for others to pick up and add to. The playfulness of the situation can encourage playfulness in thinking. Once the initial 'storm' has passed, we can then sort through the contributions and evaluate them against criteria decided by the group, e.g. practicality, aesthetics, expense.

Another strategy for idea generation is called *linking-thinking*. Linking ideas, as we have seen, is a fundamental part of creativity. There are a number of techniques that can help this 'linking-thinking' in the classroom. Relating a product in an analogous way can throw up new possibilities, e.g.:

'Packages are like...'
...nuts (strong, keep the contents safe, hard to open)
...homes (keep contents dry, secure, insulated, reflect the owner's character).

Develop the analogy for the item to be packaged:

'If my new sweet was growing on a tree, it would look like this...be displayed like this...be dispersed like this...be consumed by...' and so on.

Some children might find the visual a more powerful stimulation than words. Visual triggers might come from:

- random shapes/scribbles/doodles;
- images from photos or clippings;
- digital photos that have been manipulated;
- shapes in nature – fruits, river deltas, frost patterns.

In generating ideas, children might be asked to act out an aspect of the life of the intended user or even the intended product. Some adult designers have actually done this – dressing like a pregnant woman or visually impaired person. Examples for role-play could include:

- looking after a baby;
- coping in a classroom without bending;
- if I were a package I would be . . .;
- a day in the life of a shoe.

Social creativity in D&T

As teachers, should we concentrate on enabling individuals to be creative or should we concentrate on developing a creative classroom ethos? Siraj-Blatchford (1996) discusses how, in the classroom, children can move from being involved in 'collective design' – working as a group with support from the teacher – to, in later years, a 'design collective' in which children draw on earlier experiences and learned skills to design and make with autonomy alongside their peers. He suggests that if children are part of successful design collectives during the primary years then they are more likely to progress to challenging tasks with confidence.

One of the key findings from research into children's creativity is the central importance of peers, supportive adults and role models in inspiring and stimulating children. Our own research in this field – the Young Designers on Location project (Davies *et al.*, 2004) – suggests that the most important kinds of encounters for stimulating children's creativity are those involving practising designers, technologists, artists, architects and engineers – we will call them 'design-related professionals'. Children respond instinctively to the apprenticeship model of education offered by the designer in the classroom, rather than to the more rigid, curriculum-led attempts to 'teach children to design'. By sharing their own work practices with examples, it seemed that the designers working on the project helped to create a climate of confidence and trust, while maintaining 'high ambient levels of creative activity' through acting as 'co-workers', modelling behaviours and demonstrating practice. The professionals also demonstrated 'explicit expressions of confidence in the creative abilities of those within the environment' (Harrington, 1990) through a discussion of children's own creativity – demonstrating both a democratic view of creativity and a metacognitive dimension to their teaching. By the end of the project, when relationships had had time to establish, the interactions between children and designers were very productive. They were genuinely able to 'bounce ideas' off each other and challenge formulaic thinking.

The project above describes a situation where the distinction between the roles of adult and child had begun to dissolve. This poses the class teacher a real challenge – can this radical shift of roles be allowed to happen in a 'normal' classroom? The role of the 'more knowledgeable other' is like that suggested by Bruner (1996) in 'scaffolding' children's learning, as evidenced in the way Steve Heal works with his Year 5/6 class in helping them to prioritise design criteria (Figure 13.3). Another way forward is to consider different uses of curriculum time. Many schools have made a step in this direction through 'D&T weeks', where different ways of working can be developed and where different relationships can take hold. This different use of time, when combined with some input from those who work in the design world – perhaps in the form of an afternoon visit or short residency – can provide an ideal context for a 'creative ecosystem' to be developed.

Figure 13.3 'Scaffolding' children's prioritising of design criteria for a shelter

Creative making in D&T

We have discussed creative and generative thinking as a part of designing, yet there is more thinking to be done when making. At any point, the introduction of one of the strategies we have described above might refresh or refocus minds. D&T is an iterative process moving backwards and forwards between activities 'inside' and 'outside the head' (Kimbell *et al.*, 1991) so it is appropriate for children to employ procedures in different orders – for example by starting with making. In order to develop their creative ideas, children may find it helpful and motivating to get their hands on materials as soon as possible. This can involve play, by which we mean handling objects and exploring them in a relatively unstructured way. In a primary classroom children might be encouraged to handle objects such as the materials they will later be using (as in the wheeled vehicles example above). This will allow children to develop their knowledge of the properties of materials and will allow them to imagine how the materials might be put to use. Ideal materials that allow shapes and forms to be developed in a temporary way include:

- clay – to explore a form for a storage container, candle holder or vehicle body;
- pipe-cleaners or art straws – to allow exploration of stable shapes for a photo frame, furniture or playground equipment;
- paper – to allow exploration of card mechanisms, patterns for garments, patterns for bags or shoes;
- construction kits – to allow exploration of mechanisms for vehicles or toys, hinges for storage boxes, stable shapes, strong shapes.

The power of ICT in developing children's ideas before and during making is considerable. For example, using a site such as www.dtonline.org to explore packaging design, simple computer-aided design software such as TABS+ which allows children to make 3D models and prints out 2D nets, or 'My World' which allows young children to make a number of decisions, for example in relation to designing a house, can all help to develop creative solutions.

REFLECTIVE TASK

Should teachers give children freedom to design and make, or should they teach them skills beforehand? This question of balance between intervention and non-intervention has been at the heart of debates about teaching for creativity. In D&T there are certain skills that children can learn – to do with thinking and making. The tension between a skills-based approach to developing creativity (what Gardner, 1999) identifies as deriving from an Eastern, Confucian tradition with an emphasis on 'mastery') and one that is more 'constructive' with an emphasis on process was highlighted in our own work with 11-year-olds and 'design-related professionals' (Davies *et al.*, 2004). Those with more skills input produced outcomes of higher quality, though children who had been encouraged to reflect on their own creativity and 'follow their own path' were less conventional. This reflects research by DATA/Nuffield (2003) who advocate an approach combining skills input with 'surprise' activities to stimulate unusual solutions. The National Grid for Learning (NGfL Scotland, 2003) urges teachers to go beyond the 'creative ecosystem' to a more directive role in children's capability:

Although a creative climate and an encouraging adult are essential they are not enough to develop creativity. The teacher's role, beyond encouragement, involves intervening, actively teaching creative technqiues and strategies.

Although young children may exhibit 'preconventional' creativity (Rosenblatt and Winner, 1988) before exposure to specific D&T knowledge and skills, our own view is that 'postconventional' creativity (i.e. that which transcends convention) is associated with explicit teaching of knowledge and skills, through, for example, focused practical tasks (FPTs). Through making with a range of materials, children will develop knowledge of their properties, together with skills of cutting, fixing, joining and manipulating that will enable them to realise their creativity with fewer frustrations. There is no substitute for this first-hand experience.

Sometimes children can get 'stuck' and give up, or return again and again to making the same limited range of things. To move children on and help them transcend their existing set of ideas for solving the problem we can intervene in a number of ways:

• by introducing a new set of materials;
• by asking the child to share their project and ideas with the rest of the class;
• by showing a new technique for cutting, joining or combining.

One way in which we can support children in their development of problem-solving is to make the strategies they are using more explicit through questioning. This will promote 'self-knowledge', or 'metacognition', widely regarded as essential if you want to get better at something. For example, during an activity to design and make homes for story characters (see above) class teacher Sarah Stillie gathered the children on the carpet for a joint problem-solving session (Figure 13.4). Each pair had to present their progress and discuss their problems – plus the ways in which they had tried to overcome them – with the wider group, who made suggestions about the way forward.

Figure 13.4 A problem-solving seminar during making

PRACTICAL TASK PRACTICAL TASK **PRACTICAL TASK** PRACTICAL TASK **PRACTICAL TASK**

Another way of looking at creative teaching of D&T is to consider what a D&T teacher should *not* do (Fasciato and Rogers, 2005). Can you imagine what the most uncreative D&T teaching would be like?

A SUMMARY OF **KEY POINTS**

In this chapter, we have suggested that in order to develop children's creativity through D&T teachers should:

> develop a supportive 'ecosystem';

> be playful with ideas, spaces, time and resources;

> make connections, when planning, between learning and children's lives;

> teach skills and knowledge, but in a way that helps children to solve their own problems;

> develop cross-curricular links with other learning areas.

MOVING *ON* > > > > > > MOVING *ON* > > > > > > MOVING *ON*

After teaching some Design and Technology, a teacher will want to know if the lesson is a success. There are at least two ways of asking this: 'Did I put on a good performance and ensure the lesson ran smoothly and to plan?' *or* (and this is the key question in the context of this chapter) 'Did I teach in a way that enabled children's creativity?'

In order to answer the question next time you are evaluating a lesson, the following factors could be considered:

In the lesson, was there:

- a non-threatening atmosphere in which children were secure enough to take risks and make mistakes – or were they always looking to me for reassurance and the 'right answer'?
- opportunity for play and experimentation – did I allow the children to try things for themselves in an open-ended way?

- opportunity for generative thought – where lots of ideas were expressed and greeted openly?
- an activity presented in an exciting context – did the children find the context motivating and worthwhile?
- a chance for children to choose resources and methods?
- opportunity for critical reflection in a supportive environment – did the class appraise their own and each other's work constructively?

If you can answer yes to at least one of these questions then you are on the way to teaching design and technology that is supporting children's creativity.

REFERENCES REFERENCES **REFERENCES** REFERENCES **REFERENCES** REFERENCES

Bruner, JS (1996) *The culture of education*. Cambridge, MA: Harvard University Press.

Cambridge University (2008) *Understanding creativity for creative understanding* www.admin.cam. ac.uk/news/dp/200804290/ accessed 19.5.08.

Csikszentmihalyi, M (1997) *Creativity, flow and the psychology of discovery and invention*. London: Rider.

Davies, D, Howe, A and Haywood, S (2004) Building a creative ecosystem – the Young Designers on Location Project. *International Journal of Art and Design Education*, 23:3, 278–89.

Department for Education and Employment (DfEE) (1999a) *All our futures: creativity, culture and education*. The National Advisory Committee's Report on Creative and Cultural Education. London: HMSO.

Department for Education and Employment (DfEE) (1999c) *The National Curriculum: Handbook for primary teachers in England*. London: DfEE.

Csikszentmihalyi, M (2002) *Flow*. London: Rider.

Design and Technology Association (DATA)/Nuffield Foundation (2003) *Creativity in crisis?* Wellesbourne: DATA.

Harrington, D M (1990) The ecology of human creativity: a psychological perspective, in Runco, MA and Albert, RS (eds) *Theories of creativity*. London: Sage.

Hicks, D and Holden, C (1995) *Visions of the future:why we need to teach for tomorrow*. Stoke-on-Trent: Trentham Books.

Howe, A, Davies, D and Ritchie, R (2001) *Primary design and technology for the future: creativity, culture and citizenship in the curriculum*. London: David Fulton.

Kimbell, R, Stables, K, Wheeler, T, Wozniak, A and Kelly, AV (1991) *The assessment of performance in design and technology*. London: Evaluation and Monitoring Unit (EMU), School Examinations and Assessment Council (SEAC).

Koestler, A (1964) *The act of creation*. London: Macmillan.

National Advisory Committee on Creative and Cultural Education (NACCCE) (1999) *All our futures: creativity, culture and education* (The Robinson Report). London: DfEE.

NGfL Scotland (2003) *Creativity in education online*. See website: www.ltscotland.org.uk/creativity

Nicholl, B, McLellan, R and Kotob, W (2008) *Understanding creativity for creative understanding*. Cambridge: University of Cambridge Faculty of Education.

Orr, D (1993) Schools for the 21st century. *Resurgence*, 160 (September/October).

Roden, C (1999) How children's problem-solving strategies develop at Key Stage 1. *Journal of Design and Technology Education*, 4:1, 21–7.

Rosenblatt, E and Winner, E (1988) The art of children's drawing. *Journal of Aesthetic Education*, 22: 3–15.

14
Creativity in primary history
Hilary Cooper

Chapter objectives

By the end of the chapter you will have considered:

- **what is historical enquiry?;**
- **how psychologists' definitions of creativity link to historical enquiry;**
- **how constructivist learning theories are related to creativity and historical enquiry;**
- **why a creative approach to learning history is essential;**
- **how developing creativity through history reflects recent documentation.**

This chapter addresses the following Professional Standards for the award of QTS:
Q1, Q6, Q7(b), Q8, Q10

Introduction

This chapter will help you to understand why creative thinking must be at the centre of teaching and learning in history. A series of examples will illustrate how these points apply to practice.

What is historical enquiry?

Historical enquiry, whether for an academic historian or at a simpler level for a primary school child, involves the same process. We find out about the past from a variety of sources, through traces of the past which remain, such as photographs, paintings, objects, buildings, statistics, maps, advertisements, newspaper accounts, diaries. We need to ask questions about the source. How was it made? Who made it? Why? What did it mean to the people who made and used it (Collingwood, 1939). Often there is no right or wrong answer. We need to say, 'probably', 'I think', 'perhaps', to give reasons and to listen to the reasons of others; we may possibly change our mind. Craft (2000) identifies 'possibility thinking' as creative. And we have to recognise that some things we may never know. This involves the creative thinking as identified by the psychologists who described it as producing a rich variety of ideas and tolerating what cannot be known.

In order to try to understand people and events in the past we also need to try to see things from their perspectives and to use historical imagination, imagination rooted in evidence, as described by Cox (1986); Jones (1968); Gardner (1993); Goleman (1996); Anderson and Ryhammer (1998). Young children have a limited knowledge base but if, from the beginning, they learn how to make multiple suggestions about how people may have thought and felt they will, as they grow older, be able to make increasingly valid suggestions based on what is known, what is likely and what cannot be disproved (Cooper 2007: 194).

Finally children, like historians, need to combine what they know and can 'guess' from the sources to construct an account of a past time, or event, or for the reasons for changes over time. To do this they need 'multi-dimensional creativity'. For these do not need to be written accounts; they could be 'museum displays', role play, models, picture stories, video or audio presentations or PowerPoint presentations (DfEE, 1999a; Edwards and Springate, 1995). These interpretations may be different but be equally valid, just as historians' interpretations are, depending on particular interests, gender, ethnicity and perspectives and what is known at the time.

History also involves multi-dimensional creativity because history is an umbrella subject. It involves all aspects of societies from the past: music, art or literature which can all be integrated into a history topic. This involves not just interpreting them as sources but also engaging with the creativity within the subjects themselves.

Psychologists, creativity and historical enquiry

When, in the 1960s, psychologists attempted to define and even test creativity in an attempt to make the curriculum broader, more flexible and 'child-centred' they found it very difficult (Guilford, 1959; Torrance, 1965; Walach and Kagan, 1965). They concluded that creativity is concerned with 'divergent thinking', with producing a variety of ideas (for example imagining uses for objects), tolerating what is not known and generating imaginative interpretations of situations which may be difficult to understand. Haddon and Lytton (1968) found that children develop this kind of thinking if they are in an environment where they are encouraged to think creatively, although many teachers did not recognise creative thinking because they preferred conformity. Psychologists also investigated children's ability to see things from another person's perspective. Donaldson (1978) and Cox (1986) concluded that children had been underestimated in their ability to do this, if an activity was interesting, through role play, conversation and looking at pictures.

Jones (1968) thought it essential that thinking should be related to emotions and imagination and suggested ways in which children can be encouraged to understand both themselves and the behaviour and feelings and ideas of other societies. More recently the concepts of multi-intelligences and emotional intelligence have become familiar. Research of the 1970s and 1980s recognises that both logic and imagination are involved in creativity (Anderson and Rhyammer, 1998) and research in the 1980s and 1990s recognised the importance of social interaction in fostering creativity (Craft, Jeffrey and Leibling, 2001).

Recent neuroscience research shows that learning depends on the development of multi-sensory networks of neurons distributed across the entire brain (Goswami and Bryant, 2008). For example a concept in history, say Elizabethan or The Industrial Revolution, may depend on neurons being simultaneously active in visual, spatial, memory, deductive and kinaesthetic regions of both hemispheres.

The National Advisory Council on Creative and Cultural Education (NACCCE) sums up previous research, defining creativity as:

- multi-dimensional – involving all fields of activity (Boden, 1990; Gardner, 1993);
- playing with ideas and making unusual connections;
- involving imagination and feelings as well as thinking (Goleman, 1996).

Creativity has been seen to include 'possibility thinking' (Craft, 2000) and the ability to transfer knowledge gained in one context to another in order to solve a problem (Seltzer and Bentley, 1999, p10). Others (e.g. Edwards and Springate, 2001) have suggested that creativity is fostered through expressing ideas in a wide variety of symbolic media and encouraging integration of subject areas through meaningful topics.

Constructivist learning theories, creativity and historical enquiry

The key constructivist theorists are Piaget, Vygotsky and Bruner. Much subsequent research has developed their work. Constructivist learning theories are based on the idea that we all construct, or create, our own understandings of the world through gradually building up our own mental maps, based on our personal experiences, and through discussion with others. This is a continuing, active process. Piaget's work on reasoning (1928) applies to interpreting sources and his work on language (1926) explores how children gradually become able to make robust arguments to support their reasoning, using 'because'. Vygotsky (1978) emphasised the importance of working with others and of discussion, trial and error in order to clarify, modify and extend our understanding and learn new concepts. Craft and Jeffrey (2000) also saw creativity as linked to social interaction. Bruner (1966) emphasised the importance of presenting material in different ways, material children can explore physically (artefacts, tools, buildings, sites), visually (pictures, photographs, paintings, illustrations and diagrams), as well as through language. He argued that if material is presented in an appropriate way children of any age can ask and answer questions at the heart of a subject. Bruner argues (1963) that if children learn the methods of enquiry at the heart of a discipline they can transfer this reasoning to new contexts and so avoid mental overload. Selzer and Bentley (1999) saw this as part of the creative process.

History then can only be learned through engaging in historical enquiry. The work of psychologists and learning theorists has shown how this process involves creative thinking: making probabilistic inferences and causal arguments, discussing these with others, understanding different viewpoints and using imagination to understand how people in the past may have thought, felt and behaved. Learning history also involves creativity because it is multi-dimensional; it subsumes other dimensions of society, including art, literature and music. Constructing interpretations or accounts of an enquiry also involve multi-dimensional creativity involving different curriculum areas. Constructivist learning theory illustrates how children construct and create their own historical understanding.

Why a creative approach to history is important

Learning to ask and answer questions, to develop and defend arguments, to listen to others, to recognise that there may not be a right answer is part of social and emotional as well as cognitive development. Constructing our own histories includes family histories, local histories, histories of different places and recognising that there is no single history and that stories of the past can change. This values individuals and diversity and develops identities. Understanding how different valid interpretations are constructed is essential in a democratic society as is evident from previously Communist and Fascist countries who are trying to reconstruct their multifaceted histories, and in countries where views of the past are contested, such as South Africa and Northern Ireland.

Creativity, history and recent documentation

The *Excellence and Enjoyment* agenda (DfES, 2003) encourages us to develop history education in creative ways. It emphasises the importance of a broad, rich and meaningful curriculum and returns to teachers' professional judgement the responsibility for managing time and structuring the curriculum. *The Futures Programme* (DfES, 2005) requires teachers 'to plan creative, coherent curricula with cross-curricular links' and speaks of the need for personalisation and innovation through creative partnerships. Aims of the *Every Child Matters* agenda (DfES, 2003) include enjoyment and achievement and valuing each individual. History plays a vital part in pupils' well-being through nurturing their own culture and identity and those of others, by respecting differences, encouraging them to ask questions, interpret evidence, hypothesise, identify issues and draw conclusions through critical analysis of the past and through visiting places of historic interest (Bristow, 2007). The *National Literacy and Numeracy Framework* (DfES, 2007) is intended to be used in the context of cross-curricular work. Values are intended to underpin the subjects of *The National Curriculum* (DfEE, 1999: 10–13, 19–21); examples of this in the context of history can be found in Cooper and Rowley (2006). And R*esearching Effective Pedagogy in the Early Years* (Siraj-Blatchford *et al.*, 2002) recognises the importance of 'sustained shared thinking', through which adults with good curriculum knowledge and children develop their understandings through shared dialogue. This involves the teacher adopting 'an elaborate, conversational style, amplifying and evaluating what the child says' (Goswami and Bryant, 2008).

REFLECTIVE TASK

You are asked, because of limited time for history, to base your lessons on Elizabethan England on chapters from *Our Island Story* (Marshall, 1905, reprinted by subscription of readers of *The Daily Telegraph*, 2005). This gives a narrative account of English History from Roman to Victorian Times. What alternative approach would you suggest and how would you justify it?

Examples of developing creativity through history

History, play and creativity

In play children are motivated, they make choices, explore, are flexible and actively engaged. Imaginitive play frees a child from the immediate environment. In play children behave beyond their age and daily behaviour (Vygotsky, 1978). Through 'Let's pretend play' about oral history, myths, legends, folk tales as well as about 'true' stories from the past children construct their own accounts (QCA 2000, p25). This, in an embryonic way, is how all accounts of the past are constructed; imagining, from what is known, why people felt, thought and acted as they did. They use experimental dialogue about supposed places and people in 'alternative worlds'.

Meadows and Cashdan (1988, p39), Vygotsky (1976) and Bruner (1987) say that social interaction with adults enhances the quality of learning through play. Adults can help children to sequence, repeat and retell stories, discuss what happens next and why, using the language of time through questioning and extended shared thinking. Who lived

Creativity	Historical enquiry	Psychology	Constructivist learning Theory	Recent documentation
Multi-dimensional thinking Expressing ideas in variety of media	Creating interpretations through role play, technologies, displays, paintings, etc.	Divergent thinking, Producing a variety of ideas Multi-intelligences Logic and imagination	Bruner – Presenting material in different ways (kinaesthetic, iconic, symbolic)	*Excellence and Enjoyment* (2003): broad, rich meaningful curriculum; teachers manage time and curriculum structure.
Rational and emotional thinking	Imagination rooted in evidence	Generating imaginative solutions Understanding behaviour and feelings of others Emotional intelligence	Bruner – transferring knowledge and thinking processes to new contexts	*Futures Programme* (2005): creative, innovative, coherent curriculum with cross-curricular links.
Playing with ideas and making connections	Causal thinking	Social interaction in problem-solving		
Possibility thinking	Making inferences about sources; tolerating what cannot be known	Seeing things from perspective of others through role play, looking at pictures, conversation. Tolerating what cannot be known	Piaget – reasoning, causal argument, Vygotsky – importance of social interaction in concept development; Zone of proximal development	*Every Child Matters* (2003): enjoying and achieving, valuing individuals
Transfer knowledge and thinking to new contexts to solve a problem				*National Curriculum* (1999)
Integrating subjects	Cross-curricular links within history	A subject is learned through multi-sensory networks		*National Literacy and Numeracy Framework* literacy through subjects
Social Interaction				

Table 14.1 Synopsis: Creativity, History, Psychology, Learning Theories and Recent Documentation

in the castle? What did they wear? What did they eat? Children learn probabilistic thinking; (what if?), to hypothesise, that there is not always a right answer and that others have different ideas. Winnicot (in Bruce, 1987, p71) suggested that adults are able to relate to powerful events, hero figures, music and paintings if they have related to them through play. Bruce (1987) claims that play forms a fundamental part of fostering a child's creativity. Garvey (1977) emphasised the importance of play which reconstructs stories about the past for social and emotional growth because it explores emotions, relationships and situations beyond their direct experience.

Children, need to be involved in negotiating and organising the play (Bennett *et al.*, 1997). They need to learn to develop a story they know, sequence ideas, adopt roles and take turns. They may do this through sensitive adult intervention to extend language, model, mediate, question or to give some direction for a while. Teacher-directed activities are integrated with play through a topic approach, and through 'plan, do, review sessions', which encourage children to initiate and follow up ideas. Several aspects of the 3–5 curriculum and the Key Stage 1 curriculum can be assessed through and observing play and such conversations.

PRACTICAL TASK PRACTICAL TASK **PRACTICAL TASK** PRACTICAL TASK **PRACTICAL TASK**

Select a story set in a past time. Plan teacher-directed activities related to the story, and how you would initiate a related role-play area. List ways in which you might intervene in play in order to extend and assess thinking.

CASE STUDY

A visit to a castle: Year 6 and Year 7

This case aimed to promote continuity between Key Stages 2 and 3 and to involve pupils in the role of historians, in each stage of a pupil-initiated historical enquiry (Cooper, 2009). In session one both classes worked in their own schools. They learned, through teacher questioning and information based on a PowerPoint presentation showing the plan and photographs, the stages in which the castle was built and by whom, why it was built and why it was built where it was. Pupils then worked in groups to list questions they would like to investigate on a site visit. Their questions were then conflated into five enquiries.

- How was the castle defended; where were the weakest points?
- Which part of the castle was built by Viexpoint, Robert Clifford, Hugh Clifford? Why do you think so?
- What evidence is there of life in the castle in the days of Robert Clifford?
- How can we create a guide to the castle young children (or blind children) might enjoy.
- You are creating a TV series, romantic novel or ghost story based on locations in the castle. Record the locations which will be part of the story.

On the site visit pupils worked in groups of three Year 6 and three Year 7 pupils. They selected the evidence they needed for their investigation and recorded it using notes, drawings, digital and video cameras.

In session three they combined and interpreted their data to create accounts (interpretations) of their findings. The final session took place in the secondary school. Interpretations included role play against images of castle locations, models, television scripts, a video, an animation, a display board for young children, a toy (to encourage problem-solving and fantasy play) to be sold in the shop, an information board for younger children and a tactile tour for partially-sighted visitors.

REFLECTIVE TASK

REFLECTIVE TASK

Using the Table 14.1 on page 181 identify the ways in which the case study uses creative approaches to find out about the castle.

Cross-curricular approaches to teaching history and creating a stimulating school environment

I am conjuring up an image of a school in which I worked. It is an open plan school. The Key Stage 2 unit consists of a large space shared by four classes with a small 'quiet room' for each class and a drama studio leading off it. The history topic this term is Ancient Greece. In one corner of the unit is a kitchen area with dresser, table, chairs, sink, cooker. A group of children are preparing an Ancient Greek lunch of chick pea soup, bread, goats' cheese and olives, salted anchovies and pomegranates. The smell is delicious. In another corner a Greek Temple reaches from floor to ceiling, its pillars made from corrugated card and the steps from staging blocks. Here requests appropriate for Ancient Greek Gods can be offered to Zeus and the Gods whose stories are depicted around the walls. In a third corner a group of children are making replica Greek vases and dishes in the pottery area based on photographs. In the drama studio another group are preparing their Assembly drama, based on stories from the Odyssey; Odysseus is negotiating the Straits of Messina while pupils' poems describing the drama are read to the accompaniment of various stringed instruments and pan pipes made in a design and technology lesson. Around the walls are huge paintings of Greek vases and inferences about the stories the pictures tell. They were made by projecting slides of Greek vases onto paper then painting the images. The curtains at one of the windows are screen printed with a design of laurel wreaths and temples.

PRACTICAL TASK PRACTICAL TASK PRACTICAL TASK PRACTICAL TASK PRACTICAL TASK

Plan activities related to another history study unit and linked to study units for design and technology, art and design, music and English which will help children to take ownership of their environment.

Art and historical imagination

Visual images, paintings, sculpture, photographs, cartoons from past times are important historical sources. Arnheim (1970, p31) said that, 'Every visual pattern, be it a painting, a building, an ornament, a chair...every work of art is a statement about something which makes a declaration about the nature of human existence.' Arnheim explains how paintings and sculptures that portray figures, objects, actions in a more or less realistic style nevertheless make no sense as reports of what life was like in the past until the viewer can read what each symbolises. This requires thought, language, discussion.

Dewey (1932) said that through an expressive object the artist and the active observer encounter each other, their material and mental environments and their culture at large; it demonstrates the connections between art and everyday experience. 'To emphasise what is aesthetic,' he said 'is to emphasise ways in which an aesthetic experience is a manifestation, a record, a celebration of a civilization...and an ultimate judgement on the quality of that civilization.'

Arnheim (1970) similarly linked visual perception and thought. He said that by collecting images of kinds of qualities, kinds of objects and kinds of events the mind grasps what they have in common and so organises experience into concepts. For example we may collect and group images of power, defeat, celebrations, noble deeds, poverty, wealth across the centuries, which become categorised as abstract concepts.

Dewey (1996, p236) said that 'The imagination is the medium of appreciation in every field.' Collingwood (1939, 1942, 1946) was concerned with the definition of historical imagination. He reasoned that we can only speculate about the feelings of people in the past by speculating about the sources they leave behind. The more we know about a period the more likely are the suppositions we make.

Gombrich (1982) discusses ways in which strong feelings can be conveyed in images. For example 'The Kneeling Captive', (Bibliothèque Nationale, Paris) demonstrates, through posture, the stark contrast in the statues of Imperial Rome between authority and submission. Innumerable images of thirteenth-century saints, donors and worthies in churches, with their folded hands, evoke piety, although there is here a complex relationship between ritual and expression. Greek vases illustrate familiar narratives but nineteenth century paintings of domestic scenes tell stories about feelings – jealousy, fear, loss. Images in stained glass windows change metaphor into symbolic images. Egan (1992) emphasised the importance of forming and articulating vivid images in our teaching.

Gardner (1990. p31) having introduced his theory of multiple intelligences, concluded that the most promising way to integrate the various forms is through 'situated learning':

> *When students encounter various forms of knowing operating together in a natural situation, when they see accomplished adults move back and forwards between these forms, when they are themselves engaged in a rich and engaging project which calls on various modes of representation, when they have the opportunity to interact and communicate with individuals who evidence complementary forms of learning, these are the situations that facilitate a proper alignment amongst various forms of knowledge.*

PRACTICAL TASK PRACTICAL TASK PRACTICAL TASK PRACTICAL TASK PRACTICAL TASK

Using online sources (e.g. www.nationalgallery.org.uk; www.npg.org.uk) and in response to a specified unit of study, select the following.

- A painting which makes a statement about aspects of human existence at the time.
- A work of art you think is a celebration of the civilization which produced it.
- A work of art which expresses people's feelings at the time.
- The narrative described on a Greek vase.

- A symbolic image.

What questions might you ask children so that they can make suggestions about what each image can tell us about the time in which it was made? Cooper (2002, p101–24) suggests practical ways of using visual sources with young children.

Personal and social education through history

The *National Curriculum Handbook* (DfEE, 1999, pp10–13, 19–21) defines ways in which schools can promote core values, which include the capacity to think rationally and creatively, contributing to their sense of identity through understanding the spiritual, moral, social and cultural heritages of diverse societies in the local, national and global dimensions of their lives. Surprisingly little work has been done on how such values can be an integral part of curriculum subjects.

History is concerned with causes and effects of and motives for human behaviour. Historical enquiry attempts to understand the values and attitudes of people in the past. This involves rational interpretations, empathy and tolerance; all have creative potential. Knight (1987), Slater (1995), Husbands (1960), and Claire (2005) provide excellent examples of how teachers may help children to engage with moral issues of the past. Pupils explore questions through hot-seating, drama, poetry and oral history. Would you help an escaping negro slave? Would you hide the Frank family? What would it feel like to be on the *Kinderstransport*? They consider how governments terrorise and scapegoat a community.

Folk Tales are oral history which handed down the hopes, fears and values of daily life through a community. Two recent studies (Cooper, 2007a; 2007b) investigated whether Key Stage 2 pupils could retell traditional Turkish and Russian folk tales in contemporary contexts. Central to the Turkish tale was the importance of hospitality and also the importance of respecting the house rules of a host. The Russian tales were concerned with greed, with respect for others and with being careful about what you wish for. Children's interpretations were extremely insightful in a rich variety of familiar, contemporary contexts, suggesting that there are universal values underpinning individual differences.

In another study (Ager, 2009) children identify and evaluate, through a variety of activities, the reasons for Tudor voyages of exploration and settlement: science, trade, religious toleration, population growth, plunder, political rivalry. This small rural school booked an interactive video session with experts in the National Maritime Museum to discuss some of these issues (www.nmm.ac.uk). Another focus was on the Roanoake Settlement in Virginia, who were looking for a land of religious tolerance, the original support of the Amerindians, their ethnic differences, the pressure on food supplies and eventual conflict encompassed numerous moral predicaments.

REFLECTIVE TASK

Research the Roanoke Settlement (www.dur.ac.uk/4schools/Roanoke/default.htm). What value-laden issues arise? How might you explore them with a Key Stage 2 class?

A SUMMARY OF **KEY POINTS**

> Historical enquiry involves making inferences and deductions about historical sources and using concepts of time, cause and effect and motivation, in order to construct accounts of the past which may differ, depending on the interests of the historian, but be equally valid.

> This process is creative because it involves suggesting a variety of possibilities, it involves reasoning, emotion and imagination, in attempting to understand the feelings, thoughts and motives of people in the past.

> Learning history involves developing a sense of your own identity and of similarities and differences with others. It involves developing and defending arguments, listening to the views of others and recognising that there may be no single 'right answer'. This is part of social and emotional as well as cognitive growth.

> This reflects research into creative thinking in psychology and constructivist theories of learning.

> Finding out about the past and constructing interpretations of the past is cross-curricular; this reflects research in neuroscience.

MOVING *ON* > > > > > > MOVING *ON* > > > > > > MOVING *ON*

A checklist to ensure that your history teaching in future is creative

- Does it involve making deductions and inferences about a range of sources in order to construct interpretations of past times and changes over time in a variety of ways?
- Do sources include literature, music, statistics, art, maps and diagrams?
- Are interpretations constructed in different ways (using technologies, design and technology, art and design, literacy, mathematics, role play)?

REFERENCES REFERENCES **REFERENCES** REFERENCES **REFERENCES** REFERENCES

Ager, J (2009) Tudor exploration, in *Cross-curricular approaches in the primary school*, Rowley, C and Cooper, H (eds) London: Sage.

Anderson, AL and Ryhammar, L (1998) Psychoanalytic models of the mind, creative functioning and percept-genetic reconstruction. *Psychoanalysis and Contemporary Thought*, 21, 359–82.

Arnheim, R (1970) *Visual thinking.* London: Faber & Faber.

Bennett, N, Wood, L, and Rogers, S (1997) *Teaching through play: teachers' thinking and classroom practice.* Buckingham: Open University Press.

Boden, M (1990, second edition, 2004) *The creative mind: myths and mechanisms*. Abingdon: Routledge.

Bruce, T (1987) *Early childhood education*. London: Hodder & Stoughton.

Bruner, JS (1963) *The process of education.* New York: Vintage Books.

Bruner, JS (1966) *Towards a theory of instruction.* Harvard, MA: Belknap Press.

Bruner, JS (1987) *Making sense: the child's construction of the world.* London: Methuen.

Claire, H (2005) History, citizenship and the primary curriculum, paper presented at the History in British Education Conference, Institute of Historical Research, London 14–15 February, accessed at http://www.history.ac.uk/education/conference/claire.html last accessed 09.12.08.

Collingwood, RG (1939) *An autobiography*. Oxford: Oxford University Press.

Collingwood, RG (1942) *The new leviathan*. Oxford: Oxford University Press.

Collingwood, RG (1946) *The idea of history*. Oxford: Clarendon Press.

Cooper, H (2002) *History in the Early Years*. Abingdon: Routledge.

Cooper, H (2007) *History 3–11*. London: David Fulton.

Cooper, H (2009) Young historians visit Brougham Castle, in Cooper, H and Chapman, A (eds) *Constructing history 11–19*. London: Sage.

Cooper, H (2008) Russian folk tales: contemporary interpretations, paper presented at the International Conference Britain: History, Culture, Education, University of Yaroslavl, Russia, 28–29 May.

Cooper, H and Rowley C (2006) *Geography 3–11: a guide for teachers.* London: David Fulton.

Craft, A (2000) *Creativity across the primary curriculum.* Abingdon: Routledge.

Craft, A, Jeffrey, B and Leibling, M (2001) *Creativity in education: current perspectives on policy and practice.* London: Cassell.

Cox, MV (1986*)* *The development of cognition and language.* Brighton: Harvester Press.

Department for Education and Employment (DfEE) (1999a) *All our futures: creativity, culture and education.* National Advisory Committee on Creative and Cultural Education, (NACCCE). London: DfEE.

Department for Education and Employment/Qualifications and Curriculum Authority (1999b) *The National Curriculum: Handbook for primary teachers in England.* London: QCA.

Department for Education and Skills (2003) *Excellence and enjoyment: a strategy for primary schools.* London: DfES.

Department for Education and Skills (2005) *The futures programme; meeting the challenge.* London: DfES.

Department for Education and Skills (2007) *National literacy and numeracy framework.* London: DfES.

Dewey, J (1932) *Art as experience.* New York: Berkeley Publishing Group.

Donaldson, M (1978) *Children's minds.* London: Fontana.

Edwards, CP and Springate, KW (1995) Encouraging creativity in Early Childhood Classrooms. *ERIC Digest.* Office of Educational Research and Improvement, Washington, DC.

Egan (1992) *Imagination in teaching and learning.* Abingdon: Routledge.

Gardner, H (1990) *Art education and human development.* Santa Monica, CA: The Getty Centre for Educational Arts.

Gardner, H (1993) *Multiple intelligences: the theory in practice.* New York: Harper Collins.

Garvey, C (1977) *Play* (The Developing Child Series), Bruner, JS, Cole, M and Lloyd, B (series eds). London: Collins/Fontana.

Goleman, D (1996) *Emotional intelligence.* London: Bloomsbury Publishing.

Gombrich, EH (1982) *The image and the eye: further studies in the psychology of pictorial representation.* Oxford: Phaidon.

Goswami, U and Bryant, P (2008) Children's cognitive development and learning, primary review research findings 2/1a. *The Primary Review.* Cambridge University Faculty of Education.

Guilford, JP (1959) Traits of creativity, in Anderson, HH (ed.) *Creativity and its cultivation.* New York: Harper, pp142-61.

Haddon, FA and Lytton, H (1968) Teaching approach and the development of divergent thinking abilities in primary schools. *British Journal of Educational Psychology*, 38, 171–80.

Husbands, C (1996) *What is history teaching? Language, ideas and meaning in learning about the past.* Buckingham: Open University Press.

Knight, P (1989) A study of children's understanding of people in the past. *Education Review*, 41:3.

Jones, RM (1968) *Fantasy and feeling in education.* London: London University Press.

Marshall, HE (1905) (second edition, 2005) *Our island story.* Cranbrook: Galore Park Publishing Limited.

Meadows, S and Cashdan, A (1988) *The child as thinker: the development and acquisition of cognition in childhood.* Abingdon: Routledge.

Piaget, J (1926) *The language and thought of the child.* Abingdon: Routledge.

Piaget, J (1928) *The judgement and reasoning of the child.* Abingdon: Routledge.

Seltzer, K and Bentley, T (1999) *The creative age: knowledge and skills for the new economy.* London: Demos.

Siraj-Blatchford, I, Sylva, K, Muttock, S, Gilden, R and Bell, D. (2002) *Researching effective pedagogy in the early years*, Research Report 356. Annersley: Department for Education and Skills, (http:/ www.dfes.gov.uk/research/data/).

Slater, J (1995) *Teaching history in the new Europe*. London: Cassell.

Torrance, EP (1965) *Rewarding creative behaviour*. Prentice Hall.

Vygotsky, LS (1986) *Thought and language* (translated, revised and edited by Alex Kozulin). Cambridge, MA: Massachusetts Institute of Technology.

Wallach, MA and Kagan, N (1965) *Modes of thinking in young children*. New York: Holt, Rinehart & Winston.

15
Creativity in primary geography
Simon Catling

Chapter objectives

By the end of this chapter you should:

- **appreciate that geography is an imaginative subject;**
- **recognise that harnessing children's geographies is vital to enabling creative geographical learning;**
- **be aware of the characteristics and principles underpinning creative geography teaching and learning;**
- **be able to identify and consider how to use a variety of approaches to creativity in primary geography.**

This chapter addresses the following Professional Standards for the Award of QTS:
Q8, Q14

Introduction

Geography is an active subject, at the heart of which lies creativity. We can think of creativity in a number of ways. Commonly it is associated with imagination and being imaginative, creating new ways of looking at or making something, whether an idea or object. It is, therefore, about understanding the world about us as much as it may involve something fictional or imagined. In this context it might imply resourcefulness in the production of ideas as well as objects and can be linked to the creation and use of images. It can link, then, not only to processes but also to products, even to signs and symbols that represent ways of understanding, such as words and pictures. It can also be thought of as a frame of mind, an attitude to undertaking tasks. In many senses, creativity is a way of responding to challenges, but creativity in itself is equally challenging.

Creativity can be found in the notion of constructivist learning, how we make or create our own knowledge of the world, initiating, adapting, assimilating, and recreating learning from new contexts to revise, even reject and renew, current understandings or schema. This can be influenced by the way we perceive events, our environment and the people involved. Creativity is not, therefore, a single entity but rather it has a number of overlapping meanings. It is not straightforward, therefore, to pin down simply in terms of originality or of having purpose and value; at times creativity appears intuitive or serendipitous, as when the solution to a problem might 'spring to mind' rather than appear to be based in explicit and analytic thought. In this sense creativity is active and *generative* (NACCCE, 1999). It is about new insights, new perspectives, new alternatives and new possibilities, whether personally or for the wider world. Creativity is fundamental to learning as much as it is vital to the way disciplines or subjects evolve.

Creativity for geographers involves several different things. There are images to be created, be they maps, photographs, field sketches or models to show the world. There is the capacity to understand how the world works, the processes that create our natural and human environments and lives and the creativity that understands these processes. Where we need to provide further resources, housing or services there are problems to solve and we need to imagine how these will look and what impact they will have, as indeed we may want to consider whether or not we make these developments and changes. Geography requires the use of imagination, the capacity to innovate, and creativity (Craft, 2005).

This chapter explores some aspects of and approaches to creativity in primary geography. It considers points to do with teaching creatively as well as engaging children in learning that is creative (Craft, 2005). It has been argued that *creative teaching* is fundamentally aligned to effective teaching, that effective teaching involves dimensions of creativity, whether in opening children's eyes to new perspectives and helping them create new understandings or by involving them in developing approaches to undertake their studies and fostering insight through their self-developed activities. The latter, though, can be seen as teaching *for* creativity in that it is concerned with the empowerment of the learner, where the child is a co-participant alongside the teacher in constructing the approaches to learning. The argument is that this provides the basis for *creative learning*, exhibited through five 'behaviours': the capacities to ask questions, to make connections, to imagine what might be, to explore options and to reflect critically (Craft, Cremin and Burnard, 2008). To these we might add: to be empathetic – to understand others' perspectives and feelings. These are all elements of an enquiry approach in geography (Roberts, 2003; Martin, 2004) that can support strongly teaching for creativity and creative learning.

Children's creative geographies

This summary uses a different and 'creative' approach to identify ways in which children engage with, think and feel about the world (Catling, 2003, 2005, 2006a, 2006b). Its purpose is to enable us to recognise that children's environmental and place experience is a 'given' in their lives and there to be drawn upon variously if we construct our geography in school to do so. These worlds also represent *children's geographical imaginations*, their constructions of experience in the world.

Children's *'action world'* is the environment of their daily experiences, of going to school and coming home, of playing outside and indoors, of shopping with their parents, and of visiting their friends and relatives. It is their engagement with their environment and that enables their creative development of environmental knowledge and spatial understanding. It is the source for their mental maps of familiar places and the basis for extending their field of activity into new areas. Children associate people with places and this human interaction helps to create their sense of place. In their *'peopled world'* others influence their experiences of places, guide and encourage their environmental experience, impact on their routines and activities and provide them with information and perspectives about the world around them. This occurs both at first hand and also through the media: television, computer games, and film.

Children's perceptions and images of their own places and of the wider world are influenced by their experience and their understandings, and their feelings in turn impact on how they assimilate and appreciate new encounters with places and the wider world whether through visits or the media. Their *'perceived world'* interacts with their action and people worlds to influence how they make use of their locality and of other places and what sense they construct of other places and peoples. Children's *'valued world'* encompasses their place and environmental likes and dislikes, their attachment to or detachment from places, of where they prefer to be or are determined to avoid, of who they want to be with in particular places, of sites that are special to them – their feelings for and senses of place.

It is evident that their experience of places and the environment enables children to construct their *'information world'*, their tacit and shared knowledge of the local and wider world. Their inquisitiveness involves them with a wide variety of environmental information, which they inter-relate to create understandings about places enabling them to use places not always as adults imagine. Yet other aspects of their knowledge remain particular, partial and unconnected, an assemblage of facts and/or misconceptions. Their environmental experience enables children to develop their *'competence world'*, the range of skills they employ to make use of places. These involve refining their inquisitiveness such that their investigative skills are more directly useful, constructing their wayfinding and navigational skills, and connecting these with map making and use. Children's own experiences in their home and local area, with their family, friends and strangers, through play equipment and story and information books, and through television and computer programmes and increasingly by mobile communication technology provide their *'source world'*. It is a world that is presented to children in mediated and selective encounters. It is also a world in which children are increasingly creating their own sources, through blogs and in virtual environments such as My Space and Bebo.

A vital way in which children make sense of the world they inhabit is through their *'imagined worlds'*. Play enables children to explore the activities and actions of people, to mimic and play out what they have observed occurring in, for instance, the supermarket, alongside the use of toys or other objects as props to construct environments at their own scale or in miniature, creating a beach scene or building and role playing characters in an imagined street. Children's imagination is fired by stories set in places and about lives and events occurring there, both familiar and novel. There are connections here with children's *'future worlds'*. In noticing what places are like, the various ways in which people live in them and what they do or happens to them, provokes in children a sense of what might be. This is influenced by their own experiences with family, friends and society. From a young age children become concerned about injustice, for people and the environment – often intertwined – and desire to see change effected for a fairer world. They have a sense of a 'preferable world'. This connects with children's *'commitment world'*. Children's sense of injustice and welfare leads to more than identifying what might be alternatives for the future. It leads to a desire to act, and as such to the frustration of inactivity, not simply of their own impotence but the inactivity of others. The development of ethical awareness means for many children the move to commitment to make improvements, to take action to create a fairer and better world, focused usually on the lives of others.

PRACTICAL TASK PRACTICAL TASK **PRACTICAL TASK** PRACTICAL TASK **PRACTICAL TASK**

Consider your own experience and that of children and young people with whom you have worked in or out of school. For each of the ten *worlds* of children's geographies above provide a personal example and one you might know of or can infer from another person's experience.

Challenging children's learning

Creativity in primary geography involves harnessing and integrating both the creative subject of geography and the creative nature of children's geographies. There is an informative literature on creative teaching and learning which can be applied to teaching geography with younger children (Duffy, 1998; Craft, 2000, 2005; QCA, 2002; Bruce, 2004; Grainger and Barnes, 2006). Emerging strongly from this literature is the notion of *challenge* in pedagogy, that creative teaching is focused on challenging children in their learning. Challenge is used here not as a singular notion but in several ways.

Before exploring this a little further it is relevant to pause on some of the characteristics exhibited in pedagogical strategies by teachers in constructing creative learning contexts (Rawling and Westaway, 2003; Barnes, 2004; Craft, 2005; Grainger and Barnes, 2006; Johnstone and Halocha, 2007). These include:

- being clear about the nature and focus of the topic that is to be studied but setting it up in an open way to which the children contribute;
- providing stimulating and motivating introductions and tasks to generate interest and engagement in learning;
- setting clear structures for lessons and tasks, for instance in the use of available sources and/or materials, time limits and types of outcome;
- ensuring there is enough time to develop ideas within a time limit for undertaking the task;
- providing a safe, secure and supportive learning environment, where children can 'go beyond what is expected', not necessarily in a linear fashion;
- providing a context for the children such that they recognise the relevance and pertinence of the tasks;
- being committed to developing understanding through the tasks set which are designed to make demands on children;
- encouraging the use of discussion and sharing and the use of vocabulary and expression to explore and develop tasks and outcomes;
- ensuring that children encounter alternative approaches to tackling tasks through the example set by the teacher;
- being flexible and open to making use of the unexpected, whether this comes from the children or an outside source;
- engaging children in the use of evaluative criteria such that they can identify and explain the quality of what they have achieved.

Implicit in these pedagogical characteristics is the idea of *challenge*, not least for the teacher intending to adopt these characteristics in their teaching. So in what senses is *challenge* being employed here? There are a variety of ways in which the idea of *challenge* is used.

- The obvious characteristic of challenge is that of *making demands* on children in terms of higher order thinking skills, which involve problem-solving approaches, careful scrutiny and evaluation and well-argued and presented outcomes.
- This includes the curiosity to explore and follow lines of *enquiry* where they lead. This also means taking a questioning and critical stance in that the interest is not to accept the conventional, indeed any, response without taking a hard look at it.
- This might well require *risk taking*, where it is not clear where enquiries might lead. It involves engaging with uncertainty and the unknown and a willingness to come up with novel solutions as necessary.
- Linked closely to this is the requirement for *openmindedness*, in which children do not close off options to explore or viewpoints to examine but where they are concerned to identify as many possibilities as possible,

evaluating limitations before rejecting them, and returning to them later if circumstances warrant it.

- Another element of challenge involves a willingness to be *unconventional*, not to take the more likely option, even to follow up what will become controversial because it evokes strong and mixed responses and will need to be well-considered and argued.
- Related to these last two is another element, that of *speculation*, which is the capacity to think laterally. This is about keeping one's options open and playing around with different ideas to come up with alternatives, characterised at times as 'thinking outside the box' and links with *possibilities* thinking (Craft, Cremin and Burnard, 2008).
- A further characteristic of challenge is the capacity to identify and *make connections* and see relationships, as well as to notice the 'gaps'. Here we are involved in linking ideas and ways to generate solutions to the problems that are the subject of the enquiry.

Creative approaches to teaching and learning

There are many ways to provide opportunities for creative learning through creative geography teaching. The following illustrate a variety of approaches that can be used in pupil investigations.

ALTERNATIVE LOCALITIES

A Year 4 class began a study of their local area with group and then class discussions about what they knew about their locality, what they thought about it and how they felt about it. It became clear that they had a wide range of knowledge of the area between them, how variously they related to the area and that they had views about the state of the area. Drawing out their ideas and questions the teacher encouraged the children to work in four teams, each of which focused on a different way of looking at the locality, and each of which was to produce its own report. The four mini-topics were: 'What is good about our place', 'A clean neighbourhood?', 'What you can do here', and 'What we like here'. A variety of investigations developed. Opportunities for fieldwork were organised and many of the children were able to draw on their local knowledge and to follow up lines of enquiry outside school. Investigations involved interviews with family, friends and other local people; photographs of places liked or thought 'scruffy'; mapping local shops and other useful services; sketches of particular features and views. The children were encouraged to be creative in preparing their reports. The teams drew on leaflets, posters and such like that they had come across for inspiration. One produced a brochure to attract people to the area and emphasised what a good place to live in it is. Another provided a 'clean up our neighbourhood' poster with photographs of unkempt sites and advice on what to do. The third team made a presentation about their and other children's favourite places using maps and photographs to show the sites. The fourth team produced a map leaflet to show what services were available and where they were.

The outcome was insightful, in that it provided four differing but overlapping perspectives on the geographies of the area. The children's favourite sites did not mesh with the views of a range of adults and younger people on what was good about the locality; indeed, there was some overlap with other people's ideas of what was scruffy about the area, such as the waste ground. Being creative in geography should involve looking at places and environmental matters from more than one angle and sharing and reflecting on these, as this class did. Creativity helps us to see the world differently.

AN ARTIFACT COLLECTION

A Year 3 class were presented with a number of artifacts from another culture in another part of the world. They included cooking utensils, cleaning equipment, storage jars, children's toys and musical instruments. This set of commercially collected and sold artifacts – all were originals, not copies – were provided for the class as a stimulus to involve the children in the study of a locality in a less economically developed region. The teacher drew on an approach he had used in history, not telling the children what the objects were or where they had come from but inviting them to select two or three objects in turn and working in twos and threes to say what they could about them, who might use them, for what and when. They were required to give a reason for their comments. They were also asked to see if they could say where in the world they came from. A large globe and atlases were available. The teacher recognised that their experience was limited and that this might prove a fruitless line of guesswork. The children responded and the study of the locality went ahead. During the enquiry the teacher introduced photographs, newspaper extracts, postcards, clothing, food samples and other resources. The children pursued various lines of enquiry both self- and teacher-initiated. The creative start and use of a wide variety of resources, introduced in timely ways, engaged the children and they came away more aware and empathetic to others elsewhere.

There was one point in this study when the children were asked what else would help them know more about the place they were studying. More resources from that part of the world was one of the responses. This sparked a creative moment for the teacher. He decided that he would adjust the geography and other parts of the curriculum to run a short topic on what their own local artifacts might be. He put it to the children that since they had received a collection of artifacts from another locality it would be helpful to people there if they could make their own set of artifacts for others to use to find out about their place. This approach uses a '3 Ds' approach – *develop*, *debate*, *decide* – for the children: to develop their own ideas about what to include; to debate what might be included and why; and finally to decide what to include.

Suspending much of the intended curriculum for one week, the teacher focused the children on developing their ideas about which artifacts might tell other people about their lives in their place. Children worked in groups of four to come up with their lists and reasons why. The result was that many children brought into school one or more artifacts, including clothing, local postcards and newspapers, food packets, sweet and drink labels, photographs they or family members had taken (all labelled), as well as items similar to those they had initially been introduced to in the distant locality study, and much else. It proved not only highly stimulating but gave credibility to the risk in suspending the curriculum (an unusual practice here) and opened eyes to what the children felt was important to say about themselves and their neighbourhood.

BELONGING

Belonging (Baker, 2004) is a picture story without text. It presents the view from an upstairs window across the back garden to two local streets. Over a period of years, as child grows from babyhood to being a first time parent, it shows how the streets change. There is decline in the quality of the area, then a gradual improvement and greening of the neighbourhood. The focus of the book, Baker argues, is on the sense of belonging to the land. The story is about how communities contribute to and enhance or neglect at their peril their environment and how their nurturing creates the character of places.

Used with a mixed-age class of Years 1 and 2, the children were taken through the book by their teacher but not in one sitting. The story was introduced after the children had spent several minutes looking out of their classroom window. They were given no particular brief but when they sat down were asked what they had seen. The responses were uniformly about features. The teacher then showed the children the first picture and asked the children to say what they saw. Features and people were identified, but two children said that it looked rather tatty and another noticed the dog urinating! This led to two discussions. One was about how the area looked and what the children felt about it. The other focused on the couple in their back garden and their baby: what did the children think would happen to this family. Responses ranged from moving out to staying poor with some ideas about the place 'getting better' and that they would make a 'nice garden'. Over the rest of the week several pages at a time were shown and discussed, the children encouraged to notice what had changed, to say what they felt about the changes, what they thought might happen next and what they would like to do to improve the area. The second half of the book provides opportunities to discuss creative ways to make an area more pleasant and attractive and about how it might be used by local people, including children like themselves.

The book generated three responses from the children. One was that among different groups of children there was increased sharing of their lives at home, what they did, what they liked to do and where to go, and so forth. A second was that, spontaneously, the children started talking about the views they saw from one or more of their windows at home, commenting on the view and the features, the state of the neighbourhood, how it looked different at night and how far and what they could see. The third was to suggest ideas about how the school playgrounds and field could be 'greened'. They came back from the story and home views to the view from their classroom window and to the somewhat barren nature of the play areas they used daily in school. This sparked further discussions, resulting in the children creating their own ideas and pictures about what sort of play areas in school they would like. They were aided here by the willingness of the teacher to go with where the children were taking their learning from the story, not in any direction that she had planned but one which extended the sense of belonging to a place in the book and around home to the idea of school as a place of belonging. A creative approach to the use of the book led to opening up creative opportunities for the children, which did in the end lead to some additional resources for playtime use though not to some of the physical changes the children suggested. Creativity has an impact and can change minds and places.

These three examples, while focused on local places, illustrate how innovative and imaginative approaches to teaching geography can generate creative thinking and learning in children. Creativity and creative understanding are possibilities in all subjects; they can draw on approaches from each other. Figure 15.1 identifies forty creative approaches to teaching geography which can generate and involve children in creative geographical learning across the age range. While you may not be able to undertake a geography topic that uses a creative approach throughout because it has been pre-structured, it is possible to draw on one or more of the ideas in Figure 15.1 to initiate and develop some creative aspects in your teaching and the children's learning.

PRACTICAL TASK PRACTICAL TASK PRACTICAL TASK PRACTICAL TASK PRACTICAL TASK

Read the three classroom case studies outlined above and identify the ways in which creativity has been used in the teaching involved and what learning by the children appears to have taken place.

• give (and follow) route instructions with a map and/ or compass • use vocabulary to describe features, layouts and areas without naming them (others work it out) • make and using maps to show particular aspects of places • take, annotate and display photographs of features, sites and places • draw field sketches • make a picture postcard • make models of real or imagined places • use role play to debate an environmental change • make a video/audio tape recording about a local feature or issue • create a picture sequence with drawings or photographs to show a route or development • make a wall frieze or collage to depict the 'look' of a street • plan and follow a trail around your neighbourhood to show particular aspects of it • use thought tracking during a freeze frame in a role play to express views on an issue • write a formal report about a geographical topic or concern • write and illustrating a newspaper article about a topical local or global event	• undertake surveys and interviews about, e.g., disability access, local v. chain shops • create a website about your school's neighbourhood • write (shape) poetry and stories about or set in landscapes, urban sites, rivers • make equipment to gather data, e.g. about weather elements • organise a Planning Enquiry on a real or imagined development • make posters to encourage, e.g., using litter bins • arrange a debate about a topic environmental issue, e.g. food or water shortage • question visitors about their perception of the locality • plan, organise and undertake fieldwork in the local area or further afield • use hot seating to consider someone's viewpoint on an issue, e.g. a planner, shopkeeper, developer • use conscience alley at the end of a role play to involve the class in thinking about the views of the character walking between two rows • use drama and improvisation to act out scenes in, e.g. a meeting about a global issue like climate change • undertake a simulation exercise to explore, e.g. a traffic/parking problem • make a presentation using PowerPoint (or not) about, e.g. a place, an environmental issue	• plan how changes might be made to an area, real or imagined, that people would like to see • create a display of artifacts about the local area or another place • make playmat maps for younger children to use and trial them • arrange a meal using ingredients from around the world or a particular part of the world • link with another UK or non-UK school and exchange information about your respective places • prepare a travel itinerary to visit another locality, how to get there, what you might do • create a resource pack for your locality for use in another school • create an activity sheet to be used to investigate a specific place or environmental topic • play with environmental toys, creating a model of your own or an imaginary place • evaluate the quality of places by developing criteria using rating scales • allocate pairs of children roles, e.g. as people in another locality, who then hold an improvised conversation about their community

Figure 15.1 Examples of creative teaching activities to use to generate creative geographical learning

Features of good practice in creative geography teaching and learning

As with any effective teaching there are a number of features of creative teaching that have underpinned the strategies and learning in the three examples given above. They are impor-tant in developing geographical learning and relate to the characteristics of creative teaching that teachers use to provide the contexts for creative learning, and they provide the envir-onment for the 'principles' inherent in the meanings of *challenge* in creative teaching and learning. These features include the following.

- *Clarity of focus*: being clear about what the children can be encouraged to learn from the topic and helping them to identify what they are learning as it develops.
- *Emphasise questioning and enquiries*: involve children in devising questions about the topic they are researching, e.g. What is it like? What is life like there? How might people there want it to develop? – and in selecting and structuring their geographical questions and their investigations – using and doing enquiry.
- *Teaching approaches*: using children's perspectives, 'problematising' the topic, questioning the 'accepted', becoming aware of alternative possibilities, creating personal responses and meanings, making judgements and decisions and justifying them.
- *Focus on children doing the thinking*: on interpreting, looking critically, making deductions or inferences, giving reasons, recognising limitations; justifying their perspectives and conclusions; identifying what has been learnt – always being prepared to challenge the children's views and arguments to enable them to hone them.
- *Evaluating learning*: involve children in appreciating what they have learnt and in identifying some of the gaps and limitations to their awareness – to help them realise and recognise their geographical learning.
- *Connecting with personal futures*: engaging children in thinking about ways in which their geographical studies and their understanding about their own geographies and learning might impact on their personal lives and the lives of others around them, how they might go about things differently in their use of and/ or attitude to the environment, places and other peoples (Hicks, 2002).

A SUMMARY OF **KEY POINTS**

> Geography is a creative subject.
> Children's geographies are both created through their experience and are creative in the ways in which they are aware of, appreciate and understand the world.
> The characteristics of creative pedagogies link well with the focus on challenge in creativity that is characteristic of creative geographical teaching and learning.
> Innovation, imagination and creativity are intertwined in approaches to geography teaching and learning.
> Effective geography learning and teaching will involve creative approaches and engender creative learning within geography.

MOVING *ON* > > > > > > MOVING *ON* > > > > > > MOVING *ON*

When you have the opportunity (next) to teach a geography topic or an interdisciplinary topic which involves geography, identify the approaches you can use to provide both creative teaching approaches and for creative learning for the children. Remember that it is you who can facilitate these opportunities for creative geographical teaching and learning by accepting the challenges and taking the risks in planning creative teaching. Try one activity, then another and a third . . .

REFERENCES REFERENCES **REFERENCES** REFERENCES REFERENCES REFERENCES

Baker, J (2004) *Belonging*. London: Walker Books.

Barnes, J (2004) Geography, creativity and place, in Scoffham, S (ed.) *Handbook of primary geography*. Sheffield: Geographical Association.

Bruce, T (2004) *Cultivating creativity in babies, toddlers and young children*. London: Hodder Education.

Catling, S (2003) Curriculum contested: primary geography and social justice. *Geography*, 88:3, 164–210.

Catling, S (2005) Children's personal geographies and the English primary school geography curriculum. *Children's Geographies*, 3:3, 325–44.

Catling, S (2006a) What do 5-year-olds know of the world? – Geographical understanding and play in young children's early learning. *Geography*, 91:1, 55–74.

Catling, S (2006b) Younger children's geographical worlds and primary geography, in Schmeinck, D (ed.) *Research on learning and teaching in primary geography*. Karslruhe: Pädagogische Hochschule Karlsruhe.

Craft, A (2000) *Creativity across the primary curriculum*. Abingdon: Routledge.

Craft A (2005) *Creativity in schools*. Abingdon: Routledge.

Craft, A, Cremin, T and Burnard, P (eds) (2008) *Creative learning 3–11 and how we document it*. Stoke-on-Trent: Trentham Books.

Duffy, B (1998) *Supporting creativity and imagination in the Early Years*. Buckingham: Open University Press.

Grainger, T and Barnes, J (2006) Creativity in the curriculum, in Arthur, J, Grainger, T and Wray, D (eds) *Learning to teach in the primary school*. Abingdon: Routledge.

Hicks, D (2002) *Lessons for the future*. Abingdon: Routledge.

Johnstone, J and Halocha, J (2007) Planning for creative teaching, in Johnstone, J, Halocha, J and Chater, M *Developing teaching skills in the primary school*. Maidenhead: Open University Press.

Martin, F (2004) Creativity through geography, in Fisher, R and Williams, M (eds) *Unlocking creativity*. London: David Fulton, 117–32.

National Advisory Committee on Creative and Cultural Education (1999) *All our futures: creativity, culture and education*. London: DfEE.

Ofsted (2008) *Geography in schools: changing practice*, www.Ofsted.gov.uk

Qualifications and Curriculum Authority (2002), *Creativity: Find it! Promote it!* London: QCA.

Rawling, E and Westaway, J (2003) Exploring creativity. *Primary Geographer*, 50, 7–9.

Roberts, M (2003) *Learning through enquiry*. Sheffield: Geographical Association.

Added to the page number 'f' denotes a figure and 't' denotes a table.